Roman Law

Roman Law: An Introduction offers a clear and accessible introduction to Roman law for students of any legal tradition. In the thousand years between the Law of the Twelve Tables and Justinian's massive Codification, the Romans developed the most sophisticated and comprehensive secular legal system of Antiquity, which remains at the heart of the civil law tradition of Europe, Latin America, and some countries of Asia and Africa. Roman lawyers created new legal concepts, ideas, rules, and mechanisms that most Western legal systems still apply. The study of Roman law thus facilitates understanding among people of different cultures by inspiring a kind of legal common sense and breadth of knowledge.

Based on over twenty-five years' experience teaching Roman law, this volume offers a comprehensive examination of the subject, as well as a historical introduction which contextualizes the Roman legal system for students who have no familiarity with Latin or knowledge of Roman history. More than a compilation of legal facts, the book captures the defining characteristics and principal achievements of Roman legal culture through a millennium of development.

Rafael Domingo (1963, PhD 1987) is the Spruill Family Research Professor at Emory University in Atlanta, USA, and ICS Professor of Law at the University of Navarra, Spain. A specialist in legal history, legal theory, ancient Roman law, and comparative law, he has authored and edited more than twenty books, including *Auctoritas* (1999), *Juristas Universales* (2004), *The New Global Law* (2010), *God and the Secular Legal System* (2016), and *Great Christian Jurists in Spanish History* (2018).

"Rafael Domingo brings his considerable knowledge of Roman legal science and religion to this wonderfully clear and thorough introduction to Roman law."

Ernest Metzger, University of Glasgow, UK

Roman Law

An Introduction

Rafael Domingo

Routledge
Taylor & Francis Group
LONDON AND NEW YORK

First published 2018
by Routledge
2 Park Square, Milton Park, Abingdon, Oxon OX14 4RN

and by Routledge
711 Third Avenue, New York, NY 10017

Routledge is an imprint of the Taylor & Francis Group, an informa business

British Library Cataloguing-in-Publication Data
A catalogue record for this book is available from the British Library

Library of Congress Cataloging-in-Publication Data
Names: Domingo, Rafael, 1963- author.
Title: Roman law : an introduction / Rafael Domingo.
Description: Abingdon, Oxon ; New York, NY : Routledge, 2018. | Includes bibliographical references and index.
Identifiers: LCCN 2017056407 (print) | LCCN 2017057469 (ebook) |
ISBN 9781351111478 (ebook) | ISBN 9781351111461 (web pdf) |
ISBN 9781351111454 (epub) | ISBN 9781351111447 (mobi/kindle) |
ISBN 9780815362753 (hardback : alk. paper) | ISBN 9780815362777 (pbk. : alk. paper)
Subjects: LCSH: Roman law.
Classification: LCC KJA147 (ebook) | LCC KJA147 .D6624 2018 (print) |
DDC 340.5/4--dc23
LC record available at https://lccn.loc.gov/2017056407

ISBN: 978-0-815-36275-3 (hbk)
ISBN: 978-0-815-36277-7 (pbk)
ISBN: 978-1-351-11147-8 (ebk)

Typeset in Times New Roman
by Taylor & Francis Books

To Javier Echevarría, in memory

Contents

Preface

This textbook is designed to be an accessible introduction to Roman law for students of any legal tradition. It is based on more than twenty-five years' experience teaching Roman law at the Universities of Cantabria and Navarra in northern Spain, and at Emory University in Atlanta. The volume has been written to support a semester-long course and, thus, to be expanded on by instructors. Understanding it does not require familiarity with Latin or extensive knowledge of Roman history. More than a compilation of legal facts, the book tries to capture the essentials of Roman legal culture. I am convinced that the study of Roman law can help inoculate legal actors today against the virus of legalism and help them to make legal judgments independent of political loyalties, economic interests, and media and social pressures. Furthermore, the study of Roman law inspires a common foundation and knowledge that facilitate understanding among lawyers of different legal cultures. I admire the new efforts of contemporary socio-legal scholarship that tries to separate ancient Roman law from the Romanistic tradition, but I consider it more profitable for students to read a more institutional, even conventional, textbook deeply embedded in the Romanistic tradition.

The great Goethe rightly likened Roman law to a diving duck that "hides itself from time to time but is never quite lost; always coming up again alive."[1] The study of Roman law is emerging again in our own day because of the need, fostered by globalization, for a common legal vocabulary. As the highly refined terminology of the Roman jurists was unfailingly adopted by legal thinkers to conceptualize international law up to the eighteenth century, it should be adopted again for the conceptualization and development of a new global law. Roman law can serve today as an inspiration toward global constitutionalism, which is inherently postsovereignist, postnationalist, and postpositivist.[2] That Roman law was also intrinsically presovereignist, prenationalist, and prepositivist assists constitutionalists in eliminating from global constitutionalism any nonfoundational elements derived from a highly statist paradigm.

The subject treated in this textbook is classical law, roughly developed in the late Republic and the Principate. I have included references to post-classical and Justinian law where I have thought them beneficial for twenty-first-century students. I have said little about early Roman law because of its scant influence on modern legal systems. Many points of Roman law are still controversial, and certain questions about its historical development are especially so. I have tried, however, to avoid these disputed questions, and to lay out the most widely accepted contemporary views, even where I do not fully agree with them. That is so especially in the realms of property law and contract law.

The book is divided into two parts. The first attempts to situate Roman law within its historical context and to trace its development. I provide a brief, concentrated outline of the constitutional and social framework in which Roman law arose and was developed. The second part deals with the practice of Roman law. In selecting topics, I follow the Roman jurists who, without discounting criminal law, devoted more attention to private law. The latter– especially the law of property, the law of succession upon death, and the law of contracts– stimulated the legal imagination of Roman jurists as no other areas of the law did. Thus, as a matter of fact, private law dominated Roman legal debates, overshadowing public law. Indeed, Roman private law is one of the greatest legal accomplishments of Western culture. At the end of each chapter, I offer a bibliographic selection of books and articles on the subject. The reader, actually an English speaker, will understand my reasonable preference for books written in English. However, I have also included basic references to relevant books in other languages (German, Spanish, Italian, and French).

It will become apparent how much I owe to my beloved mentor and friend Álvaro d'Ors. I worked closely with him at the University of Navarra for more than twenty years and spent thousands of hours reading, analyzing, and discussing with him Roman legal sources. I also owe a great deal to Max Kaser. His monumental handbook on Roman law (*Das römische Privatrecht*)[3] has been for many years a lodestar when I had to deal with a contentious topic. I hope that the forthcoming German handbook on private Roman law (*Handbuch des römischen Privatrechts*, Tübingen: Mohr Siebeck), coedited by Ulrike Babusiaux, Christian Baldus, Wolfgang Ernst, Franz-Stefan Meissel, Thomas Rüfner, and Johannes Platschek, finally supersedes Kaser's still-leading handbook.

Along with Roman legal sources, especially the *Corpus Iuris Civilis* and Gaius's *Institutes*, I have also repeatedly consulted a few classical handbooks, textbooks, commentaries, and dictionaries in English in the course of writing this manuscript. By mentioning them, I want to pay tribute to the authors to whom this textbook is largely indebted: Buckland's *Textbook on Roman Law* (3rd ed., 1963), De Zulueta's commentary on the *Institutes of Gaius* (vol. II, 1953), Schulz's *Classical Roman Law* (1951), Wolff's *Roman Law* (1951), Berger's *Encyclopedic Dictionary of Roman Law* (1953), Jolowicz and Nicholas's *Historical Introduction to the Study of Roman Law* (3rd ed., 1972), Kunkel's *Roman Legal and Constitutional History* (2nd ed., 1973), Thomas's *Textbook of Roman Law* (1976), and Nicholas's *Introduction to Roman Law* (1975). Although these could be considered, in a sense, old books, they remain vital for readers interested in the institutions and development of Roman law.

I have often consulted three recent Roman law volumes in English that should also be mentioned out of my gratitude and respect to the authors: *The Cambridge Companion of Roman Law* (2015), edited by David Johnston; *Amne adverso: Roman Legal Heritage in European Culture* (2015), by Laurent Waelkens; and *The Oxford Handbook of Roman Law and Society* (2016), edited by Paul J. du Plessis, Clifford Ando, and Kaius Tuori. Although very different in style, purpose, and methodology, the three volumes provide new and fresh approaches to Roman law. I also want to mention the edition of Alan Watson's English translation of *The Digest of Justinian*,[4] and Bruce Frier's new annotated English translation of the Code of Justinian.[5] Both works are indispensable tools for teaching Roman law in English.

Unfortunately, men and women were not equal under Roman law. For this reason, I prefer to use only male pronouns when referring to general circumstances. Otherwise, an effort at courtesy and equity might have obscured some of the historical facts, such as they are. Romans had their own value system, which shaped not only the behavior of Roman citizens in society but also the Roman legal order. To teach Roman law does not, of course, imply any endorsement of their social standards or ethical principles. Slavery, misogyny, and the unrestricted power of the head of the family over the other members are some good examples of inhumane yet widely accepted social behaviors of the time. But the study of these institutions exemplifies the principle that some good can come out of evil (*ex malo bonum*). We do well not simply to judge the past, nor of course to rationalize it, but to try to understand it as well as possible, and so to learn from it.

I have incurred a number of debts in preparing this textbook. I wish to thank the students of Emory Law School who attended my courses on Roman law while I was writing the manuscript. Provocative questions and intelligent commentaries helped me to improve the text. I am deeply indebted to John Witte, Jr. for encouraging me to write this book, as well as for stimulating conversations and wise suggestions. I would like to thank Gary S. Hauk and Sherif Girgis for their constructive editing of my final text. I wish to thank Amy Davis-Poynter for her excellent work as an editor, Conchita Domingo for her self-denying support and assistance, and the anonymous reviewers for detailed comments and valuable suggestions. Lastly, I would like to thank Gonzalo Rodríguez-Fraile and the Spruill family in Atlanta for their generous support of my work.

Rafael Domingo
Atlanta, December 12, 2017

Notes

1 Johann Peter Eckermann, *Conversations of Goethe with Eckermann and Soret*, vol. 2, trans. John Oxenford (London: Smith, Elder & Co., 1850), 162.

2 See Mattias Kumm, "Constituent Power, Cosmopolitan Constitutionalism, and Post-Positivist Law," in *International Journal of Constitutional Law* 14 (2016) 697–711.

3 Max Kaser, *Das römische Privatrecht*, 2 vols., 2nd ed. (Munich: Beck Verlag, 1971 and 1975); and Max Kaser and Karl Hackl, *Das römische Zivilprozessrecht*, 2nd ed. (Munich: Beck Verlag, 1996).

4 Alan Watson (ed.), *The Digest of Justinian*, 2 vols. (revised English translation Philadelphia: University of Pennsylvania Press, 1998).

5 Bruce W. Frier (ed.) and Fred H. Blume (trans.), *The Codex of Justinian. A New Annotated Translation, with Parallel Latin and Greek Text*, 3 vols. (Cambridge: Cambridge University Press, 2016).

Abbreviations

ca.	circa (approximately)
C.J.	Code of Justinian
Const.	Constitutio
Collatio	Mosaicarum et Romanarum Legum Collatio
C.Th.	Thedosian Code
D.	Digest of Justinian
E.P.	Edictum Perpetuum
Ep. Ulp.	Epitome Ulpiani
FIRA	Fontes Iuris Romani Antejustiniani
F.V.	Fragmenta Vaticana
Gaius	Institutes of Gaius
Inst.	Institutes of Justinian
Nov.	Novels (Novellae leges)
pr.	proemium (preface)
P.S.	Pauli Sententiae
r.	reign
S.C.	senatus consultum (decree of the Senate)

Chronological tables

BCE

753	Founding of Rome
509	Expulsion of the Tarquins; beginning of Roman Republic
451–450	The Twelve Tables
445	Lex Canuleia allowed marriages between patricians and plebeians
367	Institution of praetorship
287	Lex Hortensia: equation of pleciscita with leges
264–241	First Punic War
252	Tiberius Coruncanius, first plebeian to be elected pontifex maximus
242	Institution of peregrine praetorship (over foreigners)
241	Annexation of Sicily
218–201	Second Punic War
169	Lex Voconia on inheritance of women
ca. 130	Lex Aebutia on formulary procedure
91–89	The Social War
82–79	Dictatorship of Sulla; Leges Corneliae on criminal law
44	Assassination of Caesar
43	Assassination of Cicero
40	Lex Falcidia on succession
31	Octavian defeats Antony at the battle of Actium
27	Inauguration of the Principate
18–17	Lex Julia on marriage and lex Julia on adultery
ca. 6	Birth of Jesus of Nazareth

CE

4	Lex Aelia Sentia on manumission
9	Lex Pappia Poppaea on marriage
14	Death of Augustus
114–38	Reign of Hadrian
ca. 130	Consolidation of the Edict: Edictum Perpetuum
161–80	Reign of Marcus Aurelius
ca. 161	Institutes of Gaius
212	Constitutio Antoniniana on citizenship
223	Assassination of Ulpian
284–305	Reign of Diocletian; beginning of the late Roman Empire
306–37	Reign of Constantine
313	Promulgation of the so-called Edict of Milan
379–95	Reign of Theodosius the Great
395	Division of the Empire into Western and Eastern
408–50	Reign of Theodosius II
426	Law of Citations
438	Theodosian Code
476	End of the Western Empire
506	Lex Romana Visigothorum
527–65	Reign of Justinian
529	First edition of the Code of Justinian
533	Institutes and Digest of Justinian
534	Second edition of the Code of Justinian
565	Death of Justinian

Part I

Roman law in historical context

1 Basic legal concepts and values

This introductory chapter addresses broad topics and general ideas that overarch the entire Roman legal tradition. They constitute the most distinctive representations of Roman law. Some are original to the Romans, most come from the Greeks, and a few come from other ancient civilizations. The Roman spirit and talent modulated all of them, but at no point did they remain static in Roman legal sources. With different nuances, refinements, and implications, these fundamental topics also embody the key ideas of most Western legal systems.

These basic ideas comprise the grammar of any legal culture because they deal with the permanent questions that human beings have formulated in relation to the law. This chapter's selection is discretionary and has a pedagogical purpose. It could have included many other crucial ideas: ownership, obligation, contract, and so on. These further subjects, however, I prefer to discuss in context to facilitate understanding of them. The first three sections, different in character, introduce the very idea of Roman law as such and its connection with Greek culture.

Significance of Roman law

Roman law was the legal system (*ordo iuris*) of ancient Rome from its foundation in 753 BCE, according to tradition, to the death of Emperor Justinian the Great (483–565 CE), almost one hundred years after the fall of the Western Roman Empire (476 CE). In the thousand years between the Law of the Twelve Tables (451–450 BCE) and Justinian's massive Codification (around 530 CE), the Romans developed the most sophisticated and comprehensive secular legal system of antiquity. Roman law is still at the heart of the civil law tradition of the European continent and some of its former colonies in the Americas, Asia, and Africa, and it was instrumental in the development of international law, the church's canon law, and the common law tradition. Roman lawyers created new legal concepts, ideas, rules, and mechanisms that most Western legal systems still apply.

The development of Roman law was gradual and always in line with the different stages of Roman constitutional history: the Monarchy (753–509 BCE), the Republic (509–27 BCE), the Principate (27 BCE–284 CE), and the Later Empire (284–565 CE). Roman law started as a set of rules and rituals of a central Italian city-state with a citizen body of around twenty thousand people, and it became over time the legal system of a great empire with an estimated population of sixty-five to eighty million at its greatest extent in the reign of Trajan (117 CE). Gradually, Roman law began losing its local character, becoming the common law of more than a fourth of the world's population.

Roman law represents a unique achievement in legal history. One of the most original contributions of Roman civilization to humankind, it was a characteristic product of Roman genius and probably Rome's greatest intellectual legacy. The success of Roman law derives, in part, from its universal character; the high quality and creativity of its legal science; the power of ancient Rome; and the centuries of adaptation and refinement of Roman law by the Catholic Church (the legal technique and structure of canon law are basically distilled from Roman law). The success of Roman law also lay in its ability to live in harmony with the rules and institutions of other legal systems and cultures.

Roman law reached an unprecedented balance between justice and fairness, natural and civil justice, private and public interest, moral authority (*auctoritas*) and coercive power (*potestas*), judicial flexibility and legal certainty, grammar and intention, tradition and innovation, simplicity and scholarship, and abstraction and casuistry. Roman law constitutes a perennial model for the appropriate development of legal systems for all times, as well as a foundational pillar of emerging global law. Roman law offers a good example of how a legal system can be developed and modernized based on equitable ideas and principles. For these reasons, among others, Roman law still commands the respect and admiration of independent legal thinkers and practitioners of different legal traditions as a unique tradition of legal thought.

Classical Roman law

The classical period of Roman law provides the best comprehensive framework of the development of Roman law, and it became the model for later generations of legal actors. This classical period stretched from about the last century of the Roman Republic to the end of the Principate (284 CE). It is also common to locate the beginning of the classical period in the promulgation of the *lex Aebutia* (around 130 BCE), which promoted the so-called formulary procedure, and to mark the close of this period around 230 CE, some decades before the end of the Principate, with the murders of the jurist Ulpian in 223 CE and the Emperor Alexander Severus in 235 CE. This period is called classical because of the imagination and creativity of the emerging class of Roman jurists and the harmony and elegance of their legal science. The rise of a selected group of jurists developing a refined technique of legal reasoning for the resolution of legal conflicts, and the formation and expansion of the so-called formulary procedure, are traditionally considered the two features that characterize this classical period of Roman law.

Primitive Roman law emphasized an excessive adherence to prescribed forms and rituals. Without the observance of these steady formalities, the manifestation of the will of a citizen was considered legally ineffective. It was the solemnity of the forms, the formalities, and not agreements or intentions, that produced legal consequences. A defect of will (fraud or mistake) did not affect the validity of a legal act or its legal effectiveness. Classical Roman lawyers, however, mitigated formalism and promoted an increasing flexibility. They developed a good balance between the required formalities demanded by the need for certainty, and the necessary elasticity required to protect individual or collective consent, rights, and wills.

During the classical period, Roman lawyers applied new abstract methods of thought imported from Greek culture. This allowed, for instance, the development of the idea of ownership as a right; the idea of consensual contract as a sort of legal obligation; the idea of good faith as a pillar of some reciprocal legal relations; and many other ideas and concepts at the heart of the Western legal tradition. Finally, classical Roman law also fostered the use of writing in the legal field. That happened specifically in the area of litigation with the introduction of formulary procedure, which provided a new remedial structure for the resolution of legal conflicts based on a written document (*formula*) approved by the praetor at the request of the parties. The link between the classical period and legal procedure is so strong that the classical period ended along with the fading of formulary procedure around 230 CE.

Greek impact on Roman law

The influence of Greek civilization on Roman law is clear but complex and problematic. Paradoxically, Romans began to appreciate Greek culture just as Greek civilization began to decline. Roman superiority in the military and political realms was not an obstacle to admiring the intellectual excellence and preeminence of Greek models in philosophy, rhetoric, historiography, and poetry, among other things. It is said that the Roman army conquered the Greek world, but the Greek spirit conquered the Roman soul. This mutual relationship inspired Horace's famous epigram (*Epistles* 2.1.156–57): "Graecia capta ferum victorem cepit et artis / intulit agresti Latio" (Captive Greece took captive her fierce conqueror, and introduced her arts into the rude region of Latium).

In the specific field of Roman law, according to an ancient tradition, the commission charged to draw up the Roman code of the Twelve Tables (451–450 BCE) traveled from Rome to Athens to study and analyze in depth the laws of Solon, and they actually incorporated some of those precepts. In 155 BCE, a delegation of relevant members of the Athenian Peripatetic, Academic, and Stoic schools visited and spoke before the Roman Senate. Of these schools, the Stoic was the main source of influence on Roman legal education.

Founded in Athens by Zeno of Citium in the early third century BCE, Stoic teaching was based on the idea that reason constitutes the essential nature of human beings. This idea is summed up in the famous Stoic maxim, "Live according to nature." The Scipionic circle developed this Stoic view of the world. This circle was a kind of literary society patronized by Scipio Aemilianus (185–129 BCE), extremely active in the middle of the second century BCE, and composed of philosophers, poets, and politicians who promoted Greek culture and values. The Stoic spirit also animated almost all the Roman jurists and many of the Roman thinkers during both the Republic and the Empire (Cicero, Seneca, Marcus Aurelius).

Roman jurists made little use of Greek philosophy in general, but Greek thought stimulated them, especially during the Hellenistic period of Roman jurisprudence, from the close of the Second Punic War (201 BCE) to the beginning of the Principate by Octavian (27 BCE). One of the most important intellectual tools Roman jurists received from the Greeks was the dialectical method. According to this mode of argumentation, material should be organized in an orderly system by a process of division and subdivision into genera and species. The criteria of classification were made by establishing differences, on the one hand, and analogies or affinities, on the other. The conception of the law of nations (*ius gentium*), and the aedilitian edict, with important innovations in the law of sale, are among other things, good examples of the influence of Greek law upon Roman law. Another notable contribution of Greek ideas to Roman law was the supremacy of intention or will (*voluntas*) over words (*verba*). As the jurist Celsus put it, "knowing the laws does not mean simply grasping the words, but their force and scope" (D. 1.3.17: "scire leges non hoc est verba earum tenere, sed vim ac potestatem"). Finally, the Roman concept of equity (*aequitas*) deserves mention as a concrete specification of the Greek concept *epieikeia*.

Iustitia

The Roman jurists did not develop a theory of the foundations of justice, and they did not discuss its nature, as Greek philosophers did. Although in their high moral consciousness Roman jurists captured the concept of substantive justice, they rarely appealed to the ethical foundations of justice, probably because of the simplicity of their legal style and their intuitive resistance to abstraction. In their instructional writings, they just accommodated Greek philosophy to the Roman spirit and character.

Unlike the Roman jurists, Cicero, who classified himself as a thinker working outside of jurisprudence (*Brutus* 41.151; *Pro Murena* 13, 29–30; *De oratore* 41.141), explored the idea of justice in his dialogue *De officiis* [On duties, 44 BCE], in which he considered this virtue the most distinguished of all of them (*De officiis* 1.20). According to Cicero, justice and beneficence are two categories of the same virtue (*De officiis* 1.20) that involves the idea of respect for each human being and for humanity as a collectivity. Justice has two aspects: one negative and another positive. The negative aspect demands not doing any harm to anyone, unless provoked by a wrongful or unlawful act. The positive requires using common things as common and private things as private. Any taking of private property constitutes a violation of human fellowship, and therefore it is a genuine injustice (*De officiis* 1. 21). Justice also demands treating our opponents with respect and honesty. Even those adversaries who have wronged someone must be treated morally. Vengeance and punishment must be limited. These duties of justice are to be observed even with regard to slaves, who should be treated as if they were employees (*De officiis* 1.41).

In relation to warfare, Cicero held that war must be the last resort after all negotiations have failed. The proper concern of human beings, who are not beasts, is to resolve conflicts by negotiation and not by force. For this reason, discussions to avoid war are always more desirable than the force of war itself (*De officiis* 1.34). War should be formally announced and declared, and can be justified only when one party has been grievously wronged by another. Promises made to the enemy must be faithfully kept. During war, the foe has to be treated mercifully, and after the end of the conflict, the vanquished party should be given fair treatment, including the possibility of receiving citizenship, as the Romans' forebears did with the Tusculani, the Aequi, the Volsci, or the Sabini (*De officiis* 1.35).

Relying predominantly on Stoic philosophy, and consequently on Ciceronian definitions, the jurist Ulpian defined justice as "the perpetual and constant will to give to each his or her own" (D. 1.1.10 pr = Inst. 1.1pr: "constans et perpetua voluntas ius suum cuique tribuendi"). This famous definition, promoted by Emperor Justinian in his important codification, has been largely accepted in Western legal culture into our own day.

Ius

The word *ius* is derived from Jupiter or Jove (in Latin: *Iuppiter*; genitive: *Iovis*). In ancient Roman religion and myth, Jupiter was the god of sky and thunder, the king of the gods, and the chief deity of the Roman state religion, laws, and social order. However, Hugo Grotius (*De iure belli ac pacis. Prolegomena* 13 note 3) preferred the derivation of *ius* from the word *iussum* (command), just as the word *os* (bone) was a shortening of *ossum*. Though interesting, Grotius's etymology is incorrect.

Ius is an ambiguous word that could be used in singular (*ius*) or plural (*iura*). There is no Greek equivalent for the Latin word *ius*, nor does it have an exact equivalent in English, although many English words come from *ius*: justice, jurisprudence, jurist, adjudication, jurisdiction, among others. Most of the time, *ius* should be translated as "law" (or "the laws"), in the objective sense of a legal order or whole body of norms, rules, and standards, but sometimes it can mean "right," in the many subjective senses of this English word. In the broadest sense, *ius* embraced the whole of the Roman legal system (*iura populi Romani*). *Ius* could also refer to a field of the law: public, private, natural, and so on, or even to an exceptional provision for certain groups of people (*ius singulare*). *Ius* can indicate the status of a person, whether legally independent (*sui iuris*) or under the power of another (*alieni iuris*). *Ius* also referred to the place where the praetor administers the law. For instance, the expression *in ius vocatio* (calling the defendant before the magistrate) was the technical term in Roman law for the act by which civil proceedings were initiated.

The legitimacy of *ius* lay in the tradition of the Roman community recognized by citizens. Norms, rules, standards, and statutes were not properly a new creation of the legal order but an expression of the vitality of that tradition of ideas, usages, and customs (*mores maiorum*). The Roman jurist Celsus (D. 1.1.1pr) elegantly defined *ius* as "the art of goodness and fairness" (*ius est ars boni et aequi*). This definition is close to that offered by the jurist Paul on natural law (D. 1.1.11): "what always is fair and good" (*id quod semper aequum ac bonum est*). Just as medicine is the art of healing, so law was the art of doing justice. And law, like medicine, was to be sought for its own benefit. According to the Roman jurist Ulpian (D.1.1.10.1= Inst. 1.1.3), the three basic principles of the law were: to live honestly, not to harm anybody, and to render to everyone his or her own. In this famous sentence, *ius* is synonymous with justice.

From the fourth century, the participle *derectum* (or *directum*) was introduced into legal vocabulary to describe the perfection of justice and fairness. In the term *derectum*, the moral and the juridical dimensions are indissolubly connected. *Directum* means "directed," "guided," "correct." *Ius directum* (right law) is the law that determines the right direction, the good way, the correct path for citizens to follow in social intercourse. Specifically, it referred to law that embodied the values of stoicism and, particularly, of Christianity.

From *directum* comes the English word *right*, the German word *Recht*, the Spanish word *derecho*, the French word *droit*, the Italian word *diritto*, and the Portuguese word *direito*, among others. It can be said that *ius* expresses the religious origin of law, whereas *derectum* (right) represents the inescapable relation between law and morality. In the idea of a right, the moral and legal connotations are inseparable, as rights touch upon personal claims and social order alike.

Ius publicum and *ius privatum*

The distinction between public and private law was not of any technical significance for Roman jurists, but it was a general classification rooted in Greek thought. Because of its ambiguity, the exact delimitation between public law and private law is of great complexity. Often public law meant constitutional law, that is, the foundational identity of the Romans; sometimes public law was a general expression to refer to positive law. In some texts, *ius publicum* was almost equivalent to public order, compelling law, and peremptory law.

When jurists used both public law and private law together, they were referring to the whole of the Roman legal system.

Ulpian (D. 1.1.1.2 = Inst. 1.1.4) roughly defined public law as the law that regarded the state of the Roman commonwealth (*quod ad statum rei Romanae spectat*). By contrast, he defined private law as the law governing relations between private individuals (*ad singulorum utilitatem*). In general, public law was established for the interest of the political community or the people. It covered everything that was not concerned with the private interest of individual citizens. Public law dealt with the constitution, administration, and functioning of the Roman political community. It integrated and combined religion and administration of the political community. It was concerned with magistrates, priests, and sacred things. Public law basically emanated from legislative organs: popular assemblies, the Senate, and the emperor.

While public law was a collective product of generations of senators and magistrates, private law was a manifestation of the free will of the individual. It was an expression of individual rights and freedoms, though it was not governed just by self-interest. The idea of moral duty did not disappear from it. Roman jurists devoted their interest and efforts mainly to private law, not to pubic law. The distinction between private and public law was increasingly developed beginning in the second half of the second century as a result of the elaboration of a science of administrative law by emperors and the central bureaucracy.

The most important practical difference between Roman public law and private law was that "public law cannot be changed by agreements concluded between private individuals" (Papinian, D. 2.14.38). However, at the heart of both public and private law lay the idea that public law could not eclipse or replace private law.

In Roman law, public law was an expansion of private law, and not vice versa, because the individual – the citizen – and not the political community was the center of the Roman legal system. Public law proceeded from private law. This original model of the construction of the law, from the bottom up and not from the top down, ought to be transferred to all legal spheres, including global law in our own day.

It was Roman private law, and not public law, that prevailed in the civil law tradition, especially in continental Europe, after the fall of the Roman Empire. Still, many aspects of Roman public law inspired political thinkers as well as important legal documents, including the Constitution of the United States. In our day, Roman public law constitutes a source of inspiration for global constitutionalism.

Ius civile

The expression *ius civile* (civil law) is ambiguous. Etymologically, it means the law of the Roman citizens, the law that binds only the Romans. In earlier times, civil law was a synonym of *ius Quiritium*, which was the primitive law of the Romans. *Quirites* (singular *quiris*, "spear") was the name of the citizens of ancient Rome. In this sense, civil law was the law of individuals who were full Roman citizens, the law of their rights and duties. In the Republican period, *ius civile* was often used as a synonym for private law, but in a narrow sense: civil law referred to the body of rules the Roman jurists developed by means of interpretation. The earliest treatises of civil law addressed almost exclusively topics of private law. Civil law was the body of law the jurists made, in contraposition to the sacral law (*ius sacrum, pontificium*), the praetorian law (*ius honorarium* or *ius praetorium*), the natural law (*ius naturale*), and the law of nations (*ius gentium*). Ulpian, in Digest 1.1.6, differentiated the civil law, which he considered *proprium* or local (*ius proprium, id est civile*), from a common law comprising both the law of nations and natural law.

In the Middle Ages, the expression "civil law" was identified with Roman law in contraposition to particular laws of different European territories, English common law, and canon law. Civil law and English common law would, in time, become jurisdictionally exclusive to the point that the defining mark of civil law would be that it was not common law, and that of common law that it was not civil law. English common lawyers ultimately treated all that was not properly English law (with the exception of canon law) as civil law. The chief difference between them was that while civil law developed fundamentally in the nascent universities, English common law developed out of the practices of the royal judges. The combination of canon law, feudal law, and Roman law formed the European *ius commune*, which was the common legal system of legal thought in Western Europe between 1100 and 1800. Jurists and theologians then agreed that the two aspects of justice, the divine and the human, were deeply related. Ironically, Roman law started being a law proper to the Romans in opposition to other common laws (natural law and law of nations) only to then become part of the European common law in opposition to the particular laws of different political communities.

Ius naturale

Deeply inspired by the doctrines of Plato, Aristotle, and the Stoics, Cicero provided the most complete theory of natural law. According to Cicero (*De legibus* 3.17–19), law (*ius*) could not be derived from the Twelve Tables, the praetor's edict, or other Roman legal sources, but arose from the deepest recesses of philosophy. The law could not be confined to the narrow corner of civil law. Among the most important principles of justice were that law represents rational principles, inherent in nature, that enjoin what ought to be done and forbid the opposite. Law is a natural force, the reason of the wise man, and the criterion of justice and injustice. Because there is nothing superior to reason, and reason is present in both God and humanity, there is a basic partnership between divine reason and human reason (*De legibus* 1. 23). Those who share reason share the law, and those who share the law share justice. This law, in harmony with nature, Cicero argued, is unchanging and eternal; it cannot be invalidated, nor can it be in any way amended, nor can it be rescinded altogether. No decree of the Senate or decision of the people can exempt human beings from the fulfillment of natural law, and no individual needs anyone else to explain or expound it (*De re publica* 3.33). There will not be, Cicero insisted, "one such law in Rome and another in Athens, one now and another in the future, but all peoples at all times will be embraced by a single and eternal and unchangeable law; and there will be, as it were, one lord and master of all of us – the God who is the author, supporter, and interpreter of that law. Whoever refuses to obey it will be turning his back on himself" (*De re publica* 3.33). Based on the idea of natural law, Cicero affirmed that even a statute properly enacted should not take away the most basic rights of Roman citizens, including their freedom (*Pro Caecina*, 33.95–97).

Unlike Cicero, however, Roman jurists did not develop dogmatically or systematically the idea of natural law, but they often used the concept in different fields of legal interpretation. Hundreds of texts in their legal literature referred to natural law, natural reason, the nature of things, and other expressions of this sort. According to Roman jurists, natural law does not imply any specific conception of law, or a concrete system of legal rules, but indicates a way of interpreting reality. "Natural" means what is reasonable according to the human standards of knowledge, behavior, or social expectations and therefore does not demand further evidence.

Based on natural interpretation, Roman jurists defended the idea that persons who have not yet reached puberty must be taken care of by someone else (Gaius 1.189); that an insane person could not make or accept a promise (Gaius, D. 44.7.1.12); that persons related by blood were tied together (Modestinus, D. 38.10.14.2); that individuals have the right of self-defense against an existing attack (Gaius, D. 9.2.4pr.); that no one is obliged to perform the impossible (Celsus, D. 50.17.185); that something belonging to nobody or captured in war becomes the property of the first person to take possession of it (Gaius 2.66, 69); and that the union of a man and a woman is called marriage (Ulpian, D. 1.1.1.3).

Natural law played an important role in regulating slavery, which is the primary example of an institution contrary to nature but recognized by the law of nations. By nature, and therefore in accordance with natural law, all human beings are equal and free. Because slaves are human beings, slavery is against natural law. Under civil law and the law of nations, however, slaves are considered things, not persons, and are therefore not subjects but objects of rights. Following the Stoic outlook, Ulpian affirmed that all human beings are free and should live in accordance to nature: "as far as concerns the civil law, slaves are regarded as nonexisting [persons]; not, however, in the natural law, because as far as concerns the natural law, all men are equal" (D. 50.17.32; see also Ulpian, D. 1.1.4pr.). Florentinus (D. 1.5.4pr.) also insisted that, although slavery was an institution of the law of nations, it is contrary to nature for one man to be the property of another.

Ius gentium

The general rule of antiquity was that the law of a community (civil law) was applied only to the members of that community, and that the stranger was without rights. In the absence of a treaty with a foreign community, a Roman could seize a foreigner as a slave, and foreign property belonged to the first Roman comer as goods without an owner.

It was Cicero, again, who applied the Greek philosophical system to international relations, coining the expression *ius gentium* in the process. The most significant mention can be found in the moral essay *De officiis* 3.17.69. After speaking of society in the broad sense as uniting all people with each other, Cicero referred to lesser societies made up of *gentes*, or those formed into cities. Finally, Cicero pointed out that the ancients desired two kinds of law: the law of nations and civil law – the former ideally being a part of the latter. Cicero considered the law of nations to be the juridical embodiment of nature. For him, the *ius gentium* oscillated between the two great coordinates of human justice set down by the Greek philosophers and refined by the Roman jurists: *natura* and *fides*. People should follow nature as they follow a ruler; they should observe faith and trust (*fides*) as the cornerstone of justice (*De officiis* 1.1.23).

Two decades younger than Cicero, Sallust employed the expression *ius gentium* in his famous narration of Rome's war against Jugurtha, the king of Numidia, written about 40 BCE, four years after Cicero's *De officiis*. Livy, however, offered further confirmation. He employed the expression *ius gentium* some forty times to refer, sometimes imprecisely, to the relationship between Rome and other peoples of the world through ambassadors and treaties. The prohibition of the maltreatment or killing of ambassadors (4.17.4); the possibility of noxal surrender of a legate who misbehaves in the territory where his mission takes him (5.36.6); observance of treaties (4.19.3); and lawful defense against armed attacks not preceded by declarations of war (42.41.11) – all were for Livy characteristic issues in the law of nations. The idea of *ius gentium* was especially developed in the areas of commercial law, the law of contracts, the law of treaties, the law of diplomacy, and the law of war. However, Roman law of family and succession remained basically intact.

Seneca and Tacitus used the expression *ius gentium*, as did the jurists of the second century: Celsus, Gaius, and Cervidius Scaevola. In the beginning of the third century, Papinian and Triphoninus – advisers to Emperor Septimius Severus – and Ulpian also used it. Of all these, one passage in Gaius and one in Ulpian deserve some attention because of the part they played in the history of the concept's subsequent development.

Gaius spoke of *ius gentium* at the beginning of his *Institutes* (1.1.1) and contrasted it, as did Cicero, with *ius civile*. Gaius said that civilized peoples – that is, those organized according to law and custom – govern themselves partly by their own law and partly by the law common to all people. The law proper to the city is civil law; the one established by natural reason among all people is called the law of nations because of its universal observance. Natural reason determines, in the abstract, what the law of nations is or could be, and its enforced general application among nations makes it so concretely. With Ulpian, however, Cicero's and Gaius's bipartite division becomes tripartite (civil law, law of nature, law of nations). According to Ulpian (D. 1.1.1.3), the reason for this is that the law of nations would be common only to people, whereas the natural law would in general encompass animals as well.

The application of *ius civile* throughout the Roman Empire, particularly under the Antonine Constitution of 212 CE, which extended Roman citizenship to all inhabitants of the empire, meant that the importance of the distinction between the law of nations and civil law would gradually fade. The Emperor Justinian adopted Gaius's definition of *ius gentium* and its later three-way division by Ulpian in the sixth century in his *Institutes* (1.2.1) and *Digest* (1.1.1.2). Later, these passed through the Byzantine Empire to medieval Europe with the discovery of the Digest. In the West, Isidore of Seville (560–636) was the vessel transmitting Gaius's concept of the *ius gentium*.

Ius fetiale

Precursor of the *ius gentium* was the fetial law (*ius fetiale*). Fetials were members of a college of priests, ranked just below the pontifical college and the augural college. The college of fetials was created in the Monarchy to be responsible for the religious conduct of international relations. It contained twenty lifetime members who were chosen by co-optation from noble families. The fetials upheld the fetial law, the sacral law concerning the international relations (Cicero, *De officiis* 1.36 and Livy 9.9.3). They prepared the formal demand of a foreign community for restitution of wrongs, and they acted as public ambassadors of the Roman people.

Whenever the fetials confirmed that the gods had made a judgment in favor of the Romans, they were responsible for demanding satisfaction from the foreign community. The demand was repeated three times at intervals of ten days. If restitution was not made, the college of fetials certified to the Senate the existence of a just and pious cause of war (*bellum iustum et pium*). Nevertheless, responsibility for determining war rested with the Senate. As a declaration of war, one of the fetials called the *pater patratus* threw a spear, which had been dipped in blood, into enemy territory and recited a ritual formula (Livy 1.32.13). But the fetials did not play any role in conducting the war or in accepting the surrender of an enemy city. They were only emissaries of peace. The bronze tablet from Alcántara (Cáceres, Spain), discovered in 1983 and kept at the Cáceres Museum, registers the surrender made in 104 BCE to Lucius Caesius, the governor of Hispania Ulterior, by the Spanish community of Seano. In the tablet, however, there is no mention of the fetials. Fetial law was not instrumental in the process of world domination but was important in the legitimation of international relations.

Fas

A fundamental concept in Roman religion, *fas* referred to the lawfulness of human conduct before the deities. Its antonym, *nefas,* meant the violation of a divine prohibition that could trigger the vengeance of the gods on the offender. Unlike human law and divine law, *ius* and *fas* were not opposite terms, since both expressed a permissibility of conduct in accordance with the gods. *Fas* was thus both distinct from and related to *ius*. We can find the intrinsic relationship between the two terms in the famous statement *fas et iura sinunt* (religion and law allow it) used by Virgil (*Georgica* 1.269), or in the expression *ius fasque* (lawful and proper) used by Plautus (*Cistellaria* 20).

At the core of Roman law was the strong conviction that the divine and the legal are intrinsically linked; thus, the legal order expresses only a portion of a much broader normative domain. After the first stage of the long process of secularization of the idea of *ius, ius* and *fas* began to operate in separate provinces – *fas* in the religious realm, and *ius* only in the realm of human conduct in relation to other humans. Nevertheless, the link between the human and the divine was never broken. According to the Roman approach, the gods continued supporting the process of creating the legal order although they no longer directly created the law. The idea of a religious legal system (divine law, pontifical law, sacral law, and so on) including the notion of *fas* in contrast with the secular legal system (*ius humanum*) was developed only in later antiquity (see Isidore of Seville, *Etymologiae* 5.2.12).

In Roman calendars, *dies fasti* (marked F) were the days of the month on which it was permissible to transact legal affairs, and the magistrate was allowed to give judgments. The name was further expanded to the days on which summoning the popular assemblies (*comitia*) and the Senate (*dies comitiales*) was allowed.

Jurisprudentia

Jurisprudentia is the legal science developed by Roman jurists. Inspired by Greek philosophy, it was defined by Ulpian as "the knowledge of things divine and human, of the just and unjust" (D. 1.1.10.2 = Inst. 1.1.1).

Roman legal science emerged in the middle of the Republic, grew up in the turbulent period of the late Republic, and greatly developed in the Principate, especially under the peace and economic prosperity of the administrations of Trajan, Hadrian, and the Antonine dynasty (138–93 CE). The legal science of the Principate is usually called "classical."

Rome was the first political community in which jurists emerged. The construction of Roman law was an undertaking of a relatively small and specialized group of jurists deeply involved in political affairs, administration, and legal practice. They discussed legal cases and provided legal opinions based on reasoned argument. In legal writings, it was common for jurists to cite one another's legal opinions to persuade their colleagues. These jurists were the true architects of the impressive and solid edifice of Roman law. In this sense, Roman law constituted a true jurist's law, a *Juristenrecht*, to use the German expression. Roman jurists focused on creating and developing the law, not on philosophical speculations and legal abstractions. Nor were they interested in comparative law, foreign law, or legal history.

Classical legal science applied common techniques and methods. The legal vocabulary the jurists used was consistent and homogeneous to the point that the imprint of particular jurists, even in the case of the leading jurists (Sabinus, Julian, Papinian), is barely noticeable. Individual style, however, varied: Celsus was identified for his elegant and epigrammatic style; Julian for his sober, clear, and simple style; Cervidius Scaevola for his brevity and absence of reasons for decisions; Papinian for his terseness and precision. The degree of originality was also different: Labeo, Sabinus, and Julian were extremely innovative jurists; Pomponius and Ulpian, however, were less creative than the previous ones.

The elaboration of a jurisprudential law demanded: a) instruction of new jurists by professional teachers; b) the capacity of jurists to assume ultimate responsibility for the quality of legal doctrines; c) freedom of discussion and disputation and, as a result, the existence of divergent and contradictory opinions among jurists; d) the permanent connection of jurists with the daily administration of the law; and e) the elaboration of a literature to nourish the continuity of a well-educated group of jurists with a comprehensive knowledge of the whole legal corpus.

Mores maiorum

The Romans possessed a special veneration for tradition, precedent, and authority. They esteemed ancestral customs (*mores maiorum*), the ways of their forebears, and their tradition of usages and ideas, particularly in the field of law. They kept a notable spirit of traditionalism. The Romans were reluctant to abolish any valid law, because they considered their ancestors part of the Roman people. They had a deeply rooted distaste of unnecessary changes and greatly distrusted novelty. They did not like fast innovations, hurried modifications, and revolutionary attitudes. They tried to build on what their ancestors had built, exquisitely respecting key legal decisions adopted in the past. This conservative attitude explains the preservation for centuries of the rigid and severe formalism that characterizes the primitive legal system. An edict of the censor of 92 BCE excluding the Latin rhetors (Suetonius, *De rhetoribus* 1), reveals this fundamental attitude of respect for the legal tradition: "all innovations in the usage and customs of our forefathers do not please us or seem proper." In imperial legislation, references to ancestral customs are frequent.

At the heart of the Romans' conservatism and respect for tradition lay the idea that justice, as a constant, continual, and perpetual individual and collective will, required careful and gradual historical development. The leader was the people, as an eternal community, and not this or that particular lawgiver. As Cicero explained through Cato the Elder, one of the reasons the

Roman constitution was superior to others is because it was established not by the great ability of a great man but by that of many, and not in the course of one man's life but over several ages and generations (*De re publica* 2.1.2). The Roman family was instrumental in passing along the *mores maiorum* down through the generations.

Probably because of this passionate love for their own tradition, the Romans were not easily attracted by foreign legal institutions and ideas. The Romans adopted foreign law gingerly and cautiously, and they always applied it with an evident and explicit Roman method and style. Early Roman law was customary in nature, and Roman jurists greatly appreciated all equitable usages recognized by their ancestors (*mores maiorum*). But Roman jurists did not admit customary law in the sense of customs directly binding upon judges. Custom made law only indirectly, through interpretation. It was not an autonomous source of law (see Gaius 1.2), but neither could it be neglected. Emperor Justinian accepted custom as a source of unwritten law, although probably it did not play an important role in the legal practice of his time. Nevertheless, the historical relevance of this inclusion was enormous.

Lex

Different from *ius*, but complementary to it, was the idea of *lex*. Cicero (*De legibus* 1.19) argued that *lex* comes from choosing and is an essential property of the concept. In relation to private transactions, *lex* was a particular clause of the contract or a condition imposed on a party. Expressions such as *lex venditionis* (a condition inserted by a seller in a contract of sale) or *lex donationis* (a term included by the donor in the act of donation), among others, occur frequently in legal writings.

In the public realm, the primary meaning of *lex* was a statute. The definition of *lex publica* offered by Roman jurists was simply descriptive. Ateius Capito defined the public *lex* as "a general decree of the people (*populus*), or of the commoners (*plebs*), answering an appeal made to them by a magistrate" (Gellius, *Noctes Atticae* 10.20.2). Gaius (1.3) restricted the term *lex* to "what the people order and decree," reserving the word *plebiscitum* to refer to "what the commoners (plebeians) order and establish."

In Roman law, the distinction between *ius* and *lex* was so fundamental that it has been preserved by all languages of civil legal systems: German: *Recht* and *Gesetz;* Spanish: *derecho* and *ley*; French: *droit* and *loi*; Italian: *diritto* and *legge*. The reason is that *ius* was deeply related to *auctoritas,* whereas *lex* was profoundly related to *potestas. Ius* was a product of the moral authority of the jurists, but *lex* was a product of the coercive power of the magistrates and the assemblies. English, like Greek, has no accurate counterparts to *ius* and *lex*. It can be said, however, that *ius* and *lex* are more or less related as the body of law (*ius*) is to a statute (*lex*).

The volume of Roman legal statutes on private law is particularly small in the classical period because Roman jurists maintained certain reservations concerning statutes. Classical Roman law was truly a case-law system, not a statute-law system. It was casuistic in nature. The Roman spirit, unlike the Greek one, was firmly opposed to codification. Inspired by the Hellenistic culture, Pompey and Julius Caesar were captivated by the idea of a codification, but neither proceeded with it.

During the Later Empire (284–476), legislation absorbed all sources of Roman law. As a result, *lex* began to be used interchangeably with *ius* to refer to the body of law. The Anglo-American common law tradition conceived law based on the postclassical, more expansive concept of *lex*.

Auctoritas and *potestas*

The distinction between moral authority (*auctoritas*) and constituted power (*potestas*) was mainly of social character, but sometimes it acquired legal relevance in both private and public Roman law. *Auctoritas* comes from *augere*, which means "to increase, to grow, to fulfill." *Auctoritas* is the influence that derives from personal respect, wisdom, and virtue without having the legal force of power. *Auctoritas* is a consequence not only of persuasive speech but also of the nods and gestures that accompany it (Cicero, *De senectute* 61). *Potestas* instead comes from the Indo-European lexeme *pot-* that refers to established power. Paul (D. 50.16.215) stated that "the word *potestas* has different meanings: in the person of a magistrate, it means supreme political power (*imperium*); in the person of a child, it means paternal power; in the person of a slave, ownership."

The division of roles between the *auctoritas* of augurs, jurists, judges, and senators, on the one hand, and the *potestas* of magistrates and the paterfamilias, on the other hand, served to establish not only a wise and healthy political, social, and legal balance in society but also an ontological equilibrium. Because power was considered indivisible by nature (Cicero, *De re publica* 1.38.60), power as such had to respond to something or someone beyond itself, and be limited by an external agent (i.e., by moral authority). In Rome, one person commanded and a different one authorized. Authority was, therefore, an effective check upon Roman power.

The most primitive manifestation of the distinction between moral authority and power lay in the role of the college of augurs. Augur, from *augeo* and related to "augment," denotes the idea of increasing, adding to, expanding, fulfilling what has been not yet fulfilled. The augurs were able to recognize the signs of the will of the gods in the behavior of birds, interpreting these as an indication of divine approval or disapproval of a proposed action. Before making their decisions on critical issues, the kings often asked the augural college for advice. Therefore, the sacral authority of the augural college and the political power of the kings formed a propitious unity at the beginning of Roman history. The Republican Senate expanded the role of the earlier college of augurs.

At the heart of the Roman Republican constitution, the relation between authority and power can be found again in the famous initialism SPQR

(*Senatus Populusque Romanus*): the Senate and People of Rome. The moral authority of the Senate (*auctoritas Senatus*) effectively limited and controlled the executive power of the magistrates (*potestas* or *imperium*), which was a materialization of popular majesty (*maiestas Populi*). As Cicero pointed out, "a compromise takes place whereby the power is vested in the people, but authority in the hands of the Senate" (*De legibus* 2.30). We can also find this distinction between authority and power in the dual structure of the classical Roman civil procedure or formulary system: the first stage took place before the magistrate, vested with power, and the second stage before the judge, vested with authority. We also find the distinction between authority and power in the institution of guardianship and even the solemn form of conveyance of ownership or *mancipatio*. With the start of the Principate, this well-balanced order based on the relationship between authority and power was substantially altered. Augustus's decision to rule the Republican institutions with his superior personal moral authority (*auctoritas Principis*) eventually led to the full identification of authority and power in the person of the emperor.

In some sense, the distinction between power and authority was reborn in the Middle Ages, when royal power was counterpoised by papal authority. The modern nation-state fully identified authority with political power. This is one of the reasons the distinction between authority and power has been blurred in modern languages, including English.

Dignitas

Closely associated with *auctoritas* is Roman dignity or worthiness (*dignitas*). *Dignitas* is the respect, recognition, and deference that people bestowed on the magistrates and senators. It contains the sense of elevation, eminence, admiration, and reputation. *Dignitas* referred to the high social status of those who held public offices because they were representatives of the political community who had to preserve the law, to administer justice, and to take care of all things entrusted to them (Cicero, *De officiis* 1.124).

In some sense, Cicero (*De officiis* 1.106) expanded dignity to all citizens when he considered the superiority and dignity of the human condition over that of the animals. The Romans, however, always recognized degrees of dignity as an inherent element of a stratified society. Free people had more dignity than slaves, for instance. Ulpian (D. 1.9.1pr.) stated that men had more dignity than women, and married women more than female concubines (D. 32.49.4). Cicero himself criticized democracy because it does not allow various degrees of dignity (*De re publica* 1.43).

Aequitas

Greek philosophers developed the idea of equity (in Greek, *epieikeia*; in Latin, *aequitas*) quite early, and Aristotle provided the best formulation in *Nicomachean Ethics* (5.10.1137b; see also *Rhetoric* 1.13). The strict and uncritical interpretation and application of the general law, without considering particular circumstances or the law's deepest purpose, can be a source of unfairness and hardship. As an appeal to morality, sometimes law should be corrected because it is not possible to generalize accurately. Greek equity provided the corrective and creative element that favored a more benevolent interpretation of law.

The Roman orators rendered Greek *epieikeia* into Roman *aequitas*. Cicero pointed out that every boy's teacher instructed him how to argue in different cases, sometimes for the letter of the statute, sometimes for equity (*De oratore* 1.57.244). He included *aequitas* as a part of positive law, as a criterion of correctness of law (*Topica* 5.28), and he regarded civil law as constitutional fairness (*Topica* 2.9: *aequitas constituta*).

Although the Republican jurists knew the Greek idea of equity thoroughly, the distinction between law and equity was pointless for them. The idea of Greek equity was so vague and useless that they could not justify a decision on that basis. Roman lawyers perceived that the law should be interpreted according to standards of reasonableness in any concrete case. So it was not a matter of correcting the law (*ius*) by equity (*aequitas*) but of searching for the right solution for the legal issue. For Roman lawyers, *aequum est* meant nothing else than *iustum est*, that is, the legal solution for a concrete case in accordance with justice. When a jurist in a legal opinion declared that a solution was "equal" (*aequum est*) he was confirming that it was right and just, and that such was the law, and that any other decision would be contrary to the law. The fragments of Servius (D. 3.5.20[21]pr.) and Alfenus Varus (D. 44.1.14) appealing to equity to justify the praetorian remedy seem to confirm this idea.

Since the end of the Republic, the Roman idea of *aequitas* as a founding element of law inspired many legal decisions. Sometimes, however, *ius* and *aequitas* appeared separable, with *aequitas* an external corrective element of law, according to the Greek approach. In Justinian's law, extensively influenced by Hellenism, Roman *aequitas* was identified with Greek *epieikeia* and with new Christian ideals. Ethical values of mercy, benevolence, and compassion, inspired by Christianity, were needed to correct the rigor of the law in the administration of justice.

Utilitas

In Ciceronian thought, public interest (*utilitas rei publicae*) and stability (*salus*) were the twofold aims of the law (*De inventione* 1.68). Public interest served as a principle for the legitimation of new statutes, a standard for legal interpretation, and a guideline for jurisprudential activity. Papinian (D. 1.1.7.1.) mentioned public interest as the ultimate ground for the validity of praetorian law, and Ulpian (D. 4.1.2) did not hesitate to put the idea of utilitas at the center of any legal change: "in determining new rules, there ought to be some clear advantage (utilitas) in view, as to whether a law which has been considered just for a long time is to be modified." Drawing upon Greek philosophy and the Ciceronian understanding of utilitas, classical jurists abundantly invoked the idea of utilitas (in the general sense of practicality, social interest, and sound policy) as a good reason to explain the acceptance of a concrete and pragmatic legal solution instead of another solution based on strict logical and dogmatic reasoning. They advocated for the validity of some manumissions, testaments, or stipulations as well as the institution of some remedies in cases in which strict interpretation of the law would have denied all of these things. Gaius (3.60), for instance, pointed out that it had been accepted on the basis of sound policy that, although a contract of mandate is discharged by the death of either party, if the mandatary continued to perform the duties after and in ignorance of the mandator's death, the mandatary could claim reimbursement for expenses from the mandator's heirs. On the other hand, Ulpian (D. 40.9.1) says that, based on practical grounds, Celsus had accepted the possibility that a man deaf from birth could manumit a slave, although it was obvious that the deaf man would not be able to hear the required legal words of the citizen who claimed the liberty of the slave involved. In both cases, the desire to meet the needs of legal practice led the lawyers to reach for a rationale and a solution beyond the strict application of the rules.

Fides

As a political community and as individual citizens, the Romans were proud of their integrity, honesty, and trustworthiness (*fides*). To be bound by one's word and remain faithful to it was the cornerstone of Roman justice: "Do in accordance with your words," Cicero urged (*De officiis* 1.23: *fit quod dictum est*). He considered *fides* the most sacred component in life (II *In Verrem* 3.3.6) and the very foundational element of justice (*De officiis* 1.23).

To extol the significance of *fides*, around 250 BCE the Romans built a temple dedicated to the goddess Fides on the Capitol as near as possible to the temple of Jupiter, the greatest of the Roman deities. Originally, *fides* was not an ethical concept but a religious one. It meant neither security nor moral reliability but the bondage or submission of a person to the sanctions of the deity. Later, the moral dimension of *fides* was developed further and began to refer to the ideas of trust, pledge, security, and moral responsibility against any kind of fraudulent behavior. This moral dimension was strengthened with the idea of good faith (*bona fides*) as a concrete expression of *fides* applied to contractual relations based on the reciprocal confidence of the parties.

In Roman law, the idea of *fides* illuminated at least two basic rules. First, legal norms have no retroactive force. In accordance with *fides*, legal repercussions and consequences of future human actions should be expected and certain. Second, the magistrate must be bound by his own norm. For instance, the *lex Cornelia* (67 BCE) bound praetors to their edicts.

Relations based on *fides* were abundant among the Romans. The relationship between a freedman and his patron, or between patrons and clients; the contracts of hospitality between individuals, between municipalities, or between individuals and municipalities; the relation of friendship and many contractual relations – all were deeply founded in both trust and trustworthiness. But relations based on *fides* were not just a priori limited to Roman citizens. They also were often with strangers. The concept of *ius gentium* was a legal development, probably the most relevant, of the idea of *fides* as a requirement of any international legal intercourse. This explains why in the temple of Fides the international treaties Rome adopted and other memorable state documents were placed for safekeeping.

Libertas

The Roman idea of liberty was basically conceived in negative terms, though not exclusively so. For the Romans, freedom meant, first of all, not to be owned by another. Free is the individual without owner, master, or *dominus*. *Libertas* is the status of nonslavery, the state of nondomination, the status of a free person and citizen in contrast to the slave. A free person is a master of himself or herself. A free person can serve his or her father but cannot serve a master. A free person can be limited by the power of the magistrate but always under legal guarantees.

By extension, free is the community that is not subject to the tyranny of a despotic royal power, a tyrant, or a foreign power. Historically, *libertas* emerged as a reaction to royal enslavement, particularly to the arrogance and despotic power of the Tarquins (Cicero, *De re publica* 2. 46). After the Tarquin family was sent into exile, two consuls, elected by the people and with limited terms of service, replaced the king. Roman *libertas* was an exclusive feature of the Roman Republic: all other nations could experience conditions of servitude, but not the Romans (Cicero, *Philippics* 20.20). This was the greatest rule of Rome (Cicero, *in Verrem* 2.63.163). The Roman people accepted the Principate that Augustus inaugurated because the *princeps* was not considered an absolute monarch, but a protector of Republican liberty, institutions, and practices.

In a broader and more positive sense, Cicero defined *libertas* as the power to live as you wish (Cicero, *Paradoxa stoicorum* 5.1.34: *potestas vivendi, ut velis*). In the second century CE, the jurist Florentinus (D. 1.5.4pr.), using similar terms, defined *libertas* as "the natural freedom of doing whatever one pleases unless it is banned by coercion or law." This definition was repeated in Justinian's *Institutes* (1.3.1) in the sixth century. The famous statement of jurist Paul (D. 50.17.106), that "freedom is inestimable," shows the reluctance to fix a sum on freedom in freedom proceedings.

The Romans often linked the idea of rights and the rights of the people (*iura Populi*) with the idea of liberty, and they even used the terms interchangeably. Specifically, liberty was closely related with ownership. Roman power refrained from interference with the private rights of individuals, particularly in relation to individual ownership. The institution of expropriation was, for instance, practically unknown to Roman law. Suetonius (*Augustus* 56) pointed out that Augustus made his forum narrower than he had planned because he did not venture to eject the owners of the neighboring houses. Another important consequence of this idea of liberty was that the *res publica* depended broadly on the free individual dynamism and private actions of citizens. Private spontaneous donations and individual gifts played an important role in the development of the city of Rome and other municipalities.

Humanitas

The Latin term *humanitas* (humanity) appeared for the first time in the Scipionic circle as an original Roman creation, and Cicero especially developed it. *Humanitas* revealed the Roman interest in the noblest aspects of the human being as the only living creature who participates in reason (*De legibus* 1.48). *Humanitas* was a civilizing instinct and one of the hallmarks of the Roman ethos.

The root of the concept can be found in two Greek ideas, *philantropia* (human kindness) and *paideia*, that is, the rearing and education in liberal arts and scientific disciplines to foster both active public service and a decent and fulfilling private life. The idea of *humanitas* referred to the splendor and dignity of the human being, superior to all other beings on the earth. It implied a duty of personal education and respect for others. *Homo humanus* was the well-educated citizen, familiar with Greek philosophy and culture, and submitted to the civil law as the best way to respect other people. Humanity was not only a form of human conduct but also the goal of personal striving, a personal quality that could be acquired. It required the moral development of human virtues: kindness, mercy, excellence, generosity, goodness, esteem, recognition, deference. Only those who followed and integrated these standards were really men in the full sense.

The implications of *humanitas* in Roman law were comprehensive. In the realm of constitutional law, *humanitas* demanded the rejection of any kind of tyranny because tyranny lacked humanity. The tyrant "is the foulest and most repellent creature imaginable. Although he has the external appearance of a man, he eclipses the wildest beast in the unmitigated savagery of his behavior" (Cicero, *De re publica* 2.48). In the realm of criminal law, humanity demanded that punishment would be moderated and controlled by the state; that only the guilty would be punished; and that the accused and witnesses should be protected and must not be tortured. The first salient application of *humanitas* in the penal domain was voluntary exile for the sake of escaping punishment. Voluntary exile did not come into existence by legislation but was a de facto creation. In the realm of private law, *humanitas* demanded a benevolent exercise of one's rights; respect and consideration of other citizens; mitigation of the costs of extreme adherence to formalism; and a tempering of justice with mercy, and of the rigor of the law with compassion and tenderness.

Elegantia

Etymologically, "elegance" comes from *eligere*, "to choose." In the schools of rhetoric, elegance was one of the features of good style. It demanded the correct choice of words in everyday speaking and writing. Elegance searched for harmony and simplicity, for clarity and intelligibility in language. Elegance ruled out exotic and ornamental rhetoric, and also vagueness, distraction, and uncertainty.

Cicero affirmed that, as well as an elegant style, there was a kind of elegant argument (*Brutus* 22–23; *Pro Plancio* 58). The capacity of choosing the proper argument was an important characteristic of Roman lawyers. The discussion of cases was the most natural place to display legal elegance. The jurist Maecianus (D. 46.3.103), for instance, considered Julian's opinion elegant when he argued that a payment of debt could be credited against any debt that the debtor could have been compelled to pay at the time of the payment. Cicero also referred to the elegance of his friend the jurist Servius Sulpicius Rufus (*Epistula ad familiares* 4.4). Celsus the Younger was an elegant jurist according to Ulpian (D. 1.1.1pr.), who had great sensitivity to evaluate elegance. Of the forty-six uses of the word "elegance" in the *Digest*, forty are Ulpian's.

As with the jurist, the attribute of elegance could be applied to the legislator. For instance, according to the law of nations, the child followed the status of the mother, unless legislation altered the rule. So, if a free woman cohabited with a male slave with the consent of his owner, the children were free; but according to a provision of the *senatus consultum Claudianum*, they were slaves. Gaius (1.84) wrote that Emperor Hadrian restored the rule of the law of nations and abolished this provision because of the injustice of the case and the inelegance of the law (*inelegantia iuris*). In the next paragraph, Gaius (1.85) affirmed that Vespasian also had used the same argument of inelegance against the legislation to restore the validity of the law of nations.

Pietas

Pietas was a religious attitude and a patriotic sense of duty and respect toward gods, parents, and other members of the family. Cicero defined piety as the virtue which "admonishes us to fulfill our duties to our country, our parents, and other relatives" (*De inventione* 2.22.66). *Pietas* was a distinctive and quintessential Roman ideal protected by the law and celebrated by Roman literature.

Aeneas's piety toward the gods and his family was stressed by Virgil (*Illiad*, 20.298–99; 347–48) and became paradigmatic in the Roman World. Pliny the Elder (*Naturalis Historia* 7.121), and Valerius Maximus (*Memorabilia* 5.4.7) referred to the legend of a daughter who was caught in the act of giving her breast milk to her starving and imprisoned mother. Instead of being punished, the daughter was recognized for her filial piety. Pietas Augusta appeared often in coins and inscriptions, and some Romans adopted *pius* as a family name or *cognomen*.

Roman law promoted piety. Although the paterfamilias had absolute power over his family, it had to be based on *pietas*, not savagery (Marcianus, D. 48.9.5). Emperor Trajan forced a father to emancipate his son because the father acted contrary to *pietas*. When the son died, Trajan denied the father possession of his son's property, to which he would otherwise have been entitled under Roman law (Papinian, D. 27.12.5). On the other hand, children were bound by filial duty, and to treat a parent disrespectfully, i.e., without obedience (*obsequium*) and submissive respect (*reverentia*), merited punishment. Imperial law, in general, did not allow family members to testify against each other in court (C.J. 4.20.6, 294 CE); emancipated children could sue their parent only after receiving official authorization (C.J. 2.2.2., 287 CE).

Further reading

Ando, Clifford, Paul J. du Plessis, and Kaius Tuori, eds. *The Oxford Handbook of Roman Law and Society*. Oxford and New York: Oxford University Press, 2016.

Bauman, Richard A. *Crime and Punishment in Ancient Rome*. London and New York: Routledge, 1996.

Bederman, David J. *International Law in Antiquity*. Cambridge and New York: Cambridge University Press, 2004.

Bellomo, Manlio. *The Common Legal Past of Europe (1000–1800)*. 2nd ed. Translated by Lydia G. Cochrane. Washington, DC: Catholic University of America Press, 1995.

Berger, Adolf. *Encyclopedic Dictionary of Roman Law*. Philadelphia, PA: The American Philosophical Society, 1953; reprint 1980.

Berman, Harold J. *Law and Revolution: The Formation of the Western Legal Tradition*. Cambridge, MA: Harvard University Press, 1983.

Domingo, Rafael. *Teoría de la auctoritas*. Pamplona: Eunsa, 1987.

Domingo, Rafael. *Auctoritas*. Barcelona: Ariel, 1999.

Domingo, Rafael. *The New Global Law*. Cambridge and New York: Cambridge University Press, 2010.

d'Ors, Álvaro. *Derecho privado romano*. 10th ed. Pamplona: Eunsa, 2004.

d'Ors, Álvaro. *Ensayos de teoría política*. Pamplona: Eunsa, 1977.

du Plessis, Paul J., ed. *Cicero's Law: Rethinking Roman Law of the Late Republic*. Oxford and New York: Oxford University Press, 2016.

Fiori, Roberto. *Bonus vir. Politica, retorica e diritto nel De officiis di Cicerone*. Naples: Jovene, 2011.

Giltaij, Jacob. "Greek Philosophy and Classical Roman Law. A Brief Overview." In *The Oxford Handbook of Roman Law and Society*, 188–199, edited by Paul de Plessis, Clifford Ando, and Kaius Tuori. Oxford, New York: Oxford University Press, 2016.

Hammer, Dean. *Roman Political Thought*. Cambridge and New York: Cambridge University Press, 2014.

Helmholz, R. H. *Natural Law in Court: A History of Legal Theory in Practice*. Cambridge, MA: Harvard University Press, 2015.

Honoré, Tony. *About Law: An Introduction*. Oxford: Clarendon Press, 1995.
Honoré, Tony. *Ulpian: Pioneer of Human Rights*. 2nd ed. Oxford and New York: Oxford University Press, 2002.
Iglesias, Juan. *Espíritu del Derecho romano*. 2nd ed. Madrid: Centro de Estudios Ramon Areces, 1991.
Johnston, David, ed. *The Cambridge Companion to Roman Law*. Cambridge and New York: Cambridge University Press, 2015.
Jolowicz, Herbert Felix. *Roman Foundations of Modern Law*. Oxford: Oxford University Press, 1957; reprint 1978.
Jolowicz, Herbert Felix, and Barry Nicholas. *Historical Introduction to the Study of Roman Law*. 3rd ed. Cambridge: Cambridge University Press, 1972.
Kaser, Max. *Das römische Privatrecht*. 2 vols. 2nd ed. Munich: Beck Verlag, 1971 and 1975.
Kelly, John M. *A Short History of Western Legal Theory*. Oxford: Clarendon Press, 1992.
Kingsbury, Benedict, and Benjamin Straumann, eds. *The Roman Foundations of the Law of Nations: Alberico Gentili and the Justice of Empire*. Oxford and New York: Oxford University Press, 2010.
Kunkel, Wolfgang. *An Introduction to Roman Legal and Constitutional History*. 2nd ed. Translated by J. M. Kelly. Oxford: Clarendon Press, 1973.
Levy, Ernst. "Natural Law in the Roman Period." *Natural Law Proceedings* 2 (1949): 43–72.
Nörr, Dieter. *Aspekte des römischen Völkerrechts: Die Bronzetafel von Alcántara*. Munich: Bayerische Akademie der Wissenschaften, 1989.
Nörr, Dieter. *Die fides in römischen Völkerrecht*. Heidelberg: Müller Juristischer Verlag, 1991.
Padovani, Andrea, and Peter G. Stein, eds. *The Jurists' Philosophy of Law from Rome to the Seventeenth Century*. Dordrecht, Berlin, Heidelberg, and Vienna: Springer, 2007.
Rabel, Ernst. "Private Law of Western Civilization I. The Significance of Roman Law." *Louisiana Law Review* 10 (1949–50): 1–14.
Scevola, Roberto. *Utilitas publica*, 2 vols. Padua: CEDAM, 2012.
Schiavone, Aldo. *The Invention of the Law in the West*. Translated by Jeremy Carden and Anthony Shugaar. Cambridge, MA, and London: The Belknap Press of Harvard University Press, 2012.
Schiller, Arthur. *Roman Law: Mechanisms of Development*. The Hague, Paris, and New York: Mounton Publishers, 1978.
Schulz, Fritz. *History of Roman Legal Science*. Oxford: Clarendon Press, 1946.
Schulz, Fritz. *Principles of Roman Law*. Translated by Marguerite Wolff. Oxford: Clarendon Press, 1936.
Stein, Peter. *The Character and Influence of the Roman Civil Law: Historical Essays*. London and Ronceverte: The Hambledon Press, 1988.
Straumann, Benjamin. *Crisis and Constitutionalism: Roman Political Thought from the Fall of the Republic to the Age of Revolution*. Oxford and New York: Oxford University Press, 2016.
Vinogradoff, Paul. "Sources of Law: Right and Law." *The Collected Papers of Paul Vinogradoff*, 465–478. Oxford: Clarendon Press, 1923; reprint 1963.
Watson, Alan. *International Law in Archaic Rome*. Baltimore and London: The Johns Hopkins University Press, 1993.

Watson, Alan. *The Spirit of Roman Law.* Athens, GA, and London: University of Georgia Press, 1995.

Wieacker, Franz. *Römische Rechtgeschichte: Quellenkunde, Rechtsbildung, Jurisprudenz and Rechtsliteratur* I. Munich: Beck Verlag, 1988.

Wolff, Hans Julius. *Roman Law: An Historical Introduction.* Norman, OK: University of Oklahoma Press, 1951.

2 Constitutional background of Roman law

The science of law is autonomous but not independent. It cannot live isolated from politics and culture. Law is part of a social structure, of tradition, of a collective human project. Law is a branch of politics in the noblest sense. Legal institutions, concepts, and ideas are so often a natural consequence of political ideals and values. Political revolutions many times involve legal revolutions. Therefore, to help the reader understand Roman law in context, what follows is a brief summary of the most significant aspects of ancient Rome's unwritten political constitution from the foundation of Rome in 753 BCE until the death of Emperor Justinian in 565 CE.

Foundation of Rome: the monarchy

The founding of Rome is deeply shrouded in legend and myth. There is first the myth of the Trojan prince Aeneas, epically narrated by the Augustan-era poet Virgil in his *Aeneid*, in which Aeneas leads survivors from the fallen Troy on a voyage across the Mediterranean to Italy. There, according to the myth, the son of Aeneas fathered a line of kings who ruled until the eighth century BCE. In the related Italian myth of Romulus and Remus, these twin brothers, sons of the god Mars, were rightful heirs to the throne but were exposed at birth by a usurping king. They were found on the banks of the Tiber River by a she-wolf, who suckled them until their discovery and adoption by a shepherd. While Romulus wanted to found a new city on the Palatine Hill, Remus preferred the Aventine Hill. They agreed to determine the location through augury, but they disagreed on how to interpret the signs they were given, and consequently Romulus killed Remus. According to a popular legend, Romulus eventually founded Rome on 21 April 753 BCE, the day of the sacred festival to Pales, the goddess of shepherds.

For more than two centuries, kings ruled Rome. The king was the supreme lawgiver, the chief executive, and the judge of the community. He was Rome's leader in war and its chief priest. He was its official representative in religious relations with the gods and in political relations with foreign communities. As Rome's first king, Romulus laid the political foundations of the city by establishing the Senate and dividing the people into three great tribes, probably ethnic in origin: the Ramnes, the Tities, and the Luceres. Each tribe consisted of ten *curiae*, or assemblies of men. Under the curiae were the patrician-led family clans (*gentes*), and under them, individual families. Members of the same clan were united by a common name and a common cult. It is probable that patrician land belonged to the collective ownership of the gentes.

The curiae formed the basic political unit of primitive Rome. Their members took an oath of allegiance to the king at his inauguration; they took part in some of the king's religious activities, and they delegated their power (*imperium*) to senior magistrates. At no time were they a legislative body. The curiae did, however, play an important role in military organization. Each curia provided (at least originally) one hundred infantrymen (*centuria*) and one squadron of knights (*equites*). Here lay the origin of the *comitia centuriata*, a popular assembly with military functions but no political ones, whose creation has been attributed to king Servius Tullius. This king carried out an important reform in Roman organization that was instrumental to the development of republican institutions: the Servian constitution. Tullius divided the city into four geographical districts (thus abandoning ethnic criteria), each encompassing a single tribe. He also instituted a census of every male citizen, gathering information about each man's wealth, military duties, and tax liabilities.

The Senate was the royal council and consisted of aristocratic patricians. Senators gathered when called together by the king, who appointed them in accordance with tradition (*mos maiorum*). The number of senators increased gradually, until three hundred senators were fixed as the maximum. After the death of the king, supreme power rested in the Senate until the election of a new one. In the meantime, a senator appointed as *interrex* assumed the charge of all public affairs for a period of five days. After this short deadline, if the new king was not yet elected, a new interrex was designated.

Of the seven kings whose names we know, the last three – Tarquin the Elder (Tarquinius Priscus), Servius Tullius, and Tarquin the Proud (Tarquinius Superbus) – formed the Etruscan dynasty, which is certainly historical, not mythical. This dynasty expanded royal power, functions, and influence. Legend attributes to the Etruscans the development of the royal insignia to dignify the figure of the king: the golden crown, the ivory scepter, the *curule* chair, the *toga praetexta* (white robe with purple borders), the twelve lictors, and so on.

According to Roman tradition, Tarquin the Proud, son or grandson of Tarquin the Elder and son-in-law of Servius Tullius, was a cruel tyrant. Tarquin the Proud brutally murdered Servius Tullius and established a despotic government based on terror. Many senators were put to death during his reign. After the rape of an aristocratic woman named Lucretia, or Lucrece, by Tarquin's youngest son, Sextus, a group of senators, led by Lucius Junius Brutus, raised a revolt and expelled the Tarquin family from Rome. The hateful Etruscan dynasty was overthrown, and the Roman Republic was established (in 509 BCE by tradition). With the inauguration of the Republic, the king was replaced by two magistrates called consuls.

With the expulsion of the Tarquins, the figure of the king, now degraded to that of an oppressor, a despot, and a tyrant, became a sort of political trauma in the memory and imagination of Rome. Owing to its wide and sudden impact, the rape of Lucrece turned into a major theme in European music, literature, and art. As William Shakespeare put it at the end of his narrative poem on this rape: "The Romans plausibly did give consent / To Tarquin's everlasting banishment" (*The Rape of Lucrece*, lines 1854–55).

Constitution of the Roman Republic

Rome never had a written constitution, and it never was a democracy in the sense of modern democracies. Rather than a single text, Rome's constitution was a living and nimble set of legal and political norms. It was a long, ongoing, and complex process of constituting the republic by creating and developing institutions, political powers, principles and rules, practices and functions, as well as mutual institutional relations. The constitution of Rome was never reduced to a document; largely unwritten and evolving over time, the Roman constitution was based on tradition, but not on obsolete precedents. The annual election of two consuls, the existence and functions of the Senate, and the gathering of different popular assemblies for different purposes all were elements of the constitution but were unregulated by written statutes.

The Roman constitution accommodated changing circumstances with new ideas and arguments (Cicero, *De imperio Pompei* 60). For this reason, the Roman constitution was inescapably controversial, intrinsically political, and always opens to testing in public debate. Romans were proud of the superiority of their constitution because of its stability, balanced structure, clear assignment of functions, and solid discipline (Cicero, *De re publica* 1.70). The great Greek historian Polybius (1.1.5) associated Roman military success with the perfection and greatness of Rome's constitution, which enabled Rome to bring almost the whole of the Mediterranean world under its dominion within a mere fifty-three years.

Polybius and Cicero understood the Republican constitution as a mixed constitution. It combined elements of aristocracy (the Senate) with democracy (the people) and monarchy (the consuls). According to Cicero (*De re publica* 1.69), such a constitution has an extensive component of equality; it provides harmony and stability, and it prevents corruption. Simple constitutions lead to corrupted versions of each kind of rule, producing a despot instead of a king, an oligarchy instead of an aristocracy, and a chaotic mob instead of a democracy. On the contrary, the Roman constitution was a system of checks and balances based on a combination of powers and vetoes of magistrates, and of political control of the magistrates by the Senate and the people. The greatness of the Roman constitution was reflected in a very short phrase: "the Senate and the People of Rome" (*Senatus Populusque Romanus*, abbreviated as SPQR).

Populus Romanus

The English word "people" derives from the Latin word *populus* and conveys much of the original Latin meaning. *Populus Romanus* was the organized community of all Roman citizens, including both patricians and plebeians (but originally only patricians, who formed a class of privileged citizens). Between the small number of noble families (*patricii*) and the mass of the Roman people (*plebs*) was an enormous social gulf: marriages between patricians and plebeians were prohibited until 445 BCE, when they were allowed by a *lex Canuleia*. The plebeians were also excluded from the magistracies for centuries and from some priesthoods at all times. An important, although not final, result of the long struggle between patricians and plebeians was the enactment of the *lex Hortensia* (287 BCE), which made all resolutions passed by plebeians (*plebiscita*) binding on all citizens, including patricians. Over time, legal differences between the classes were mitigated through legislation.

The Romans did not elaborate a theory of the populus. As a supreme political organ of the Republic, the people legitimized with their decisions the most salient political processes (electoral, legislative, judicial, and so on). That was their political function; nothing more and nothing less. The idea of a nation-state is a modern abstraction quite contrary to the Roman spirit. For according to the Romans, power was always personal – not impersonal, as we think of it (cf. the power of the state). During the Roman Republic and even during the Principate, "populus Romanus" was the technical expression to refer to the Roman political community. Without populus, there could be no community, that is, a truly united body of citizens with a unified political purpose.

Politically, the populus was invested with *maiestas* (majesty), probably the most fundamental principle of the Roman Republic. Maiestas was an original concept, with no equivalent word in Greek. Neither is it equivalent to the modern idea of sovereignty, since sovereignty presupposes the nation-state. Maiestas was inclusive, uniting people; sovereignty, on the contrary, is exclusive, uniting particular territories and therefore excluding others.

Maiestas comes from *maior* (greater) and expresses the idea of the superiority and greatness of the Roman people. In virtue of its superiority, Rome demanded respect and submission from other peoples, although this requirement did not imply a rejection of others' liberty. Indeed, liberty of other peoples was considered a necessary condition of Roman maiestas. The Romans' talent for bringing "the whole world under their sway" while preserving liberty lay, according to Polybius (6.50.6; 6.5.9), in the greatness of the republican constitution. The transference of majesty from the populus to the emperor began with Augustus (see Horace, *Epistulae.* 2.1.258), and it was completed by the beginning of the Later Empire, at the end of the third century. Consequently, as the emperor's majesty grew, republican structure declined.

Res publica refers to the affairs and the property of the Roman people. Attribution of property to the populus did not imply common ownership, however. *Res publica* was not a technical description of the political community as such. *Res publica* meant "republic" in the modern sense only when writers used the expression in opposition to the power and authority of the emperor.

Popular assemblies

According to tradition, the Roman people exercised their power in popular assemblies called *comitia* (from *com-ire*: to come together). These assemblies were basically constituted for legislative and judicial purposes, as well as for the election of magistrates. Comitia met originally in an open-air public space (*comitium*), located in front of the meeting house of the Roman Senate (curia), and they celebrated the day determined by the auspices. Only male adult citizens had the right to participate. There were also comitia in municipalities (*municipia*) and colonies (*coloniae*) for the election of local magistrates and the enactment of local legislation.

The comitia voted only on proposals made by the presiding magistrates, without the opportunity to debate the proposal or make amendments during formal meetings. True public debates and political discussions of important issues took place in informal gatherings (*contiones*). The popular assemblies consisted of different units (e.g. military and residential), and each unit voted as a bloc; votes of individuals were not counted. The decadence and eventual disintegration and disappearance of the comitia were closely related to this system of organizing votes, which easily degenerated into corruption. As a result, the patrician farming class continued to exercise exclusive control over all important issues.

The oldest assembly was the aforementioned comitia curiata, which became insignificant during the Republic period. The only functions of the comitia curiata in the Republic were in the realm of sacral law. The second type of popular assemblies was the comitia centuriata, which became one of the most important assemblies under the republican constitution. Military in origin, they were political in practice. The comitia centuriata chose the highest magistrates (consuls, praetors, and censors); they passed statutes on the proposal of the consuls and made formal decisions on war and peace. They were also involved in political trials in which the life of an accused citizen was at stake. The comitia centuriata gradually lost legislative functions in favor of the tribal assemblies (*comitia tributa*).

The tribal assemblies were the last established popular assemblies. Civil in character, the comitia tributa distributed the citizens, both patricians and plebeians, in accordance with the different territorial districts, called tribes (like the old primitive institution under the kings, but not connected to it). This system strongly favored landowners. Landless citizens were confined to the four urban tribes, strong in numbers of individuals but weak as voting units, while the landowners controlled the growing rustic tribes. In 241 BCE there were thirty-one rural and four urban tribes. The comitia tributa elected lower magistrates, enacted laws, and imposed fines for violation of statutes.

As a political body, the plebeians were organized in plebeian assemblies or councils (*concilia plebis*) based also on tribes. These councils included the greater part of the citizenry, but not the whole people. A plebeian magistrate, either a tribune or an aedile, convened and presided over plebeian assemblies. Resolutions passed by the plebeian councils bound only the plebeians themselves. However, the *lex Publilia* of 339 BCE validated plebeian resolutions for the whole people if they were ratified either by the Senate or by another assembly. The aforementioned *lex Hortensia* of 287 BCE made plebeian resolutions equivalent to statutes passed in the comitia centuriata or tributa. The plebeian council elected the tribunes and the plebeian aediles, and it acted as an appellate judicial body for fines imposed by them.

Republican magistrates

The magistrates were the officials of Rome elected by the people and vested with executive power (*potestas*) to fulfill their functions. They embodied the firm sense of order, power, and discipline of the Roman spirit. The comitia centuriata elected consuls, praetors, and censors. Aediles and quaestors were chosen in the tribal assemblies.

Every magistrate had potestas, that is, the power to fulfill the rights and duties connected to his office. In addition to the general potestas, consuls and praetors (as well as the dictator and his main lieutenant) possessed a supreme power called *imperium* (command). The imperium included the power to represent Rome in its relations with foreign communities, to command the army, to take the auspices, to exercise civil and criminal jurisdiction, to call for the Senate and popular assemblies, and to issue edicts and proclamations. The insignia and impressive apparatus associated with imperium were an inheritance from the royal period. The imperium was effective both outside and inside the city. Inside the city, however, the imperium was limited by the right of citizens to appeal to the popular assemblies in case of imposition of a corporal or capital punishment. The magistrate's power to impose fines was also restricted by law.

Characteristic elements of the magistracies in general were their collegiality, temporality, and gratuity. These three elements limited magisterial power and acted as constitutional checks. Collegiality meant that two (or more) magistrates (*collegae*) could simultaneously hold the same office and have the same power (Ulpian, D. 50.16.173pr.). Collegiality did not require that magistrates act in unison. As a matter of fact, to avoid conflicts, colleagues usually separated their activities, or they applied the principle of alternation. Any magistrate could obstruct the activity of another magistrate with equal or lower magisterial power. In the case of equal power (e.g., by a consul to his colleague), the veto (*intercessio*) would be interposed just when the colleague had already partially begun accomplishing his action, neither before its initiation nor after its completion. In the case of a veto to a magistrate of lower power (e.g., by a consul against a praetor), the superior magistrate could prohibit the lower magistrate from taking the specific action or even remove him from office altogether.

The second limitation of magistracies was temporal. All magistrates held office for a fixed and short term. The more absolute or exceptional the power of the magistrate was, the shorter his term was. The consuls and most of the ordinary magistrates held office for one year. The dictator's term, however, could not exceed six months. Once his term had expired, the magistrate had to wait ten years to serve in the same office again. In exceptional circumstances (e.g., amid a serious war, as during the Second Punic War, 218–211 BCE), the term could be extended. Ex-consuls and ex-praetors were entrusted with the administration of provinces by an extension of their imperium (proconsul or propraetor). In the case of a magistracy becoming vacant (for instance, upon the death or resignation of a magistrate), a new elected magistrate held the office for the rest of the term. Between the term of magistracy and the election for a superior office, an interval of at least two years was required.

The last principle was gratuity. No salary was expected to be paid to any magistrate. To be a magistrate was considered a form of public recognition (*honos*), since the magistrate assumed the role of the city as such (*persona communitatis*). For this reason, only wealthy people or citizens supported by wealthy people could hold the office of magistrate.

Functions of the magistrates

At the top of the government of the Roman Republic were two consuls. As supreme Roman magistrates, consuls inherited the primitive royal powers. They possessed the highest imperium, except when a dictator was appointed. Years were named after them until Emperor Justinian abolished that system of dating in 537 CE. Originally, both consuls were patricians. However, beginning with the *lex Licinia Sextia* of 367 BCE (actually a plebiscite), one of them could be plebeian, and after the *lex Genucia* of 342 BCE, at least one of the consuls had to be plebeian. Owing to the influence of the patricians, however, this change did not become effective until 172 BCE.

The most important consular function was military command. To relieve the consuls of ordinary administration and jurisdiction, a praetorship was created in 367 BCE. As a junior colleague of the consuls, the praetor was vested with the same imperium as the consuls, but the praetor could not veto the consuls. In the beginning, there was only one praetor, but by 242 BCE a second one was added. Later, the functions of the praetors were divided: the urban praetor exercised jurisdiction over citizens; the peregrine praetor exercised jurisdiction over foreigners or between foreigners and Roman citizens. Since the administration of provinces was in the hands of praetors, the number of praetors gradually increased. Praetors were instrumental to developing Roman law by issuing edicts and introducing legislation.

In 367 BCE the patrician aedileship was created. Tradition maintained that two plebeian aediles had long existed as assistants of the plebeian tribune. Aediles oversaw public order and security in Rome. They supervised streets, buildings – specifically temples (*aedes*) – bridges, aqueducts, markets (weights and measures), and market transactions (sales of slaves and animals, among other things). They arranged public games, and they also had some criminal jurisdiction in minor offenses.

The quaestorship was probably established at the beginning of the Republic. Quaestors were magistrates who supervised the treasure of Rome. Originally, they served as assistants of the consuls in finance and administrative matters domestically and abroad. Since the quaestors managed the finances of the provinces, the number of quaestors increased constantly during the Republic. Julius Caesar raised the number of quaestors to forty. The Senate supervised the distribution of quaestors, but magistrates seem to have had some discretion in selecting quaestors as subalterns. Quaestorship was the lowest of the magistracies and used to be the initial office in a magisterial career.

In 443 BCE, the censorship was established as a temporary magistracy with the purpose of creating a census of Roman citizens to count and rank the Roman people and register their properties. The comitia centuriata, presided over by the consul, elected the two censors once every five years, and they held office for eighteen months (so for three and a half years there were no censors). Despite the lack of imperium in the censorship, Roman citizens considered the office to have the highest dignity. As a result, only former consuls were ordinarily elected to this magistracy. The censors made up the list of senators and fixed the tribe and class to which each citizen belonged. Vested with strong discretionary power, the censors became the supervisors of and took responsibility for public morality, especially of the upper class. Toward the end of the Republic, the censorship disappeared.

The nomination of a dictator (also called *magister populi*) was entrusted to the consuls. The dictatorship was an extraordinary magistracy appointed for a maximum term of six months in times of extreme internal or external difficulties. The dictator commanded the army and took care of civil emergencies. He had supreme power and jurisdiction and could not be called to account for his actions. The dictator appointed a master of the horse as a lieutenant to assist him. Although other magistrates remained in office, they answered to the dictator.

One of the most famous and popular dictatorships was that of Lucius Quinctius Cincinnatus (Livy, *Ab urbe condita* 3.26–29; Dionysius of Halicarnassus, *Roman Antiquities* 10, 23–25). He was a Roman aristocrat (born around 519 BCE) and a citizen of outstanding leadership, consul in 460 BCE, and dictator in 458 BCE and, according to legend, again in 439 BCE. The Romans admired him because he defeated Rome's enemies, relieved the besieged consul Municius, and then returned to his farm, all within sixteen days. (The first American president, George Washington, was sometimes called the "American Cincinnatus" because he retired to his farm at Mount Vernon after defeating the British army and declining the offer of quasi-monarchical powers.) The last constitutional dictatorship was appointed in 201 BCE, the last year of the Second Punic War. Afterward, Rome ceased to appoint dictators. The dictatorships of Sulla (82 BCE) and Julius Caesar (49 BCE) had a different constitutional character.

The office of the plebeian tribunes, which was originally not strictly a magistracy, was established in 494 BCE in the course of the first secession of the plebeians in the so-called conflict of the orders (494–287 BCE), in which the plebeians sought equality with the patricians. The aim of the office was to protect the plebeians against the abuses and arbitrary use of the imperium of the Roman patrician magistrates. Tribunes were elected by the plebeian assemblies and later by the comitia tributa. In 457 BCE, the number of tribunes was increased from probably five to ten. According to the *lex Valeria Horatia* (449 BCE), the person and the office of a tribune could not be violated (*sacrosanctitas*). As a result, anyone who attacked a tribune or injured him in the performance of his duties might be freely killed by anyone.

The power of the tribune was opposed to the power of the magistrates. In fact, it was the most important check on the power of the magistrates. By virtue of their tribunician power, individual tribunes could veto any activity of the magistrates, to whose imperium plebeian tribunes did not submit. Plebeian tribunes could convene and preside over the plebeian assemblies, attend the meetings of the Senate, propose legislation, and prosecute criminals before the comitia centuriata. They could even pronounce the death penalty. Patricians could become tribunes only by previous adoption into a plebeian family. This was the case, for instance, with Clodius, the bitter political enemy of Cicero. In 59 BCE Clodius was adopted into a plebeian family and was elected tribune for 58 BCE. Gradually the tribune of the plebs became indistinguishable from other magistracies, although it never lost its radical flavor and populist character. In the late Republic, the office of the tribunes was terminated and assimilated into the other magistracies.

A number of magistrates of low status were appointed every year by the people, and a number of magistrates were elected occasionally when they were required for the good of the Roman Republic.

The Senate

Along with the assemblies and the magistrates, the Senate (*senatus*, from *senex*, "old man") was the third component of the republican constitution and the institution that symbolized both political stability and political discussion. During the Republic, the Senate was basically an advisory council of ex-magistrates, not a legislative body. However, it became the most important governing body of international affairs and internal policy. The Senate exercised supreme control of all political and administrative matters, and the resolutions of the Senate embodied the most influential political decisions. However, the initiative for senatorial decisions had to come from the magistrates, who were also free to accept or reject those decisions. Ordinarily, the magistrates followed the advice because they had no interest in conflicting with the Senate.

Holding their positions for life, senators were originally divided into *patres*, who were patricians, and *conscripti*, or plebeians enrolled in the Senate. After the *lex Licinia Sextia* (367 BCE), however, this division became obsolete. The ordinary number of senators was three hundred, though in 81 BCE, Sulla raised the number to six hundred, and under Caesar the number grew to nine hundred. Augustus restored the number to six hundred. The Senate was organized in classes according to rank: ex-consuls (called *consulares*), ex-praetors, ex-aediles, and so on. The decline in the influence and power of the Senate pointed to the decline of the Roman Republic.

The powers of the Senate and its relations with popular assemblies and the magistrates were not defined by statutes but were rather based on an accumulated tradition. Over several centuries, the Senate became active in the realm of foreign affairs, public finances, and religion. Although the ultimate decisions on both declaring war and peace and concluding treaties rested with the popular assemblies, in practice the opinion of the Senate was decisive. Only a rash and unwise consul would bring these important questions before the popular assemblies without previously consulting the Senate. The Senate appointed the emissaries for missions abroad, and only after having concluded negotiations could the result be submitted for approval to the people. The Senate managed the public finances, authorized the imposition of taxes, and fixed the taxes the provinces had to pay. It collected money for the army, the construction and maintenance of public works, and public games. The Senate also controlled state religious life, specifically the approval of new deities' cults.

In case of extreme public danger, the Senate had the power to declare a state of emergency, ordering the consuls to defend the Roman Republic and authorizing them to apply extraordinary measures, including the temporary suspension of some constitutional institutions (the so-called last decree: *senatus consultum ultimum*). The first application of this exceptional remedy took place during the Gracchi movement (121 BCE).

The Principate

This was the first period of the Roman Empire, from the beginning of the reign of Augustus to Diocletian (27 BCE–284 CE). During the Principate, the powers of the emperors increased gradually as they made efforts to preserve the old republican institutions and aspirations. The political effect was the transformation of the Roman Republic into an absolute monarchy and, ultimately, the destruction of the remains of the Republic.

The name "Principate" comes from the title of *princeps*, which means the preeminence of the first citizen. This title was first assumed unofficially by

Octavian (63 BCE–14 CE) in 27 BCE. In a solemn meeting of the Senate on January 13 of that year, the constitutional powers of the new princeps were regulated after Augustus laid down all his powers as a triumvir and transferred control of the state to the Senate and the people of Rome (*Res gestae* 34.1). Augustus accepted no magistracy for himself that ran against the traditional republican constitution. However, he accepted proconsular power for ten years, and he received the tribunician power for life. He also retained consulship until 23 BCE. The proconsular imperium involved control of the imperial provinces (Spain, Gaul, and Syria) and authority over the promagistrate of public or senatorial provinces. As a tribune of the plebs (a title conferred on him in 36 BCE), Augustus retained the right of inviolability and veto power, the authority to convene the Senate, and the right to bring bills before the plebeian assemblies.

Augustus preserved the old constitutional organs (magistracies, the popular assemblies, and the Senate) while he secured supreme power. It was by virtue of his personal prestige (*auctoritas Principis*) based on tradition and mos maiorum that Augustus claimed supremacy and preeminence for himself over the Senate and the people. Augustus wanted to be the greatest of the citizens, the protector of the republican institutions, and the guardian of the most genuine Roman traditions. As a princeps, he had the task of building up a strong system of government and a powerful body of administration that would preserve and protect Rome, Italy, and the empire. Tacitus pointed out that the republic was renovated not by a king or a dictator but by the authority of the princeps (*Annales* 1.9).

Augustus reorganized the equestrian order. Lower in rank than the senatorial class, the *equites* (originally cavalrymen) had become a distinct and wealthy social class. They had obtained their wealth from commerce (forbidden to senators) and farm taxes. Gradually, during the Principate, the most important positions in the administration of the emperor were occupied by persons of the equestrian rank. After the important reforms of Hadrian, the leadership and reputation of the equestrian order grew still more. The golden ring, a distinction worn during the Republic by both the senators and the equites, became an exclusive distinction of the equestrian order.

During the Principate, the consulship remained but increasingly became a merely honorary function. From time to time, the emperors themselves took on the consulship. The praetors, however, retained the same civil and criminal jurisdiction they had enjoyed in the late Republic. The popular assemblies were not abolished but gradually stopped functioning. By contrast, the Senate considerably extended its powers, and senatorial legislation replaced popular legislation. Even the Senate, however, was losing supreme control of political activities to the emperor, who belonged to the Senate as its senior member (*princeps senatus*). The senatorial decrees became a simple expression of the imperial will – so much so that the speeches of the emperor to the Senate were called senatus consulta. While the emperor rarely attended the meetings of the Senate, an imperial magistrate read the messages of the emperor, which were approved by praise, rounds of applause, and flatteries. The most critical changes in the Senate took place during the reign of Hadrian, who established a new administrative bureaucratic system and made important modifications to the judicial system.

The primary legal activity of the emperor was judicial. Suetonius (*Augustus* 33.1) wrote that Augustus spent many hours on the tribunal, often well into the night. Tiberius also sat as judge. With their councilors, the emperors heard appeals to assure some degree of uniformity in the administration of justice. As a judge, for instance, Emperor Claudius was accused of arbitrary behavior (Suetonius, *Claudius* 15). On the other hand, Hadrian was so interested in legal matters that he preferred to cross-examine witnesses personally (*Historia Augusta. Hadrian* 16.8; 20.3; 21.1). Caracalla, by contrast, according to Cassius Dio, seldom sat in court (Cassius Dio 77.17.3).

During the Principate, the old republican state treasury was replaced by a new financial administration of the imperial treasury (*fiscus Caesaris*). The revenues of the treasury came basically from the rental or sale of public land in the provinces; from periodic payments from the imperial provinces and, to some extent, public or senatorial provinces, pastures, woods, mines, custom duties, and other indirect taxes; and from legacies left to the emperor.

The most fragile aspect of the Principate was the question of the succession of the princeps. Since the constitutional position of the princeps was grounded in political ideology and not in the old principles of the republican constitution, the death of each emperor was a critical moment for internal stability. The political struggles after the deaths of Nero and Commodus were paradigmatic. Since the end of the first century, the practice was that the princeps adopted one of his collaborators and then designated him as a successor. That happened with some salient emperors such as Trajan, Hadrian, Antoninus Pius, and Marcus Aurelius, among others.

The later Roman Empire

The later Roman Empire (also known as the Dominate, from *dominus*, "lord") emerged with the reign of Diocletian in 284, after the great third-century crisis (235–84). Although Diocletian's attitude was in some sense conservative, he broke away from the republican tradition; he destroyed the institutional façade of the Principate, becoming the founder of a new political order. Diocletian abandoned the appearance of the Republic by taking the government of the cosmopolitan empire completely into his hands and those of his reordered bureaucratic administration. He transformed the imperial power into a monarchy in accordance with the splendor of the oriental model. The idea of the emperor was then understood as an incarnation of the majesty of the people, no longer as a first citizen. However, the term princeps or the associated adjective principalis did not disappear. They continue prominently in imperial legislation. The emperor was an absolute ruler to whom all inhabitants of the empire had to submit. In many respects, the Diocletian reform was completed by Constantine the Great (r. 306–37 CE).

During the later Roman Empire, political institutions of the city of Rome lost political leadership. Diocletian lived mainly in Nicomedia, the metropolis of Bithynia (in Asia Minor), which was made the capital of the eastern part of the empire in 286. After becoming the sole ruler of both the West and the East, in 330 Constantine established Constantinople (ancient Byzantium) as the capital of the empire: the New Rome. Western emperors lived in different cities (Treves, Milan, and Ravenna). Beginning with Emperor Constantius II, there were two imperial senates: one at Rome and one at Constantinople.

The later Roman Empire also witnessed the geographic division of power among several emperors to make it more effective and prevent problems of succession. Each part of the empire (the Latin West and the Greek East) had both a main emperor (called Augustus) and a deputy emperor (called Caesar), who was supposed to be the successor of the former. In the eastern part of the empire, the Greek culture and language were dominant, while the West remained Latin in culture and language.

The imperial administration rested on an enormous, well-organized, and hierarchical bureaucracy entirely disconnected from the military command. The distinction between public (or senatorial) and imperial provinces disappeared completely. At the top of this administrative structure were four *praefecti praetorio*, two for the West and two for the East. These were the chiefs of the four administrative prefectures into which Diocletian divided the empire: the two Eastern prefectures, Oriens (Egypt and the provinces of Asia and Thrace) and Illyricum (Macedonia and Dacia), and the two Western prefectures of Italy (including Africa) and Gaul (including Spain and Britain). The prefectures were divided into dioceses governed by vicars, and these into provinces governed by presidents (*praesides*).

The Christianization of the empire occurred during the later Roman Empire. The Edict of Toleration by Emperor Galerius, issued in Serdica (now Sofia) in 311, attempted to put an end to the official persecution of Christians throughout the empire. Very controversial is the so-called Edict of Milan (313), issued by emperors Constantine and Licinius. The term Edict of Milan is a modern construct used to describe a document preserved in divergent forms by two contemporaries of Emperor Constantine: Lactantius (*De mortibus persecutorum* 48.2–12) and Eusebius of Caesarea (*Historia Ecclesiastica* 10.5.2–14). The original intent of the document, its nature, and its provenance are still contentious questions. The Edict of Milan seems to have been the outcome of a political agreement concluded in Milan between Constantine and Licinius in early February 313, with the aim of granting liberty of worship to all religions, including Christianity, and the restoration of properties confiscated from Christians during the persecutions beginning in 303. In June 313, Licinius published at Nicomedia an epistolary version of the Edict of Milan for the eastern part of the Empire, from which Lactantius made his copy. Eusebius probably made his copy from the publication of the epistolary version of the edict in Palestine.

On February 27, 380, Emperors Theodosius, Gratian, and Valentinian II issued the imperial constitution *Cunctos populos,* also known as the Edict of Thessalonica (C.Th. 16.1.2). This edict marked the end of a great fourth-century religious controversy by declaring Nicene Trinitarian Christianity to be the only established imperial religion and the only one that could be called Catholic as such.

On the death of Emperor Theodosius in 395, the empire was formally divided into two parts. Theodosius left the East to his son Arcadius, who was about eighteen years old, and the West to his son Honorius, who was about ten. This partition of the mainly Greek-speaking East from the Latin West was to have far-reaching repercussions in later centuries. The Roman Empire was never reunited, and the destinies of the two halves of the empire were vastly different. Great hordes of Germans invaded the Western Empire. In 410 the Goths sacked Rome, and in 476 the last Western emperor, Romulus Augustulus, was deposed by the Germanic Odoacer, who became the first king of Italy. In the Eastern Empire, the conception of a Roman Empire embracing the whole Mediterranean area, both eastern and western, endured until the death of Emperor Justinian, in 565. The Eastern Empire persisted through Late Antiquity and the Middle Ages in the form of the Byzantine Empire, until it fell to the Ottoman Turks in 1453 at the beginning of the modern era.

The provinces

The province was the largest territorial and administrative Roman unit outside Italy until Diocletian. Rome began expanding beyond Italy during the First Punic War (264–241 BCE). It was precisely then that the term "province" was first applied to a territorial unit under Roman control. The first provinces to be annexed to Rome were Sicily, in 241 BCE, and the province of Corsica and Sardinia, in 237 BCE. In 197 BCE, the province of Hispania Citerior, along the east cost of the Iberian Peninsula, and the province of Hispania Ulterior, along the southern cost of the Iberian Peninsula, were annexed.

Under the Roman Republic, the power to organize a new province rested with the Senate. The provincial laws (*leges provinciarum*), none of which have come down to us, were probably the basic statutory decrees issued by the general who conquered the province and ratified by a senatorial commission. Besides these leges, the jurisdiction of the governor of the province was constrained by the provincial edict he issued after his appointment as a governor and by the city charters held by various colonial or municipal communities inside the province. The famous letter Cicero wrote to his friend Atticus (*Ad Atticum* 6.1.15), when Cicero was the governor of Cilicia in 51 BCE, provides the best evidence for the existence of a provincial edict during the Roman Republic. During the reign of Emperor Hadrian, the jurist Salvius Julianus fixed the content and structure of the provincial edict, following the structure of the edict of the urban praetor. Remaining portions of the jurist Gaius's commentary on the provincial edict confirm the connection between the structure and contents of the city edict and those of the provincial edict.

During the reign of Augustus, provinces were divided into two classes: imperial provinces, under the emperor's jurisdiction, and public (or senatorial) provinces, under the control of the Senate. Imperial provinces were those not pacified despite being under strong military control. They needed the presence of the Roman army. The emperor directly appointed the governors (*legati Augusti*, but also procurators or prefects), and they remained in the province until the emperor himself recalled them. The soil of the imperial provinces belonged to the emperor, and all taxes and revenues of the imperial provinces went to the imperial treasury.

Public (or senatorial) provinces, in contrast, were those that had been long annexed and pacified by the Romans. They were often along the Mediterranean Sea (Achaea, Hispania Baetica, Sicilia, Africa, and so on). The governors of these public provinces were proconsuls (especially in the provinces of Asia and Africa) or propraetors (in the rest of the provinces) appointed by the Senate and under its instructions. Though the Senate appointed proconsuls, the emperor, by virtue of his "supreme proconsular power," had the right to intervene tactically in the appointment of senatorial governors. The soil of the public provinces belonged to the Roman people. The emperor had the authority to order the change of a province from one category to another. In 68 CE, of a total of thirty-six provinces, eleven were public, and twenty-five were imperial. Of the imperial, fifteen were under legati, and ten under procuratores or praefecti.

During the reign of Diocletian, the division of the empire into prefectures and dioceses was connected to the creation of more and smaller provinces than those of the Principate. Diocletian divided the empire into almost a hundred provinces, including Italy. The provinces were combined into thirteen dioceses, and the dioceses, in turn, were grouped into four prefectures. The governors of the dioceses were the representatives to the prefects. This new administrative structure marked the beginning of the process of the division of the Roman Empire, which culminated in 395 CE with its formal partition.

Italy

Italy represented a privileged part of the Roman power and dominions. According to Roman tradition, the *foedus Cassianum* (493 BCE) was a treaty between Rome and the league of Latin cities after the legendary victory of the Romans in the battle of Lake Regillus. This treaty established that Rome must be considered equal to the members of the Latin League (but not a member of it), and that each party should give assistance in war to the other. From a legal point of view, Rome bestowed on the Latin cities some rights that until then had belonged only to the Roman citizens. The most important right was the possibility of becoming a Roman citizen by permanent residence in Rome. Another important right was the *ius conubii*, that is, the recognition of marriages between Latins and Romans. Finally, Latins had the right to commerce, which was the right to benefit from the solemn form of conveyance of ownership in Rome (*mancipatio*).

After the Latin revolt of 340 BCE, the Latin League was dissolved. Some cities received full Roman citizenship while maintaining their local government; others acquired the same rights and duties (military and financial burdens) that the Romans had, with the exception of the right to vote or be elected to a magistracy. Others remained as allies, retaining the right to commerce and probably the right to marry Romans. For the rest of Italy, Rome followed policies similar to those that applied to the Latins. The Romans continued using these ius Latii to expand Romanization through Italy and the empire. Thus, Latinity became a privileged status of non-Romans with some specific rights, including the possibility of becoming Roman citizens.

In general, allied communities enjoyed full autonomy. They had their own territory, their own local government, their own law. Rome usually signed a treaty of friendship, peace, and alliance with these allied cities to bind the parties to reciprocal military support in case of war. When the allied city instead recognized expressly the supremacy of Rome in its treaty of alliance and demanded Roman military assistance, the allied community was obliged to obey the orders of the Roman government.

During the Social War (91–88 BCE) between the Roman Republic and several cities of Italy that had been Roman allies for centuries prior to the war, two laws were approved and passed: the *lex Julia de civitate Latinis danda* (90 BCE) and the *lex Plautia Papiria* (89 BCE). Introduced by the consul Lucius Julius Caesar, the lex Julia offered Roman citizenship to all citizens of Italian municipalities who had not yet revolted against Rome in the Social War. The lex Plautia Papiria was a plebiscite proposed by two tribunes that offered the possibility of acquiring citizenship to any person domiciled in Rome who gave his or her name to the peregrine praetor. After the submission of all Italian cities because of the Social War, citizenship was extended quickly to all cities of Italy. This extension expanded the application of Roman law to all of Italy and introduced a kind of double citizenship that became the rule in Italy. After the Social War, all Italian communities became municipalities.

In 42 BCE, the province of Cisalpine Gaul was abolished, thus extending Italy to the north up to the southern edge of the Alps. During the reign of Augustus, Roman Italy was officially created as the administrative division of the Italian peninsula. It was not a province, but a territory of Rome with a special status. For administrative purposes, Augustus divided Italy into eleven regions. It was the first time in history that the Italian peninsula was united under the same name. This system continued without substantial changes until the reign of Diocletian, when the three islands of Corsica, Sardinia, and Sicily were added to Roman Italy, which acquired the status of diocese: the diocese Italiciana.

Colonies

Colonies (*coloniae*) were originally fortified settlements founded by Rome in conquered territories for military or political reasons. They were like an extension of Rome. In the earliest period, according to the status of the colony and the political rights of the settlers, there were two kinds of colonies: those of Roman citizens founded by Rome and those of Latins, founded in collaboration with the Latin allies. The Roman colonies (e.g., Ostia, Rimini) were usually settlements of Roman veteran soldiers, often established in pre-existing towns. The Latin colonies (e.g., Brindisi) were considerably larger than the more numerous Roman colonies. Three hundred was the ordinary number of Romans sent out to a Roman colony (Livy *Ab urbe condita* 8.21.11). The Latin colonies, instead, were populated by several thousand.

During the early Republic, the founding of a new colony demanded a special statute (lex) enacted by the popular assemblies. During the late Republic, however (especially under the dictators Sulla and Julius Caesar), many colonies were founded without passage of a special law. Octavian, Antony, and Lepidus based their prerogative of founding colonies on the statute that established the triumvirate (*lex Titia*). Under the empire, the founding of a new colony was a prerogative of the emperor. Colonies began to be founded outside the Italian peninsula beginning in 118 BCE, the year in which the colony of Narbo Martius (modern Narbonne), in Gallia Narbonensis, was established. Caesar and the triumvirs established about forty colonies in the provinces (e.g., Metellinum in Spain and Hippo and Thapsus in Tunisia). Provincial colonies were usually subject to the burdens of provincial land.

The *lex Ursonensis*, the founding city charter of the colony of Urso, modern Osuna (Seville, Spain), provides important information about colonies. The city of Urso supported Pompey during the Civil War (49–45 BCE) and was finally conquered by Dictator Caesar. Following resolutions of the Senate and the popular assembly, the founding of the colony was confirmed by a *lex Antonia* of Mark Antony, after Caesar's assassination (44 BCE). The inscription on bronze (first discovered in 1870–75, the last fragment in 1999) is a Flavian copy of the original city charter, consisting of nine tablets and comprising more than 140 chapters, of which only about fifty complete or nearly complete chapters are extant. The remnants are kept in the National Archaeological Museum in Madrid.

Municipia

Unlike the colonies, the municipia (singular *municipium*, a municipality, town, or city) were not settlements of veteran soldiers but conquered towns of the Italian peninsula incorporated by Rome. The category was also used in the provinces to describe cities that followed Roman law but were not colonies. Municipalities ranked below colonies in status because the colonies were more autonomous in local affairs than the municipalities. This explains why many provincial municipalities begged the emperor to be transformed into colonies and not vice versa. Still, the difference between colonies and municipalities is not always clear.

The creation of municipalities constituted a decisive mechanism of Roman expansion and control of Italy and, later, of the provinces. The inhabitants of the municipalities could receive full Roman citizenship with all the rights enjoyed by a native citizen, including the right to vote, or a restricted citizenship (Latin rights). Citizens of municipalities had to fulfill all military and tax duties of Roman citizens. According to Pliny the Elder (*Naturalis historia* 3.30), for instance, the province of Baetica (modern Andalusia, Spain), created in 27 BCE, had 175 cities. Of these, nine were colonies, ten were municipalities for Roman citizens, twenty-seven were municipalities with Latin rights, and the other 129 were allied cities (120 tributary cities, six tax-free cities, and three treaty cities). After Vespasian granted the Latin rights to the whole of Spain, probably in 73–74 CE, all Spanish foreign cities were promoted to municipalities.

A city charter determined the functions of the local government and the law to be applied. Since 1861, we have had substantial fragments from some Andalusian city charters (Salpensa and Malaca), which became municipalities with Latin rights at the end of the first century during the Flavian dynasty. Six of ten bronze tablets of the city charter of Irni (*lex Irnitana*) in El Saucejo (near Seville), discovered in 1981, provide more information than any other city charter of the Roman Empire. The *lex Irnitana* (91 CE) is now the most complete copy of a general model of municipal charters by the Flavian dynasty (*lex Flavia municipalis*). The text of the Flavian municipal law came from Emperor Augustus to a significant extent (chapter 91 *lex Irnitana*), and was most probably taken from general municipal legislation for Italy.

Putting together the bronze tablets of the *lex Malacitana* and the *lex Irnitana*, which follow the same common Flavian model, we have at least two-thirds of the city charters of the Flavian municipalities of Spain. The structure of the lex Flavia municipalis covers provisions and rules of the local assemblies, the local magistracies (two *duumvirs* and two aediles), the decurions (members of the local Senate), annual elections, financial and administrative law, and civil jurisdiction. Criminal jurisdiction, however, remained in the hands of the governor of the province.

Tributary cities and tax-free cities

In provinces, though not in Italy, there were two kinds of allied cities in accordance with their tax relation with Rome: tributary cities and free cities. Tributary cities were allied cities that regularly paid fixed land taxes and other tributes and exactions to Rome. Free cities, in contrast, were allied privileged cities that, owing to military assistance to Rome or for other reasons, did not pay fixed contributions to Rome. Free cities were not always free from other kinds of tax impositions by provincial governors, however.

Most provincial cities were tributary cities. Spain alone had 291 tributary cities at the beginning of the first century of our era. Free cities were the exception. In the entire Roman world, there were around two hundred free cities (of these, thirty-nine in Africa, and thirty-five in Asia). Freedom could be granted to a city by a treaty (foedus), a decree of the Senate, or a statute. Athens, Rhodes, and Marseilles were examples of free cities established by treaties. The Pisidian city of Termessos, in modern Turkey, was a free city established in 71 BCE by plebiscite (*lex Antonia de Termessibus*). By contrast, the city of Stratonicea (modern Eskihisar, Turkey) was established by a decree of the Senate (c. 81 BCE). The Romans could change the rights of free cities, whether or not they had a treaty with Rome, when these cities were not loyal. For instance, Tyre, in modern Lebanon, the birthplace of the Roman jurist Ulpian (see D. 50.15.1), was a free city under the Republic, lost its privilege as a free city under Augustus, and later recovered it.

Further reading

Abbott, Frank Frost. *A History and Description of Roman Political Institutions.* 3rd ed. Boston, New York, Chicago, and London: Ginn and Company, 1911.

Abbot, Frank Frost, and Allan Chester Johnson. *Municipal Administration in the Roman Empire.* Princeton, NJ: Princeton University Press, 1926.

Ando, Clifford. "The Administration of the Provinces." *A Companion to the Roman Empire,* edited by David S. Potter, 177–192. Chichester: Wiley-Blackwell, 2006.

Barrandon, Nathalie and François Kirbihler. *Administrer les provinces de la République romaine.* Rennes: Presses Universitaires de Rennes, 2010.

Barrandon, Nathalie and François Kirbihler. *Les gouverneurs et les provinciaux sous la République romaine.* Rennes: Presses Universitaires de Rennes, 2011.

Berger, Adolf. *Encyclopedic Dictionary of Roman Law.* Philadelphia, PA: The American Philosophical Society, 1953; reprint 1980.

Bispham, Edward. *From Asculum to Actium: The Municipalization of Italy from the Social War to Augustus.* Oxford and New York: Oxford University Press, 2007.

Coleman-Norton, Paul Robinson, and Frank Card Bourne. *Ancient Roman Statutes.* Austin, TX: University of Texas Press, 1961.

Crawford, Michael H. *Roman Statutes* I. London: Institute of Classical Studies, 1996.

d'Ors, Álvaro. *La ley Flavia Municipal.* Rome: Pontifical Lateran University, 1986.

Edwards, *Religions of the Constantinian Empire.* Oxford, New York: Oxford University Press, 2015.

Everitt, Anthony. *Augustus: The Life of Rome's First Emperor.* New York: Random House Trade Paperbacks, reprint 2006.

Gibbon, Edward. *The History of the Decline and Fall of the Roman Empire. (1776–79).* Edited by David P. Womersley. London and New York: Penguin Classics, abridged edition, 2001.

Goldsworthy, Adrian. *Augustus: First Emperor of Rome.* New Haven, CT: Yale University Press, 2014.

González, Julián. "The Lex Irnitana: A New Copy of the Flavian Municipal Law." *Journal of Roman Studies* 76 (1986): 147–243.

Jolowicz, Herbert Felix, and Barry Nicholas. *Historical Introduction to the Study of Roman Law.* 3rd ed. Cambridge: Cambridge University Press, 1972.

Kunkel, Wolfgang. *An Introduction to Roman Legal and Constitutional History.* 2nd ed. Translated by J. M. Kelly. Oxford: Clarendon Press, 1973.

Kunkel, Wolfgang, and Roland Wittmann. *Staatsordnung und Staatspraxis der römischen Republik II. Die Magistratur.* Munich: Beck Verlag, 1995.

Lintott, Andrew. *The Constitution of the Roman Republic.* Oxford and New York: Oxford University Press, 1999.

Lintott, Andrew. *Imperium Romanum: Politics and Administration.* London and New York: Routledge, 1993.

Metzer, Ernest. "Agree to Disagree: Local Jurisdiction in the lex Irnitana." In *Judge and Jurists: Essays in Memory of Lord Rodger of Earlsferry*, edited by Andrew Burrows, David Johnston, and Reinhard Zimmermann, 207–225. Oxford and New York: Oxford University Press, 2013.

Mommsen, Theodor. *The History of Rome.* 4 vols. (1854–56). Translated by William Purdie Dickson. Cambridge and New York: Cambridge University Press, 2010.

Mommsen, Theodor. *The Provinces of the Roman Empire.* 2 vols. Translated by William P. Dickson. London: Macmillan, 1909.

Mommsen, Theodor. *Römisches Staatsrecht.* 3 vols. 2nd ed. Leipzig: Verlag Von S. Hirzel, 1876–88.

Richardson, John. *The Romans in Spain.* Oxford: Blackwell, 1996.

Richardson, John. "Roman Law in the Provinces." In *The Cambridge Companion of Roman Law*, edited by David Johnston, 45–58. Cambridge and New York: Cambridge University Press, 2015.

Richardson, John. "Provincial Admnistration." In *The Oxford Handbook of Roman Law and Society*, 111–123, edited by Paul de Plessis, Clifford Ando, and Kaius Tuori. Oxford, New York: Oxford University Press, 2016.

Roselaar, Saskia T. "Local Administration." In *The Oxford Handbook of Roman Law and Society*, 124–136, edited by Paul de Plessis, Clifford Ando, and Kaius Tuori. Oxford, New York: Oxford University Press, 2016.

Sherwin-White, Adrian Nicholas. *The Roman Citizenship.* Oxford: Clarendon Press, 1973.

Siecienski, A. Edward, ed. *Constantine: Religious Faith and Imperial Policy.* London, New York: Routledge, 2017 (esp. chapter 2 on "The Significant of the Edict of Milan," written by Noel Lenski).

Sirks, Boudewijn. "Public Law." In *The Cambridge Companion of Roman Law*, edited by David Johnston, 343–349. Cambridge and New York: Cambridge University Press, 2015.

Swain, Simon. "Italy: From Augustus to Theodosius: Invention and Decline." In *The Oxford Illustrated History of Italy*, edited by George Holmes, 1–27. Oxford and New York: Oxford University Press, 2001.

Syme, Ronald. *The Roman Revolution*, especially 313–524. Oxford and New York: Oxford University Press, reprint 2002.

Willens, Pierre Gaspard Hubert. *Le Sénat de la République romaine: Sa composition et ses attributions.* 2 vols. Louvain: Peeters, 1878; reprint Aalen: Scientia Verlag, 1968.

Williamson, Callie. *The Laws of the Roman People: Public Law in the Expansion and Decline of the Roman Republic.* Ann Arbor: University of Michigan Press, 2005.

Wolf, Joseph Georg. "Jurisdiction in Urso." In *Judge and Jurists: Essays in Memory of Lord Rodger of Earlsferry*, edited by Andrew Burrows, David Johnston, and Reinhard Zimmermann, 307–323. Oxford and New York: Oxford University Press, 2013.

3 Sources of Roman law

This chapter addresses the origin and development of Roman legal sources – that is, the methods and procedures for establishing new legally binding rules, standards, and norms. The source of a legal norm gives it ultimate validity. Legal sources can be classified in many different ways. In this chapter the classification will be based on the distinction between power (potestas) and authority (auctoritas) because this is probably the most comprehensive way to understand the legal implications of Rome's transformation from the Republic to the Principate and then to the later Empire.

During the Republic, the legal sources produced by individuals or institutions vested with power (popular assemblies and magistrates) were basically the statutes (*leges* and *plebiscita*) and the edicts of the magistrates. On the other hand, the legal sources produced by individuals or institutions vested with moral authority (*auctoritas*) were the legal opinions (*responsa*) of the jurists and the resolutions of the Senate (senatus consulta). The Principate brought a major alteration in the system of legal sources when the authority of the jurists and senators was subordinated to the power of the emperor. The emperor granted legislative power to the Senate. As result, senatorial resolutions became, in practice, legislation, that is, a source of coercive power instead of a source of moral authority. On the other hand, the responsa of the jurists were submitted to imperial influence, opening the door to imperial rescripts, elaborated by the imperial chancellery under the direct control of the emperor.

During the later Empire, all sources of law ended up being mere expressions of the imperial power (imperial constitutions). The authority of jurists and senators ceased to be a constitutional limit on imperial power. Moral authority and imperial power were entirely identified in the person of the emperor, whose will had the force of a statute.

The Twelve Tables

The Twelve Tables (*lex duodecim tabularum*), the earliest Roman collection or set of fundamental rules of customary law, constituted the foundational text of the entire Roman legal system, a model, symbol, and paradigm of statutory law. Little is known of Roman law before this "codification." The Roman historian Livy (*Ab urbe condita* 3.34.6), probably imbued with republican patriotism, wrote that the Twelve Tables were the source of the entire body of public and private law: *fons omnis publici privatique iuris.* Despite unquestionable Greek influences, the Twelve Tables were indeed an archaic but genuine product of the Roman spirit and character. They show the important role of general legislation as an imperative source of certainty and equality among citizens.

Written with a lapidary simplicity and compressed archaic Latin style, at many points obscure, the provisions of the Twelve Tables consisted of brief commands and prohibitions in the fields of legal proceedings, private law (family law, the law of inheritance, property, contracts, torts), sacral law, and criminal law. The code was composed by a commission of ten men from 451 to 450 BCE, hence the name *leges decemvirales* – "laws of the ten men." The Centuriate Assembly ratified the code in 449 BCE, and it was engraved on twelve tables and attached to the rostra (a platform for speakers) before the curia in the Forum of Rome. It is probable that the final two tables were added later (Livy, *Ab urbe condita* 3.34).

The publication of the Twelve Tables constituted a new stage in the conflict between patricians and plebeians that marked the early Roman Republic. The Twelve Tables fixed the customary law that for a long time the patricians had interpreted and administered in their own interest. The code did not regulate public institutions, public offices, or the state religion, but only the individual rights and duties of Roman citizens, to protect them against abusive practices of the patricians in their legal relations with the plebeians and in their administration of justice. The code reflected the image of a transitional patriarchal and firmly aristocratic society that was trying to establish a more egalitarian political structure. The code implied private vengeance as a right of a harmed party, but with limitations. The political community inflicted public punishment only when a crime was directed against the community itself (e.g., high treason).

It is said that the original tables were destroyed during the devastating sacking and burning of Rome by the Gallic Celts in 390 BCE. It is possible, however, that some copies survived the great fire, since Cicero (106–43 BCE), centuries later, pointed out that during his school days, students had to learn to recite the Twelve Tables by heart (*De legibus* 2.59). No ancient copies have survived to our day. However, Roman writers – such as Cicero, Livy, Aulus Gellius, Festus, and Pomponius – provided good information about their contents, including a number of direct quotations. Some jurists, such as Labeo and Gaius, wrote commentaries on the Twelve Tables. Some fragments of the tables have been preserved in Justinian's Codification and have been instrumental to the partial reconstruction of the structure and content of the Twelve Tables. Often, the legal meaning of the fragments is uncertain, ambiguous, and controversial. The reconstruction of the Twelve Tables remains a work in progress, far from being complete. After the codification of the Twelve Tables, the Romans did not codify law again until the Theodosian Code (438 CE).

In some sense, the Twelve Tables played a similar role in Roman law to the Magna Carta in English law, or Las Partidas in Spanish law. Although none of the provisions of the Twelve Tables were directly applied in the classical period, they were integral to the inspiration of new legal ideas and concepts, as well as the construction of the legal system.

Leges and *plebiscita*

Lex and plebiscitum were the statutes of the Republican period. Lex was the enactment of the popular assemblies (*comitia centuriata* or *tributa*) on the proposal of a magistrate who convened and presided over the assembly. The magistrate submitted bills to the popular assemblies only after receiving the approval of the senators (*auctoritas patrum*). Plebiscitum was the enactment of a plebeian assembly on the proposal of the plebeian tribune, who also convened the assembly. Plebiscites did not need the approval of the Senate. Once plebiscites were assimilated into the leges, after the Hortensian Act of 287 BCE, they also were often called leges, even by their own jurists (see Ulpian, D. 9.2.1.1). The great majority of statutes were passed by the plebeian assemblies as plebiscites, which in specific instances were the most influential statutes for the development of private Roman law (e.g., *lex Aquilia de damno; lex Cincia de donis et muneribus*).

Statutes were recognized under the name of the magistrate or tribune who submitted the bill to the popular assembly (e.g., *lex Julia, lex Falcidia*). When two magistrates submitted the bill (e.g., the two consuls), the names of both were mentioned (e.g., the consuls Caninius Callus and Fufidius Geminus sponsored the *lex Fufia Caninia* on manumissions in 2 CE). We know about eight hundred leges and plebiscita, but we have only a few of them in the original inscription in bronze or stone.

Depending on the nature of the sanction (*Ep. Ulp.* 1.2), statutes establishing prohibitions could be "perfect" (*lex perfecta*), "less than perfect" (*lex minus quam perfecta*), or "imperfect" (*lex imperfecta*). A perfect or complete statute that forbids an act invalidates the forbidden act if it is done. A less-than-perfect statute does not invalidate the forbidden act but imposes a penalty against the person doing it. Finally, an imperfect or incomplete statute that forbids an act neither invalidates the forbidden act nor imposes a penalty for doing it, but the statute allows the magistrate to grant some remedies to protect the injured person. Originally, Roman statutes were imperfect or less than perfect. Only beginning in the later Republic were perfect statutes passed as a more effective way of implementing the purpose of the statutes and the intentions of the lawgivers. The oldest *lex perfecta* was probably the misogynistic *lex Voconia* (169 BCE), which limited the inheritance rights of women.

The *lex Cincia* (204 BCE) on donations provides a good example of an imperfect statute. The plebiscite prohibited donations exceeding a certain amount; however, a donation surpassing that maximum was not invalid. On the other hand, if a donor promised a donation exceeding the limit, and the promisee sued the donor to collect the promised sum above the limit, the praetor could protect the donor with the *exceptio legis Cinciae*, which reverted to the limit imposed by the statute. The famous *senatus consultum Macedonianum* under Emperor Vespasian was another example of an imperfect statute. It prohibited loans to sons under paternal power. If a lender loaned an amount to a son under parental power, the transaction was not void, but the son could be protected against the claim of the lender by an *exceptio senatus consulti Macedoniani*.

An example of a less-than-perfect statute was the *lex Furia testamentaria* (about 180 BCE), the earliest statute setting limits for legacies. It fixed the maximum amount for legacies at one thousand asses, except for legacies to the testator's closest relatives. If a person received a legacy for more money than the statute allowed, he had to pay fourfold the value of the surplus, but the legacy was considered valid. Finally, an example of *lex perfecta* was the *lex Falcidia* (40 BCE), which allowed the testator to dispose of three-quarters of his estate through legacies, but prohibited him from depriving his heir of the remaining fourth. The part of the legacy exceeding three-quarters was considered void. Something similar can be said of the *lex Aelia Sentia* (4 CE), which laid down conditions for the validity of manumissions; any manumission made in violation of its rules was void from the start.

The edicts of the magistrates

All the higher magistrates could issue edicts (*ius edicendi*) at any time of their magistracy to provide notice of their orders and intentions in the performance of their duties. A *lex Cornelia de edictis* of 67 BCE strictly bound the magistrates by their own edicts. For the development of Roman law, the praetorian edict, that is, the comprehensive proclamation of policy made by an urban praetor or a peregrine praetor on entering office, as an exercise of his annual jurisdiction, was essential because it was the means by which the civil law was implemented. Unfortunately, we know little of the peregrine edict since no vestige of it remains, and the few indirect sources of knowledge we have do not tell us much. We also know little about the so-called provincial edict, issued by the provincial governors to extend the Roman praetor's edict to citizens living in provinces. The fact that Gaius wrote a commentary on the provincial edict probably means that a central component of the edict applied to all provinces.

The praetorian edict was the main vehicle for the development of Roman law from about 130 BCE (*lex Aebutia*) to its final consolidation around 130 CE. The urban praetor's edict consisted of individual pronouncements, or edicts, establishing the circumstances under which the praetor would grant new remedies (*actiones*) and defining the "formulae," or patterns or models, of these remedies. The praetorian edict was published in the Forum on tables of wood painted white. For this reason, the edict of the praetor was also called *album* (white color). Each praetor naturally tended to adopt his predecessor's edict, incorporating only small changes with the help of jurists.

A new praetor would drop obsolete clauses and formulae, change existing clauses, and incorporate new ones from time to time. The earliest reference to a permanent addition to the edict was that made by Publius Rutilius Rufus around 118 BCE to protect the purchaser of the property of a bankrupt debtor. Aquilius Gallus (praetor in 66 BCE) introduced the formula concerning deceit to protect those who had suffered loss through another person's bad faith.

Gradually, the praetorian edict was improved with important innovations. By the end of the Republic, however, the edict became standardized, even though the praetor technically retained the authority to change it within his discretion. Such changes and additions were possible because of the interaction between praetors and jurists.

During the Principate, the praetorian edict waned in importance because of the increasing centralization of lawmaking power in the hands of the emperor. The praetor would incorporate changes only based on new resolutions of the Senate that were inspired by the emperor. By order of Emperor Hadrian, about 130 CE, the jurist Salvius Julianus, one of the greatest Roman jurists, was commissioned to prepare a revised and definitively fixed version of the praetorian (and the aedilitian) edict: the so-called *edictum perpetuum*. This conclusive version of the Edict was approved by a resolution of the Senate that established that from then on, modifications could be made only by the emperor (*Constitutio Tanta* 18). After Julianus's consolidation of the edict, the publication of edicts by praetors became a mere formality. Only the emperor could exercise legal creativity.

Ius honorarium

The new law that the magistrates introduced through edicts to adapt civil law to new circumstances and needs of the political community was called honorary law (*ius honorarium*), so named because *honores* were the dignity and privileges inherent to the office of the magistrate. The most important part of the ius honorarium was by far the law made by the praetors, both the urban and the peregrine (praetorian law). The legal contribution of the aediles, though also relevant, was more limited and modest.

In the first book of his *Institutes* (D.1.1.8), the jurist Marcianus wrote that the ius honorarium itself was the "living voice" (*viva vox*) of the civil law. The key to honorary law lay in the fact that the magistrate controlled remedies, and his primary legal function was to grant remedies in individual cases. Honorary law thus essentially consisted of procedural remedies developed within the Roman legal system to operate side-by-side with the civil law.

Papinian (D.1.1.7.1) explained that the role of honorary law was to "support, supplement, and correct" the civil law. Sometimes, praetorian law supported an existing civil right by providing a new, more effective remedy. This was the case, for instance, with the praetorian remedy called *actio Publiciana*, which allowed the time needed to acquire ownership of something through possession to be fictitiously asserted. Sometimes the praetor granted the actio

Publiciana in favor of a civil owner who had lost possession, simply to avoid the difficulties of proving ownership in accordance with the formalistic standards required by the civil remedy. In this case, praetorian law supported civil law by lightening the plaintiff's evidentiary burden. Likewise, for the sake of legal expediency, a civil heir might request a provisory remedy from the praetor instead of requesting a remedy by civil law.

Often praetorian law did not simply support an existing civil right but supplemented it, that is, extended it to new circumstances. This was another effect of the actio Publiciana, which was often requested by noncivil owners (praetorian owners) who had paid the purchase price of an item but without fulfilling all civil formalistic requirements for acquiring it. In such cases, praetorian law could free the plaintiff of some of those requirements for acquiring property under civil law. Sometimes, however, the praetor ruled in favor of a plaintiff even against a defendant who had the civil law on his side. In these cases, the praetor, that is, praetorian law, was not just supporting or supplementing civil law but correcting it. This was also true of the actio Publiciana when it was used to protect a noncivil owner against a civil owner (not just against a noncivil owner, as in the aforementioned case). That happened when the plaintiff did not receive the thing in dispute in accordance with the formalistic requirements of civil law. By vindicating the plaintiff, the praetor was truly changing civil law by ruling against the civil owner and for the party colloquially called the praetorian owner.

In another example, praetorian law modified civil law when the praetor protected the inheritance rights of an emancipated son even against the civil law. Civil law based inheritance rights not on blood kinship but on domestic paternal power (*patria potestas*). According to civil law, only sons who were under their father's paternal domestic power until his death could be his heirs. The civil rule, however, became obsolete in the later Republic when economic development called for a new status for emancipated young people. As a result, the praetor began to consider emancipated sons legitimate civil heirs by granting them possession of the estate over civil heirs. The praetor protected the emancipated sons by an order (*interdictum*) he issued at their request.

The original dualism between praetorian law and civil law determined to varying degrees the development of Roman law until the codification of the edict, when the distinction between civil law and praetorian law became meaningless. The great period of the ius honorarium was the convulsive last century of the Roman Republic, in which social and economic changes challenged the legal system. The birth of the formulary process allowed the praetor to take the lead in developing the law, concentrating legal power in the hands of the praetor. Political changes in the Principate reflected new ways, new systems, and new procedures for administering justice, and they ultimately replaced the formulary procedure with a new procedure (*cognitio*), displacing praetorian power by the power of the emperor.

Senatus consulta

During the Republic, the Senate had no legislative power. Its resolutions (senatus consulta, abbreviated SC or plural SCC) were based on the moral authority of the senators, and they did not go beyond an advisory function. To achieve legal relevance and force, these proposals had to be embodied in a statute approved by the popular assemblies or in an edict issued by the magistrate.

During the Principate, the emperor granted the Senate legislative power replacing the old forms of legislation of the popular assemblies, but this shift was gradual. This is probably why Gaius (1.4), in the second half of the second century CE, wrote that the legal force of the senatorial decrees was long disputed. The *S.C. Silanianum* (10 CE), for instance, condemned to torture, and eventually to death, all slaves living together when a master of slaves was assassinated by an unknown murderer (Tacitus, *Annales* 14, 42–45). We know that the *SC Silanianum* was put into effect by adding a new clause (or edict) in the Edict of the Praetor (Lenel, *E. P.* §364). Otherwise, it would never have obtained legal force.

What seems clear is that during the reign of Hadrian, after the consolidation of the edict, senatorial resolutions obtained direct legal force of their own. The *S.C. Tertullianum* under Hadrian (Inst. 3.3.2), which granted civil law rights of succession to a mother whose child had died intestate, was the first indisputable senatorial resolution with civil legal force.

Senatorial resolutions constituted a salient source of law during the first two centuries. In the field of private law, for instance, the *S.C. Largianum* (42 CE) established the order of succession for inheritances of the so-called Latini Juniani, who were the slaves manumitted in violation of the provision of the *Lex Aelia Sentia* (4 CE); the *SC Velleianum* (around 46 CE) forbade women to assume responsibility for other people; the aforementioned *SC Macedonianum* (47 CE) prohibited the giving of loans to sons still under paternal domestic power. The *S.C. Neronianum* and *S.C. Trebelianum* under Emperor Nero, *S.C. Pegasianum* under Vespasian, and *S.C. Juventianum* under Hadrian, all made important reforms in the regulation of bequests. And so on. The *SC Orficianum* (178 CE), once the edict was fixed, gave a woman's children preference in her inheritance over her brothers and sisters. At the end of the second century, the resolutions of the Senate were identified with the speech of the emperor to the Senate, which was read out at the Senate session on his behalf by a subordinate magistrate.

We know about more than two hundred senatorial resolutions of the Republic and the Principate. The original inscription in bronze of the famous *S.C. de Bacchanalibus* (186 CE), establishing some regulations against the so-called Bacchanalian conspiracy, has been preserved. It was discovered in 1640 at Tiriolo (southern Italy) and is kept in the Kunsthistorisches Museum in Vienna. The resolutions of the Senate were often named after one of the consuls of the year who proposed them (e.g., *S.C. Orficianum*, 178 CE), but they were also named after the emperor who proposed them (e.g., *S.C. Claudianum*) or after the occasion of the S.C. (e.g., *S.C. Macedonianum*).

Responsa prudentium

The foremost activity of Roman jurists was to provide legal opinions or legal answers (responsa) to questions asked not only by private individuals but also by magistrates and judges, who ordinarily were not experts in law. Responsa could be oral or written answers, and they could be given formally or with elegant informality. They could also be given prior to or during a trial. Cicero (*De oratore* 3.133), for instance, stated that Manius Manilius, one of the founders of civil law, used to walk across the Forum to give all citizens the possibility of consulting him orally upon any legal subject. Jurists were focused only on questions of law, not on questions of fact. "This is not for us; to Cicero" (*nihil hoc ad ius, ad Ciceronem*) used to be the response of the jurist Aquilius Gallus, Cicero's friend, when someone brought to him a case that involved a question of fact; Cicero himself shared this view (*Topica* 12.51). Cicero was considered an orator, not a true jurist, since he had the ability to argue both for and against any proposition.

The jurists held no official position and received no remuneration for their services. Their work only gave them public recognition and celebrity. The legitimation of their opinions rested exclusively on their personal moral authority and reputation in the court of public opinion. (Originally, however, the responses of the pontifices, or high priests, in pontifical jurisprudence based on the earliest opinion were binding precedents.) Cicero (*De oratore* 1.45.198) complained about the new practice because some jurists, after gaining distinction and respect with their opinions, prevailed in new cases rather more by their moral authority than by their talents and arguments.

The responsa were the meeting point between the legal science and the legal practice of ordinary life, and they contributed deeply to the development of Roman society. At the end of the Principate, the responsa ceased to be instrumental for the development of Roman law. We know many responsa because they were frequently mentioned in the Digest of Justinian (e.g. Scaevola, D. 3.5.34; Paul, D. 42.1.41pr, or Proculus, D. 50.16.125).

Ius respondendi

Augustus granted some distinguished jurists the privilege to provide opinions (responsa) on legal questions, not only on the strength of their private reputation and authority but by the public authority of the emperor (Pomponius, D. 1.2.2.49). Through the *ius respondendi*, Augustus created a circle of prominent jurists who supported the politics of the Principate and were able to have a powerful impact on the legal order. After being granted the privilege, jurists were divided between recognized and nonrecognized. Nonrecognized jurists could continue giving responsa in accordance with the republican pattern, but not based on the highest authority, that of the emperor.

The ius respondendi was in strict accordance with the character of Augustus. On the one hand, the measure supported and promoted a republican practice, the responsa of the jurists; on the other hand, it contributed to improving imperial control over lawyers. Emperor Tiberius was the first who granted the privilege to a jurist of the equestrian class, the famous jurist Masurius Sabinus (Pomponius, D.1.2.2.48). It is possible, therefore, that Augustus originally accepted only senators for the privilege. Under the emperors, the equestrian order constituted an aristocratic order second only to the senatorial order.

The jurists with ius respondendi did not receive an official position, nor were their opinions binding on judges and magistrates. There was no sanction for judges or magistrates who ignored the legal opinion of the authorized jurists. It was reasonable, however, for judges and magistrates to accept legal opinions that enjoyed imperial support and recommendation.

Many salient lawyers (Labeo, among others), in opposition to the new character of the Principate, never asked for the ius respondendi, especially under Emperors Claudius and Caligula, who disliked lawyers. Emperor Hadrian, probably to promote the equestrian order, is said to have strongly recommended not granting the privilege to senators who were not really experts in the legal science. He also ruled that when the opinions of jurists with the privilege were all in agreement, they bound the judges. After Emperor Hadrian, the practice of granting the imperial privilege gradually declined.

Rescripta Principum

Rescripts were written answers prepared at the imperial chancellery and given by the emperor upon a written petition from a citizen (sometimes communities or officials) confronted with a problem. From a legal point of view, rescripts formed a single category regardless of the petitioner. Originally, the emperor himself was involved in the legal decision-making process of the rescript. For instance, on the occasion of a rescript of Marcus Aurelius and Luius Verus, Ulpian (D. 37.14.17pr.) referred to a discussion of the emperors with the lawyers of their council. Later, in the third century, the emperor delegated the elaboration of rescripts to his secretary of petitions.

Rescripts were issued on the physical petition itself in the form of a subscript: the imperial decision and signature were written in under the petition addressed to the emperor. The citizen could ask for specific protection, a privilege, or a benefit, and the emperor would write his answer beneath the request. The various contents of a petition are called *preces*. The rescripts were publicly displayed, and the petitioner received a copy only by request. After the publication of the rescripts, judges were bound by the imperial decisions they contained, thus establishing a binding precedent for the future. The rescripts did not deal with matters of fact, but only with matters of law.

Therefore, the judge had to ascertain the facts before applying the rescript to support his judgment.

From Hadrian to Diocletian, rescripts were the most important source of law. They contributed enormously to the development of Roman law, but they also contributed to the decline of Roman jurisprudence. The legal profession had been one of the most honorable professions because of its independence and freedom. Now, however, the legal profession was under the control of the imperial administration and bureaucracy.

Most of the rescripts we know survived in Justinian's Code and come from collections of rescripts made by jurists during the reign of Diocletian, specifically the Codex Gregorianus and the Codex Hermogenianus. Over twenty-five hundred private rescripts were given in the name of the emperor during the third century. A chronological list of these rescripts from 193 to 305 CE was carefully compiled by Tony Honoré (*Emperors and Lawyers*, 2nd ed., 1994).

Imperial constitutions

Constitution is a general term including all categories of imperial enactment. According to Gaius, an imperial constitution was "what the emperor ordains by decree, edict, or letter" (Gaius 1.5). The argument Gaius made to defend the same binding force for imperial constitutions and other legislative sources was that the emperor's powers derived from a lex, the *lex de imperio*, and therefore imperial constitutions ultimately rested, like the statutes, on a popular decision. Underlying the imperial will was the popular will. Ulpian (D. 1.4.1pr) repeated the same statement: "What the emperor ordained has the legal force of a statute" (*quod Principi placuit legis habet vigorem*).

Emperors appropriated the right to issue edicts based on their personal imperium. Imperial edicts were unrelated and miscellaneous, and were addressed to the general public. They covered topics of private law, criminal law, administrative law, privileges, land law, and so on. They remained in force during the life of the emperor, and they continued tacitly in force unless the following emperor abolished them. The *Constitutio Antoniniana* (212 CE) of Caracalla, which granted Roman citizenship to all free individuals of the empire, and the Edict of Milan (313 CE) of Constantine and Licinius, granting toleration and freedom of worship for all religions, including Christianity, are probably the most famous imperial edicts (although it is still debated whether there was a formal Edict of Milan).

Imperial decrees were judicial decisions on civil and criminal matters pronounced after an oral proceeding before the emperor's court. Pliny the Younger provided a good account of these imperial procedures (*Epistulae* 4.22; 6.22; 6.31). Although the emperor was advised by his council, he made the final decision. Paul, in his book three on imperial decrees (D. 29.2.97), explained that, in a case on inheritance, the emperor eventually decided to follow the opinion of Papinian instead of Paul's view. The emperor's decisions bound the parties, but when published by the emperor they could be considered precedents, and they achieved general validity. Callistratus (D. 4.2.13) provided a part of a decree of the emperor Marcus Aurelius imposing on creditors the obligation of claiming what they believed to be due to them through the intermediary of a judge. According to this decree, a creditor who forced the debtor to pay without a judicial hearing lost the claim.

Imperial letters (*epistulae*) included all imperial communications. They provided the emperor's answers, by a separate letter, to questions, petitions, or requests for advice by officials, provincial governors, and provincial assemblies. The correspondence between Emperor Trajan and Pliny the Younger (c. 112 CE) regarding the Christians during his governorship of Bithynia (modern Turkey) provides a good example of the value of an epistle. Rescripts could be considered a specific type of imperial letter.

Gaius did not include the *mandata principum* in the imperial constitutions, but the Justinian Code (C.J. 1.15) mentioned them. Mandates were general instructions or judicial and administrative rules issued by the emperor to provincial governors. When the content of a mandate affected the inhabitants of a province, the governor of the province would issue an edict to publicize the imperial instruction.

The *Constitutio Antoniniana*

One of the great landmarks of Roman history, the *Constitutio Antoniniana*, was an edict of Emperor Antoninus Caracalla of 212 CE that expanded Roman citizenship to all free men and women of the empire with the minor exclusion of some prisoners of war. A surviving papyrus from Egypt, at the University Library of Giessen, in Germany (P. Giessen 40 I), seems to preserve the original text of the constitution. Because it contains gaps, however, it provides only a general idea of the purpose of the constitution. The jurist Ulpian, master of requests under Caracalla, also left us details in his commentary on the edict: "Everyone in the Roman world has been made Roman citizens as a result of the constitution of the Emperor Antoninus" (Ulpian, D. 1.5.17). In this text, however, there are no restrictions.

The ultimate reasons for and effects of the constitution are disputed. The Roman consul and historian Cassius Dio (78.9), also contemporary with and hostile to Caracalla, implied that the real purpose of the grant was the imperial desire to grow revenues by increasing the numbers of citizens liable for taxes (specifically inheritance taxes and taxes on manumissions of slaves). Religious reasons (e.g., to win new devotees to Roman gods) have also been alleged based on the papyrus. Saint Augustine (*De civitate Dei* 5.17) highlighted the humanitarian character of the decree. What is indisputable is that the impact of the constitution in the long run was enormous: the constitution stimulated in both the eastern and the western parts of the empire a uniform legal system, forged a spirit of identification with the empire, and increased the consciousness of being a Roman.

The Gregorian and Hermogenian Codes

The Gregorian and Hermogenian Codes are two collections, consisting mainly of rescripts, published around 300 CE. The two collections were probably the first legal works to appear in the form of a codex, a book constructed of a number of sheets of vellum, papyrus, or similar materials bound together, rather than the traditional scroll format. Unfortunately, neither the Gregorian nor the Hermogenian Code survived. We know parts of them basically through the Justinian Code. The Gregorian Code consisted mainly of private rescripts from Hadrian to Diocletian (until 290), while the Hermogenian Code consisted almost entirely of private rescripts between Diocletian and his colleagues issued in 293 and 294. Both codes remained in circulation until the publication of the Justinian Code in 528, which incorporated many of their laws.

We have no information about the author of the Gregorian Code beyond that the code used his name: Gregorius or Gregorianus. We know, however, that the Hermogenian Code was collected by Hermogenianus, a prominent lawyer of the Diocletian court, probably Dioclecian's *magister libellorum* (master of petitions) from the beginning of 293 to the end of 294. After 294, Hermogenianus probably served Western co-emperor Maximinian in the same capacity, and he completed the code in Milan in 295. Around 300, Hermogenianus published six books of *Iuris epitomae* (Summaries of law), a digest or synopsis that tried to offer the basic law and legal principles of his time in an easy format to legal practitioners.

The Gregorian and Hermogenian Codes are relevant for the history of Roman law because they spread imperial law around the empire in a systematic and comprehensive way and in accordance with the practical needs of governors, officials, lawyers, and Roman citizens in general. The codes also confirmed the dominance of the imperial creation and interpretation of normative legal sources.

The Theodosian Code

The *Codex Theodosianus* consisted of a body of around twenty-five hundred imperial constitutions created from 306 to 437, or from Constantine to the Eastern emperor Theodosius II (r. 408–50), who promulgated the code in 438. It took effect in the eastern part of the empire on January 1, 439. A little later, the code was also published and took effect in the Western Roman Empire under Emperor Valentinian III (r. 425–55). The code was acclaimed by the Senates of both Constantinople and Rome.

Theodosius II intended to harmonize the law in both parts of the empire, eliminating forgeries, reducing the bulk of laws, and providing an elegant, clear, and well-adjusted *corpus iuris* for the use of legal actors and practitioners. In 429, he set up an initial commission in Constantinople to collect the general imperial constitutions from Constantine up until then, put them in chronological order under headings, and shorten them so that only the operative parts remained (C.Th. 1.1.5). The commission also had the ambitious task of gathering related jurisprudential sources, but this did not happen. After this first stage was completed, in December 435, Theodosius charged a new and enlarged commission (C.Th. 1.5.6) with editing the material and completing the work. The emperor authorized the commission to make additions, emendations, and alterations. All original imperial constitutions lost validity after the publication of the code. The leader of both commissions and chief architect of the Theodosian Code was the high official (quaestor, praetorian prefect, and consul) Antiochus Chuzon, a lawyer from Antioch. When the code was promulgated, he was praised as "extraordinary in all things" (*cuncta sublimis*, Nov. Th. 1.39).

The Theodosian Code was written in Latin and consisted of sixteen books divided into titles according to subject matter. Each constitution contained an inscription with the name(s) of the emperor(s) who enacted it and the addressee, the text of the constitution, and a subscript at the end with the place and date of the enactment. Some constitutions were divided and located under different sections of the code. The date of each constitution was important for resolving conflicts between laws, as a later constitution prevailed over an earlier one. Theodosius and succeeding emperors continued to legislate by promulgating new imperial constitutions, also called novels (*novellae constitutiones*). The last novel was a constitution by Emperors Leo and Anthemius in 468.

The Theodosian Code was in force in the East until Justinian abolished it with the first edition of his code in April 529. Justinian included much of the content of the Theodosian Code in his own code. In the West, a large extract of the Theodosian Code was included in the *Lex Romana Visigothorum* or Breviary of Alaric (506). This was a collection of Roman law ordered by Alaric II, king of the Visigoths, and applied to the Hispano-Roman and Gallo-Roman populations.

Books 6–16 of the Theodosian Code survive more or less intact; the recovery of the first five books was possible through combining the extract of the Breviary of Alaric, which provided the skeleton of the legal body, and Justinian's Code, which provided the content of the laws. Theodor Mommsen made the best edition of the Theodosian Code (Berlin, 1905). Years later, Paul Krüger again edited the first eight books (Berlin, 1923 and 1926). Clyde Pharr translated the Theodosian Code into English (1952).

The Law of Citations

With the aim of regulating the use of classical precedents in court, an imperial constitution was issued in November 426 by Western Roman Emperor Valentinian III (or, rather, by his regent mother, Galla Placidia). The constitution, however, was operative in both parts of the empire. This imperial constitution made the work of five jurists primary authorities: Papinian, Paul, Ulpian, Modestinus, and Gaius. The Law of Citations was an attempt to reduce the difficulties judges faced in dealing with the large bulk of classical legal literature, by creating a canon of authoritative legal works of classical jurisprudence.

It is widely believed that the constitution issued in 426 was subjected to a revision in 438 on the occasion of the promulgation of the Theodosian Code (C.Th. 1.4.3). Probably the original constitution only recognized and confirmed the primary authority of the writings of the five great aforementioned jurists. In all likelihood, the reason for distinguishing these five lawyers was not only their reputation but also the wide availability of good manuscripts of their work. In case of differences of opinions among them, the view of the majority was to be followed; in case of equal voting, the opinion of Papinian was to be decisive.

The revised version of the Law of Citations, published in 438, confirmed not just the authority of the works of the five primary jurists but also the authority of those legal works quoted by the five principal jurists, such as the works of Scaevola, Sabinus, Julian, and Marcellus. These legal works, however, because of their antiquity, needed to be presented anew with a collation of manuscripts. This new version of the Law of Citations continued applying the same rules of preference. When conflicting opinions were cited, the majority opinion prevailed. If numbers were equal, Papinian's opinion prevailed. If Papinian was silent, the judge had to make his own judgment. This expansion of the original rule generated uncertainty among judges because of the vast number of quotations and the difficulties of confirming the authenticity of the manuscripts.

The Law of Citations reflects the decadence of Roman jurisprudence in the Late Empire. On the one hand, it based legal conclusions not on the quality of the associated legal arguments but on the personal authority of the jurist; on the other hand, by reducing judges' room to form independent judgments, it prevented the evolution of legal theory.

Further reading

Berger, Adolf. *Encyclopedic Dictionary of Roman Law*. Philadelphia: The American Philosophical Society, 1953; reprint, 1980.

Bleicken, Jochem. *Lex Publica. Gesetz und Recht in der römischen Republik*. Berlin and New York: Walter De Gruyter, 1978.

Brennan, Corey T. *The Praetorship in the Roman Republic*. Oxford and New York: Oxford University Press, 2000.

Buraselis, Kostas. *Theia dorea. Das göttlich-kaiserliche Geschenk. Studien zur Politik der Severer und zur Constitutio Antoniniana*. Vienna: Österreichische Akademie der Wissenschaften, 2007.

Comá Fort, Jose María. *Codex Theodosianus. Historia de un texto*. Madrid: Dykinson, 2014.

Crawford, Michael H. *Roman Statutes*. 2 vols. London: Institute of Classical Studies, 1996.

Domingo, Rafael, ed. *Textos de Derecho romano*. 2nd ed. Cizur Menor: Thomson Reuters Aranzadi, 2002.

Harries, Jill, and Ian Wood, eds. *The Theodosian Code: Studies in the Imperial Law of Late Antiquity.* 2nd ed. London: Bristol Classical Press, 2010.

Honoré, Tony. *Emperors and Lawyers.* 2nd ed. Oxford: Clarendon Press, 1994.

Humbert, Michel, ed. *Le dodici tavole. Dai decemviri agli umanisti.* Pavia: IUSS Press, 2005.

Ibbetson, David. "Sources of Law from the Republic to the Dominate." In *The Cambridge Companion to Roman Law,* edited by David Johnston, 25–55. Cambridge and New York: Cambridge University Press, 2015.

Johnson, Allan Chester, Paul Robinson Coleman-Norton, Frank Card Bourne, and Clyde Pharr, ed. *Ancient Roman Statutes.* Austin: University of Texas Press, 1961.

Jolowicz, Herbert Felix, and Barry Nicholas. *Historical Introduction to the Study of Roman Law.* 3rd ed. Cambridge: Cambridge University Press, 1972.

Kaser, Max. *Das römische Privatrecht.* 2 vols. 2nd ed. Munich: Beck Verlag, 1971 and 1975.

Kelly, J. M. "The Growth-Pattern of the Praetor's Edict." *Irish Jurist* 1 (1966): 341–355.

Kunkel, Wolfgang. *An Introduction to Roman Legal and Constitutional History.* 2nd ed. Translated by J. M. Kelly. Oxford: Clarendon Press, 1973.

Lenel, Otto. *Das Edictum Perpetuum. Ein Versuch zu seiner Wiederherstellung.* 3rd ed. Leipzig: Tauchnitz, 1927; reprint Aalen, 1956.

Matthews, John. *Laying Down the Law. A Study of the Theodosian Code.* New Haven, CT: Yale University Press, 2000.

Pharr, Clyde. *The Theodosian Code and Novels and the Sirmondian Constitutions: A Translation with Commentary, Glossary, and Bibliography.* Princeton, NJ: Princeton University Press, 1952.

Rotondi, Giovanni. *Leges publicae Populi Romani.* Milan: Società Editrice Italiana, 1912.

Rudorff, Adolf Friedrich. *De iuris dictione edictum. Edicti perpetui quae reliqua sunt.* Edited by Rafael Domingo. Pamplona: Eunsa, 1997.

Schiavone, Aldo. *The Invention of the Law in the West.* Translated by Jeremy Carden and Anthony Shugaar. London and Cambridge, MA: The Belknap Press of Harvard University Press, 2012.

Schiller, Arthur. "Senatus Consulta in the Principate." *Tulane Law Review* 33 (1959): 491–508.

Sirks, Boudewijn. *The Theodosian Code. A Study.* Friedrichtsdorf: Editions Tortuga, 2007.

Tuori, Kaius. "The ius respondendi and the Freedom of Roman Jurisprudence." *Revue internationale des droits de l'Antiquité* 51 (2004): 295–337.

Volterra, Edoardo. "Senatus Consulta." *Novissino Digesto Italiano* 16 (1961): 1047–1178; new edition by Pierangelo Buongiorno, *et al.* Stuttgart: Franz Steiner Verlag, 2017.

Watson, Alan. *Law Making in the Later Roman Republic.* Oxford: Clarendon Press, 1974.

Watson, Alan. *Rome of the Twelve Tables: Persons and Property.* Princeton, NJ: Princeton University Press, 1975.

Westbrook, Raymond. "The Nature and Origin of the Twelve Tables." *Zeitschrift der Savigny-Stiftung für Rechtsgeschichte. Romanistische Abteilung* 105 (1988): 74–121.

Wieacker, Franz. *Römische Rechtgeschichte. Quellenkunde, Rechtsbildung, Jurisprudenz und Rechtsliteratur* I. Munich: Beck Verlag, 1988.

Wolff, Hans Julius. *Roman Law: An Historical Introduction.* Norman: University of Oklahoma Press, 1951.

4 The jurists and the legal science

This chapter addresses the spirit, style, and character of the Roman jurists, the true architects of the Roman legal system. They formed a distinct group within Roman society, and their existence constituted a phenomenon specific to Roman culture. The original Roman jurists were priests. In the third century BCE, however, they began to develop a secular jurisprudence. They cultivated a sophisticated and practical legal science and produced a substantial literature in the field of law: commentaries on civil law and on the praetorian edict, collections of legal opinions or legal distinctions, monographs on legal topics, and so on.

Unlike the Greeks, Roman jurists spent little time on philosophical abstractions. They were primarily concerned with finding fair solutions in individual cases. Their interest in philosophical issues was peripheral. They did not develop a general theory of justice, law, the state, or political administration. They simply accommodated Greek philosophy when necessary for their legal purposes. Roman jurists were concerned with the daily practice of law, probably because most of them were public men involved in politics and interested in legal issues (without any remuneration) only as a part of their political careers. The development of legal science was a matter of disputation over interpretations of law. In this process, there emerged two groups, or schools, of jurists, the Sabinians and the Proculians, following different legal formulations, techniques, and methods.

The history of Roman legal science is inherently linked to the history of Rome. During the Republic and the early Principate, the number of jurists was small. They usually came from senatorial families. Legal education and expertise often remained within particular families (as with, for example, Mucius Scaevola, Labeo, Neratius Pricus, and Celsus). The Principate favored jurists as a group. Augustus tried to make some opinions more authoritative than others and granted some jurists the privilege to hand down opinions publicly, based on the emperor's authority (*ius respondendi*). The development of the ius respondendi is still unclear. A century later, Emperor Hadrian considered that the opinion of privileged jurists had the force of law and bound judges. He also reorganized imperial administration, investing a great number of Roman jurists with equestrian status. The extension of Roman citizenship to all inhabitants of the empire by Caracalla in 212 demanded new legal developments and opened the door to the last generation of classical jurists, many of them of provincial origin.

The best source of knowledge about Roman jurisprudence is the Digest of Justinian, a compilation of excerpts from the works of Roman jurists. The account of the history of Roman jurisprudence given by Pomponius in some surviving fragments of his textbook (D. 1.2.2) provides important information about the early periods. Literary sources, especially the writings of Cicero, offer abundant material, too, about the work of jurists at the end of the Roman Republic.

Cicero classified his work as falling outside the field of jurisprudence (*Brutus* 41.151; *Pro Murena* 13, 29–30; *De oratore* 41.141), although in his youth he received legal instruction from Quintus Mucius Scaevola Augur (159–88 BCE) and Quintus Mucius Scaevola Pontifex (died 82 BCE). Cicero was not a jurist in the strict sense but a successful advocate and a legal orator, as well as a statesman, a philosopher, and a writer. Legal oratory and advocacy demanded some knowledge of public and private law but not the legal expertise required to become a true jurist. The jurist Servius Sulpicius Rufus, Cicero's friend, was an orator before becoming a jurist. For orators, the law was the subject matter of their speeches but not the purpose of their profession.

Early history of jurisprudence

Originally, Roman jurisprudence was in the hands of the high priests (*pontifices*) who took care of state religion, public worship, and sacral law. They were the creators of the first intellectual and technical elaboration of the law. Like a religious liturgy, early law was uniform, formal, and self-consistent. According to Cicero, no practice could be more excellent than that of entrusting both religious worship and the highest interests of Rome to the same people, namely to the most honorable and eminent citizens (*De domo sua* 1.1). This unbreakable link between religion and law in early Roman law afforded the pontiffs an important position in legal matters.

The pontiffs constituted a body, the Pontifical College, that grew from three members to fifteen or even more. They organized the Roman calendar and watched over the forms preserved in the archives of the Pontifical College. They were the experts and guardians of rules and sacred rites. Until the third century BCE, the Pontifical College had a monopoly on the law and legal proceedings. As the keepers of the legal forms and rites that had to be applied in legal procedures, the pontiffs were therefore the interpreters of the law.

Tradition attributes the breakdown of the monopoly to the fact that Gnaeus Flavius, a secretary of Appius Claudius Caecus (censor in 312 BCE), compiled and published with Appius's consent the first collection of legal forms of civil actions (*ius Flavianum*) around 300 BCE. Tiberius Coruncanius, consul in 280 BCE and the first plebeian *pontifex maximus*, or chief priest, was also the first who offered public consultation on legal issues (Pomponius, D. 1.2.2.35), thereby transforming jurisprudence into a legal profession. According to Pomponius (D. 1.2.2.38), the earliest major work of legal literature was the *Tripertita* of Sextus Aelius Paetus, consul in 198 BCE. The *Tripertita* consisted of an edition of the Twelve Tables, an interpretation of this law, and formularies for litigation and legal transaction. The *Tripertita* still existed in Pomponius's time, and it was called "the cradle of the law."

The founders of the civil law

According to Pomponius (D. 1.2.2.39), the founders of the civil law were Manius Manilius, Marcus Iunius Brutus, and Publius Mucius Scaevola. They were called founders probably because they published the first books containing legal arguments, and they created new legal formularies.

A member of the Scipionis circle, Manius Manilius (consul in 149 BCE) was the author of a collection of clauses applicable to sales. Varro (*De re rustica* 2.3.5) specifically praised the quality of Manilius's stipulation guaranteeing the health and good conditions of goats that were going to be sold. Manilius enjoyed a high reputation because of the quality of his opinions (responsa) and his generosity in helping others with his legal knowledge (Cicero, *De oratore* 3.133). A legal eminence but also an enigmatic figure, Marcus Iunius Brutus, praetor in 142 BCE, was the author of a work on civil law containing a dialogue with his son on legal issues and his responsa, perhaps as a posthumous appendix.

We possess more information about the third founder of civil law: Publius Mucius Scaevola (died 113 BCE). Tribune in 141 BCE, consul in 133 BCE, and later pontifex maximus, Publius Mucius Scaevola was the son of the consul of 175 BCE and a member of an important family of jurists, including his brother (by adoption), Licinius Crassus Mucianus, who was also consul in 131 BCE and pontifex maximus, and his cousin Quintus Mucius Scaevola Augur, consul in 117 BCE. The most distinguished jurist among the Mucii was Quintus Mucius Scaevola Pontifex, perhaps the leading lawyer of the Roman Republic.

Quintus Mucius Scaevola Pontifex

Quintus Mucius Scaevola Pontifex (sometimes called Q. Mucius, sometimes Q. Scaevola), son of Publius Mucius Scaevola, was born about 140 BCE. He was quaestor in 110/109 BCE, tribune of the plebs in 106 BCE, curule aedile by 100 BCE, praetor by 98 BCE, consul in 95 BCE, and governor of Asia afterwards. As a consul, Scaevola passed a controversial statute (*lex Licinia Mucia*) with his colleague Lucius Licinius Crassus, creating a criminal tribunal against aliens falsely enrolled as Roman citizens. In his position as governor of Asia, he issued an edict on provincial administration that became a model for later governors. In 89 BCE he was appointed pontifex maximus, the last jurist known to have held that office. In 82 BCE, Marius the Younger, Scaevola's son-in-law, gave orders to the urban praetor Lucius Junius Brutus Damasippus to kill all those who were likely to support Sulla's return, including Scaevola. He was killed by the Marians in the Temple of the Vestals, and his body was thrown into the Tiber River.

A deep legal thinker and excellent interpreter of the law, Quintus Mucius was the most eloquent jurist (equitable, dispassionate, and also brief in his speeches) but not the most brilliant orator (Cicero, *Brutus* 39, 145–46). Greatly influenced by Greek dialectic, Quintus Mucius wrote the first systematic legal treatise on civil law in eighteen books, which later jurists such as Gaius and Pomponius commented on in the second century. His treatise is considered the most relevant work of republican jurisprudence. Based on the Twelve Tables, Quintus advocated using legal categories (*genera* and *species*). A single fragment of his original work on civil law survived, quoted literally by Aulus Gellius (*Noctes Atticae* 6.15.2): "If anyone has used something that was entrusted to his care, or having borrowed anything to use, has applied it to another purpose than that for which he borrowed, he is liable for theft." Scaevola also wrote a handbook of short rules and explanations on legal terms called *Horoi* (definitions), which was used in Justinian's Digest.

Quintus Mucius was the creator of the famous *cautio Muciana*, which allowed a widow who was left a legacy by her husband on the condition that she not remarry to benefit from the bequest. He was also the designer of the *praesumptio Muciana*, which established that all that a wife possessed was given to her by her husband, unless she could prove the contrary.

In 93 BCE, Scaevola confronted his former colleague Lucius Licinius Crassus, the greatest orator of his time, in the famous *causa Curiana* (Cicero, *De oratore* 1.180–81). It was a trial before the centumviral court on the validity of a will written by a certain Coponius. Coponius appointed his as-yet-unborn son as his heir and Manius Curius as substitute heir, so that Curius could succeed to the estate in the event that Coponius's unborn son died before reaching majority (pupillary substitution) and, therefore, without being able to make a testament himself. When Coponius died, he had neither a son nor an unborn son on the way. The question was whether the estate should go to Manius Curius, who claimed it as a substitute, based on a reading of the simple substitution into the will's provision for pupillary substitution, or to Marcus Coponius, who claimed it on behalf of the intestate heirs. Scaevola appeared for Coponius, and Crasssus for Curius. Scaevola defended the strict literal interpretation of the wording of a will (a simple substitution was not explicitly contained in the will) against the opinion of Crassus, who insisted that the will should be interpreted according to the testator's intention based on the ordinary use of the language and on equity. Crassus persuaded the court in favor of his client Manius Curius.

Quintus Mucius had many pupils (Volcacius, Lucius Balbus, and probably Cornelius Maximus), but the leader among them was Aquilius Gallus. Aquilius was praetor in 66 BCE and a good friend of Cicero, his colleague as praetor. An original and innovative lawyer, Aquilius Gallus was the creator of the so-called Aquilian stipulation (Inst. 3.29.2 and D. 46.4.18.1), which afforded a legal means of granting a general discharge of claims that one party had against another. He was also the designer of the action for fraud (*actio de dolo*), which protected persons who suffered loss through the bad faith of another. Aquilius's speed at giving responsa was legendary (Cicero, *Brutus* 42.154).

Servius Sulpicius Rufus

A pupil of Aquilius Gallus, Servius Sulpicius Rufus (c. 105–43 BCE) was the most influential jurist of the generation after Scaevola. In 78 BCE, Servius went to Rhodes with Cicero to learn dialectic and philosophy. He became a full orator but, lacking the talents of an orator (Cicero, *pro Murena* 10.23), decided at some point to study law under Lucilius Balbus and, especially, Aquilius. According to Pomponius (D. 1.2.2.43), the true reason Servius became a lawyer was out of an emotional reaction against a severe reproach by Quintus Mucius for his ignorance of the law.

Servius held the offices of quaestor in 75 BCE, praetor in 65 BCE, and consul in 51 BCE. In 49 BCE he joined Pompey the Great in opposition to Julius Caesar, though without enthusiasm. Caesar forgave him and, in 46, appointed Servius proconsul of Achaia (in Greece). Servius stayed there until 45 BCE. He died while working as an ambassador to Mark Antony in January 43 BCE, and he was honored with a public funeral. The *Ninth Philippic* (February 4, 43), published only a month after Servius's death, was Cicero's eulogy to him.

We know the content of the two celebrated letters Servius wrote to his friend and rival Cicero (Cicero, *Ad familiares* 4.5 and 4.12), one on the death of Tullia, Cicero's daughter, and the other informing Cicero of the assassination of Marcus Claudius Marcellus, who was consul the same year as Servius. Servius wrote many works, among them a commentary on the Twelve Tables and the first commentary on the praetorian edict. He left a large collection of responsa and instructed many students, including Alfenus Varus (consul in 39 BCE) and Aulus Ofilius, friend of Julius Caesar.

Other republican jurists

Beyond the circle of the pupils of Servius, three distinguished jurists flourished at the end of the Republic: Aelius Tubero, Aulus Cascelius, and Trebatius Testa. A pupil of Ofilius, Aulus Tubero was the son-in-law of Servius Sulpicius Rufus (Pomponius, D. 1.2.2.51) and, as a result, the natural link between Servius's circle and the other jurists. He wrote on the Senate and on the duties of judges. Cascelius, pupil of Volcatius, was an independent mind and a strong supporter of traditional republican ideals. He held the office of quaestor (c. 74 BCE), and he rejected Augustus's offer to become consul (Pomponius, D. 1.2.2.45). When friends urged him not to speak so freely against the new order instituted by Augustus, he replied that two things gave him complete freedom of speech: his old age and childlessness (Valerius Maximus 6.2.12). The last jurist, Trebatius, pupil of Cornelius Maximus, enjoyed so much attention in Cicero's works that Cicero dedicated his famous *Topica* to Trebatius and recommended Trebatius as a legal adviser to Julius Caesar. Trebatius also enjoyed the favor of Emperor Augustus, who suggested that informal codicils could be recognized as valid (Inst. 2.25). Trebatius was the teacher of the top jurist of the age of Augustus: Marcus Antistius Labeo.

Jurists of the early Principate

The jurists from the reign of Augustus up to the reign of Hadrian were divided into two opposing groups (*scholae* or *sectae*): the Proculians, founded by Antistius Labeo (see section below), and the Sabinians, founded by Ateius Capito. A rival of Labeo (Tacitus, *Annales* 3.75) and pupil of Ofilius, Capito became consul in 5 CE. He was *curator aquarum* (superintendent of the water supply) from 14 until his death in 22. Highly esteemed by his contemporaries, he was conservative in law but a supporter of Augustus, unlike Labeo. None of his works (on constitutional law, sacral law, and criminal law) have survived, and he is mentioned only once by another lawyer.

The Proculians took their name from Proculus, Labeo's successor at the head of the school. A powerful man of senatorial rank, perhaps from Spain, Proculus emphasized legal consistency. The Sabinians took their name from Masurius Sabinus, who headed the group after Capito's death in 22. Later Sabinians were known as Cassians, after Sabinus's student Gaius Cassius Longinus (consul in 30).

We possess no information about the teaching methods and the organization of these groups. We know that many jurists belonged to one or the other, and we know the names of many of their leaders. Distinguished Sabinians after Masurius Sabinus and Cassius were Caelius Sabinus, Javolenus Priscus, Gaius, and Julian. Among the Proculians, after Labeo and Proculus, stand Nerva pater, Nerva filius, Pegasus, Celsus pater, Celsus the Younger, and Neratius Priscus.

Several sources, including Gaius, reported more than twenty disputes between the schools, based probably on disputes between individual jurists. The differences and rivalries between the two schools were both doctrinal and personal. Proculians, for instance, argued that puberty, and therefore legal capacity, occurred when a child reached the age of fourteen. The Sabinians, however, argued that the age of puberty varied from person to person and thus demanded case-by-case evaluation (Gaius 1.196). The Proculians held that the addition or removal of a guarantor did not affect obligations or justify novation. The Sabinians, in contrast, argued that obligations with a guarantor differed from those without one, and therefore the addition or removal of a guarantor implied novation (Gaius 3.177–78).

Marcus Antistius Labeo

The leading jurist in the time of Augustus was Labeo, who was born about 50 BCE into a plebeian family of Samnite origin. His father, Pacuvius, also a lawyer, was killed in 42 BCE defending republican principles and ideals. Following the family tradition, Labeo was a staunch opponent of the new Octavian regime and a firm defender of the Republican constitution. In his public career, he was appointed praetor, but he decided not to go further, to avoid any political collaboration with Augustus. He refused the consulship Augustus belatedly offered him (Pomponius, D. 1.2.2.47).

A pupil of Trebatius, but also instructed by his father and other jurists, Labeo was a virtuoso not only in law but also in many other areas: grammar, literature, history, dialectic, and language. He applied his broad learning and original mind to solving the most intricate cases (Aulus Gelius, *Noctes Attticae* 13.10.1). Labeo divided his year fifty-fifty between teaching his students and giving answers (responsa) one semester in Rome, and writing in the country the other semester. He wrote about four hundred books (scrolls), among them a commentary on the Twelve Tables; a large commentary on the praetorian edict with an appendix to the peregrine edict; *Pithana* (*Probabilia*), which was a collection of decisions of cases that Paul had summarized in the third century; and a posthumous collection of cases in forty books that Javolenus Priscus had summarized (*Libri posteriores*). More than five hundred citations of Labeo's works have survived.

Labeo's originality was legendary. He was intrigued with legal definitions and distinctions among legal concepts. For instance, he recognized that the constitutive element of the private offense of injury (*iniuria*) was the insult (*contumelia*) (D. 47.10.15.46). Labeo probably introduced the technique of analogy into legal argumentation, and the idea of *regula* (rules) into legal discourse. Labeo thought that the law, like language, was inherently ordered and governed by rules. Rules promoted systematization, consistency, and certainty in the Roman legal system. In textual interpretation, he identified and separated cases affecting the interpretation of a concrete legal text (statute, will, contract, legal action) from those affecting unwritten law. He was rigorous in the application of the law. He favored confining legal concepts and tools to the spheres in which they should be applied, and avoiding strained or unjustified extensions.

Masurius Sabinus

Despite coming from a family with no wealth, probably from Verona, in North Italy, Masurius Sabinus was one of the leading jurists of the first half of the first century CE and head of the school of jurists founded by Capito. He was the first nonsenatorial lawyer Tiberius honored with the privilege of giving legal opinions based on the emperor's authority (*ius respondendi ex auctoritate Principis*). A distinguished consultant and excellent legal teacher,

Sabinus was one of the instructors of Cassius Longinus. Sabinus attained equestrian rank late in life, when he was about fifty. He probably never held a magistracy, and it was said that he relied on gifts from pupils for his financial support. His most celebrated work was his systematic treatise on civil law in three books, divided into four parts: inheritance, obligations, persons, and things. Late jurists such as Pomponius, Paul, and Ulpian wrote extensive commentaries to Sabinus's treatise. He also wrote a commentary on the praetorian edict, a commentary on the writings of the jurist Vitellius, a monograph on theft, and a collection of legal opinions.

Sabinus was pragmatic and antiformalistic, and more tied to tradition than his Proculian rivals. For him, legal interpretation should try to find a reasonable and well-argued solution in controversial cases rather than an airtight logical and technical argument. He did not hesitate to appeal to natural reason when necessary or to extend the scope of available legal remedies. For instance, Sabinus extended the concept of theft to provide a remedy for the winner of a competition against the unmeritorious holder of the prize who refused to hand it over, even though the winner was neither the owner nor the possessor (Ulpian, D. 19.5.17.5). Sabinus thought that intentions should prevail over words. According to him, for instance, a legacy of wine included whatever the testator thought should be included in this category, in accordance with the usage of men: that it should include not only wine but also vinegar, zythum (ancient Egyptian beer), and ale (Ulpian, D. 33.6.9pr).

Jurists of the second century

Beginning near the end of the first century CE, and especially in the second century, the leading jurists were involved in the imperial administration. This was true, for instance, of Javolenus Priscus, Titius Aristo, and Neratius Prisco. Javolenus Priscus was one of the most influential jurists of his time and leader of the Sabinians after Caelius Sabinus. He was consul in 86 CE and governor of Germania Superior, Syria, and Africa. Titius Aristo was a member of Trajan's council, and Neratius Priscus, head of the Proculians, was consul in 97 CE and a member of the councils, probably those of Trajan and Hadrian.

As mentioned earlier, Emperor Hadrian reorganized the administration, giving jurists new opportunities to develop a legal career. This restructuring required improvements in legal education, and during this time celebrated new teachers emerged, such as Gaius and Pomponius. Jurists also were more devoted to casuistry than before. The most distinguished jurists of this time were P. Juventius Celsus, the son of a great lawyer of the same name (Celsus pater), and Salvius Julianus. They were the heads of the two principal rival schools: Celsus the Younger of the Proculians, and Julianus of the Sabinians. The greater of the two was Julianus, whom many legal historians consider the most talented and superlative of all Roman jurists, including Papinian.

Celsus the Younger

Having the same name as his father and, like his father, leader of the Proculian School, Publius Iuventius Celsus was praetor in 106 or 107 CE, twice consul (the date of the first time is unknown, but the second time was in 129 CE), governor of the provinces of Thrace and Asia, and a member of the advisory legal council (*consilium Principis*) of Emperor Hadrian. As consul in 129 CE, he passed through the Senate the *senatus consultum Iuventianum* on the liability of heirs in an inheritance. This senatorial resolution made a distinction between possessors in good faith and those in bad faith.

A prolific writer, Celsus the Younger cultivated a concise and elegant style, coining famous legal maxims, including "law is the art of the good and the fair" (D. 1.1.1pr.); "to know the laws is not just a matter of sticking to their words but a matter of grasping their force and purpose" (D. 1.3.17); "it is not proper to judge or to counsel based on a particular part of the statute, without taking into consideration the whole statute" (D. 1.3.24); and so on. Celsus was a man of independent mind and choleric character (Plinius, *Epistulae* 6.5.), and the beginning of his strong answer to his client Domitius Labeo became famous: "Either I do not understand what you are saying, or your inquiry is very stupid" (Celsus, D. 28.1.27). Celsus's most celebrated work is the Digest, a collection in thirty-nine books of case discussions in accordance with the praetorian edict. More than 140 extracts of this work can be found in Justinian's Digest.

Salvius Julianus

Salvius Julianus came from Hadrumentum (Hammamet) in Tunisia. Leader of the Sabinian School after his teacher Javolenus Priscus and a member of the legal advisory council of Hadrian, Julian was appointed quaestor at double the regular salary, with the aim of consolidating the praetorian edict, which was enacted by a resolution of the Senate in 131. According to his own account, he served as praetor (D. 40.2.5), and we know he was consul in 148, governor of the provinces of Lower Germany (Germania Inferior) under Antoninus Pius, and of Nearer Spain (Hispania Citerior) and Africa under Marcus Aurelius and Lucius Verus. Julianus died around 170–80 CE. He taught many students, among them Caecilius Africanus and Volusius Maecianus, the legal teacher of Marcus Aurelius.

An original and independent thinker and an elegant and clear writer, he was renowned for his rich casuistry. His most distinguished work is the Digest in ninety books, written after the consolidation of the edict. His extensive work was annotated by Marcellus, Cervidius Scaevola, and Paul, among others, and extensively used in Justinian's Digest. In the Law of Citations of 426, he is mentioned only as a secondary authority; however, Justinian praised him as the most acute author of legal writings and of the perpetual edict (Constitution *Tanta* 18).

Sextus Pomponius

A teacher and prolific writer under Hadrian, Antoninus Pius, and Marcus Aurelius, Pomponius is known only by his legal works and from quotations by other Roman jurists. More than five hundred passages of Pomponius survived in Justinian's Digest. Pomponius probably held no office, and he did not give public answers (responsa). His introduction to law (*enchiridium*), written around 131 CE, was the first, and for a long time only, work on legal history. The compilers of Justinian's Digest excerpted a long fragment of it (D. 1.2.2). He was the author of large commentaries on the works of Quintus Mucius and Sabinus, an extensive commentary on the praetorian edict, and monographs on various topics (stipulations, senatorial resolutions, trusts, and so on). Although he was not a creative jurist, he made an important contribution, founding the pillars of legal history and consolidating the structure of private law.

Gaius and his *Institutes*

The famous and enigmatic provincial legal teacher and modest jurist of the second century, Gaius is known only by his praenomen. He held no office, and he probably never had the privilege of the ius respondendi. Most likely an adherent of the Sabinian group during his instruction in Rome, he was teaching and writing in the East, perhaps in Berytus (Beirut). Although the exact date of his death is unknown, we know it occurred after 178 CE because he wrote a commentary on the *senatus consultum Orfitianum* of that year (D. 8.17.9). Unlike Pomponius, who surpassed him in acuity, Gaius was entirely ignored by classical jurists. He was mentioned, however, in the Law of Citations of 426, and for compilers of the Digest Gaius was a popular author. Justinian affectionately called him "our Gaius" (Constitution *Omnem* 1).

Gaius was a legal writer with a clear and lucid style who emphasized systematization and classification. He authored an introduction to the law (*res cottidianae*), some commentaries, and monographs on trust, manumissions, verbal obligations, and so on. Among his commentaries are one on the Twelve Tables and the only known commentary on the provincial edict. Gaius is best known, however, for his celebrated *Institutes,* a teaching course in four books for law students delivered around 161 CE but probably not published by him. The date for this work is derived from references to Emperor Antoninus Pius (died 161) in book one and the first part of book two as if he were still alive (Gaius 1.53, 1.74, 1.102, 2.120, 2.126, 2.151a), while in book 2.195, Gaius mentions the emperor as if he were departed ("divus Antoninus").

The importance of the *Institutes* lies in at least three facts. First, it is the only work of a classical jurist that has survived in its original state. Second, the Institutes of Justinian were mainly based on those of Gaius. Thus, in comparing both works, we can know Justinian's contributions and thus distinguish classical from postclassical law. Third, the *Institutes* of Gaius provide new and sound information on legal procedure. The *Institutes* thus are an extraordinarily valuable means for learning and understanding Roman law and subsequent legal history. The main division of Gaius's *Institutes* into persons, things, and actions formed the basis of civil law systems and international law until the nineteenth century and was instrumental for the development of common law systems.

Quintus Cervidius Scaevola

One of the greatest jurists of the later second century, perhaps a pupil of Sextus Pomponius, Cervidius Scaevola came from Carthage. A popular consulting jurist and a casuist par excellence, Scaevola was chief of police in Rome in 175 and legal adviser of Marcus Aurelius. He taught Paul and Tryphoninus. He was the author of, among other things, a celebrated Digest (probably published posthumously) in forty books, and six books of responsa. He also annotated the Digests of Marcellus and Julian. Modestinus (D. 27.1.13.2) considered Scaevola one of the leading jurists, along with Ulpian and Paul. More than three hundred fragments of his work survived in Justinian's Digest.

The late classical jurisprudence

The last period of classical jurisprudence coincided with the reign of the Severan dynasty, which ruled the Roman Empire between 193 and 235 CE. During this period, jurists were completely involved in imperial administration. Septimius Severus created new posts for jurists in the administration of justice. Additionally, the promulgation of the Antonine Constitution of 212 multiplied legal advice and casuistry in the provinces. The great jurists of this period belonged not to the senatorial order, like the jurists of the first century CE, but to the equestrian order, and they often occupied high equestrian positions (as praetorian prefect, a sort of minister of justice). Many jurists had provincial origins and developed their activity in the eastern part of the empire.

Among the jurists of this period worthy of mention are Claudius Tryphoninus, Callistratus, Tertullianus, Aelius Marcianus, and especially Papinian, Paul, Ulpian, and Modestinus.

Aemilius Papinianus

Papinian is the most famous jurist of Roman jurisprudence, posthumously becoming the definitive authority on Roman law. The Law of Citations of 426 gave him the leading position among the authoritative jurists (Paul, Ulpian, Modestinus, and Gaius) and the deciding vote when their opinions were equally divided on a particular point of law. His name became popular even among students in the East, who called third-year law students Papinianists because they had to study Papinian's work.

A celebrated lawyer of the Severan age, Papinian was a close friend and collaborator of Emperor Septimius Severus. Nothing with certainty is known about his origin. He was probably born around 150 CE to a family from Africa or Syria. He likely received legal instruction from Cervidius Scaevola. Assistant to the praetorian prefect, probably under Emperor Commodus, and chief of the secretary of petitions under Septimius Severus, Papinian was appointed in 205 CE to succeed Gaius Fulvius Plautianus as praetorian prefect. In that capacity, Papinian accompanied Emperor Septimius Severus to Britain in the military campaign of 208–11 CE. After Severus's death in February 211 at Eboracum (modern York, England), Antoninus Caracalla removed Papinian from office. In 212 Papinian was executed by the orders of Caracalla because, according to one version of the story, he refused to compose an apology justifying before the Senate and the people the murder ordered by Caracalla of his youngest brother and co-regent, Geta, in December 211. Papinian's legendary answer was, "To accuse an innocent man who has been murdered is a second act of murder" (*Historia Augusta. Caracalla* 8). For centuries, Papinian was regarded as a martyr of justice, and he was considered the pinnacle of Roman jurists. Modern researchers ordinarily rate him less highly, placing him third, after Labeo and Julian.

Justinian's compilers recorded sixty-three books written by Papinian. His most celebrated works were casuistic: the thirty-seven books of *quaestiones* (legal issues) and the nineteen books on *Digesta responsa* (ordered legal opinions). He also wrote two books on *definitiones* (legal rules) and two works on adultery – one a monograph on Augustus's legislation on adultery, and the other a two-volume collection of legal opinions on adultery. His style was concise but obscure at times, and his criticism of rival opinions was well-balanced and temperate. He always took into consideration the most elevated ethical values when he wrote.

Julius Paulus

An original lawyer of high reputation, a popular legal teacher, and a prolific writer, Julius Paulus (known also as Paul) held the highest imperial offices. A pupil of Cervidius Scaevola, Paul was assessor to Papinian as praetorian prefect under Septimius Severus, and a member of his emperor's council at the same time as Papinian. He was also praetorian prefect under Alexander Severus. Emperor Gordian III referred to Paul as a "very wise man" (*vir prudentissimus,* Justinian's Code 5.4.6). The Law of Citations of 426 named him as one of five jurists whose works had authority.

Over eighty-five works in more than three hundred books may be credited to him. His most important works are probably his large commentary on the praetorian edict in seventy-eight books and his commentary on Sabinus in sixteen books. He was also the author of twenty-five books of quaestiones and twenty-three books of responsa, both following the order of the digest system. The famous *Pauli Sententiae*, published at the end of the third century and endorsed by Emperor Constantine as genuine, is a spurious work that uses the name of Paul to enhance its reputation and value. More than two thousand fragments of Paul's voluminous works survived in Justinian's Digest, some 17 percent of the whole Digest. After the promulgation of the Antonine Constitution, and influenced by Stoic philosophy, Paul contributed, along with Ulpian, to accommodating the Roman legal system to the new demands of a cosmopolitan society. Paul survived his contemporary Ulpian.

Domitius Ulpianus

A leading lawyer, writer, and imperial office-holder of the Severan dynasty, Ulpian is considered the most influential Roman jurist. Because of his clarity, well-documented and comprehensive works, and proximity in time to Justinian, Ulpian's writings were the main source for the Digest: more than two-fifths of the material selected by the compilers came from Ulpian. Sixty percent of the titles of the Digest begin with a fragment from the works of Ulpian. He was also one of the five authoritative jurists mentioned in the Law of Citations of 426. His pupil Modestinus (D. 27.1.13.2) mentioned him, along with Cervidius Scaevola and Paul, as one of the pinnacles of Roman jurisprudence, and twice Modestinus referred to his beloved teacher as "the excellent Ulpian" (D. 26.6.2.5 y D. 27.1.4.1).

Ulpian came from Tyre (Syria). He was secretary of petitions under Septimius Severus; *praefectus annonae* (supervisor of the grain supply), possibly under Elagabalus (at the beginning of 222); and praetorian prefect under Alexander Severus the same year. Mutinous guards assassinated him, probably in 223. An inscription from Tyrus set up in his honor was discovered in 1988.

Ulpian wrote two extensive commentaries: one on the praetorian edict (*Ad edictum praetoris*) in eighty-one books and another on Sabinus's civil law (*Ad Sabinum*) in fifty-one books. Ulpian also wrote some teaching works, including an elementary introduction to the law (*Institutiones*) and a work on *disputationes* in ten books. Ulpian wrote many short works on private law, administrative law, criminal law, and tax law. Some spurious works were attributed to him, for instance the *Six Books on Ulpian's Opinions* (*Ulpiani Opinionum libri VI*), produced around 330 CE.

Ulpian combined pragmatic solutions to legal problems with a good intellectual and theoretical approach. He understood law both as an appropriate technique for doing justice and as a real theoretical science based on principles. His philosophical views, deeply influenced by Stoicism, were egalitarian, and they helped resolve the new legal challenges arising from the extension of citizenship by the Antonine Constitution (212 CE). Ulpian tried to convert Roman law into a more cosmopolitan legal system in accordance with the needs of a multicultural society and based on the values of liberty, dignity, universality, and equality. In this sense, Tony Honoré considers him a pioneer of the human rights movement.

Herennius Modestinus

A jurist and a legal teacher of the first half of the third century, Modestinus is considered the last representative of the classical Roman jurists, and in some sense a transitional figure between classical and postclassical jurisprudence. Modestinus was mentioned in the Law of Citations of 426 CE among the five jurists with authority. We have scant information about his life. A pupil of Ulpian, Modestinus was living in Dalmatia, where he sought legal advice from his teacher (Ulpian, D. 47.2.52.20). He held the office of chief of police in Rome from 226 to 244. He wrote nine books on *differentiae* (legal distinctions), ten books on *regulae* (rules), and twelve on *pandectae* (encyclopedia). He was also the author of a Greek treatise in six books on exemptions from guardianship. Justinian's compilers used over three hundred passages from his work.

The end of classical jurisprudence

After the middle of the third century, classical jurisprudence declined. Classical legal works ceased being produced and were replaced by works in the nature of compendia or epitomes. Some pseudo-epigraphic works were published by unknown authors under the names of late classical jurists (e.g., *Pauli Sententiae*). Only in the rescripts of Diocletian (r. 284–305), written in the imperial chancellery, can vestiges of classical jurisprudence still be seen. Legal officers in the imperial administration took the place of the intellectual elite of independent jurists, and legal activities moved into the hands of a growing imperial bureaucracy.

The quaestor of the sacred palace, an office created by Emperor Constantine (r. 306–37), became the chief legal advisor of the emperor, a sort of minister of justice and legislation. This officer exercised great influence in the development of imperial law by preparing drafts of legal provisions; in many areas, however, he had neither legal expertise nor juridical sense. Legal style came to be decorated with pompous imperial rhetoric and lost its original brevity and terseness, while its content tended toward the simplistic. Laws of general application (*leges generales*) that stabilized and petrified the natural development of the legal science replaced private rescripts for specific cases. The only valid law was statutory law. Legislation replaced jurisprudence. Jurisprudence probably no longer achieved again the classical standards of excellence.

Hellenization and Christianization influenced the development of the law during this period. Greek influences were present in legal terminology, which borrowed Greek terms, as well as in the theory of sources of law (based on the tension between equity and law), in the distinction between written and unwritten law, in the promotion of the idea of natural law and *humanitas*, and in new abstract legal categorizations and definitions. The Christianization of the Empire led to systematic moderation in the severity of the law; the legal system was also illuminated by moral values and principles such as love (*caritas*), benevolence (*benignitas*), and mercy (*clementia*), especially in relation to women and slaves; and the church gained legal status. On the other hand, emperors, in their eagerness to defend the church and orthodox doctrine, enacted constitutions and special laws against pagans, heretics, Jews, and schismatics, and sexual wrongdoings were punished with severe penalties. Caesaropapism became the dominant political doctrine, which justified imperial control over ecclesiastical hierarchy.

Further reading

Bauman, Richard A. *Lawyers and Politics in the Early Roman Empire: A Study of Relations Between the Roman Jurists and the Emperors from Augustus to Hadrian*. Munich: Beck, 1989.

Bauman, Richard A. *Lawyers in Roman Republic Politics: A Study of the Roman Jurists in Their Political Setting, 316–82 BC*. Munich: Beck, 1983.

Bauman, Richard A. *Lawyers in Roman Transitional Politics: A Study of the Roman Jurists in the Political Setting in the Late Republic and Triumvirate*. Munich: Beck, 1985.

Berger, Adolf. *Encyclopedic Dictionary of Roman Law*. Philadelphia, PA: The American Philosophical Society, 1953; reprint 1980.

Domingo, Rafael, ed. *Juristas universales I. Juristas antiguos*. Madrid: Marcial Pons, 2004.

Frier, Bruce W. *The Rise of Roman Jurists: Studies in Cicero's Pro Caecina*. Princeton, NJ: Princeton University Press, 1985.

Harries, Jill. *Cicero and the Jurists: From Citizen's Law to the Lawful State*. London: Duckworth, 2006.

Honoré, Tony. *Emperors and Lawyers*. 2nd ed. Oxford and New York: Oxford University Press, 1994.

Honoré, Tony. *Gaius*. Oxford: Clarendon Press, 1962.

Honoré, Tony. *Ulpian. Pioneer of Human Rights*. 2nd ed. Oxford and New York: Oxford University Press, 2002.

Honoré, Tony. Entries on "Papinian," "Paul," and "Ulpian." In *The Oxford International Encyclopedia of Legal History*, edited by Stanley N. Katz. Oxford and New York: Oxford University Press, 2009.

Honoré, Tony. Entries on "Aemilius Papinianus"; "Antistius Labeo"; "Aquilius Gallus"; "Cerviodius Scaevola"; "Domitius Ulpianus"; "Gaius"; "Herennius Modestinus"; "Iulius Paulus"; "Iuventius Celsus"; "Julianus"; "Masurius Sabinus"; "Mucius Scaevola, Quintus" (in collaboration with Ernst Badian); "Proculus, Sempronius"; "Roman Lawyers"; "Sextus Pomponius." In *The Oxford Classical Dictionary*, edited by Simon Hornblower, Antony Spawforth, and Esther Eidinow. 4th ed. Oxford: Oxford University Press, 2012.

Lenel, Otto. *Palingenesia Iuris Civilis*. 2 vols. Leipzig: Tautniz, 1889; 2nd ed. Aalen: Scientia Verlag, 2000.

Liebs, Detlef. *Die Jurisprudenz im spätantiken Italien (260–640 n. Chr.)*. Berlin: Duncker & Humblot, 1987.

Liebs, Detlef. *Römische Jurisprudenz in Africa: mit Studien zu den pseudopaulinischen Sentenzen*. Berlin: Akademie Verlag, 1993.

Liebs, Detlef. *Hofjuristen der römischen Kaiser bis Justinian*. Munich: Bayerische Akademie der Wissenschaften and Beck Verlag. 2010.

Kunkel, Wolfgang. *Die römischen Juristen. Herkunft und soziale Stellung*. 2nd ed. Reprint Cologne: Bohlau Verlag, 2001.

Nörr, Dieter. *Rechtskritik in der römischen Antike*. Munich: Beck, 1974.

Padovani, Andrea, and Peter G. Stein, eds. *The Jurists' Philosophy of Law from Rome to the Seventeenth Century*. Dordrecht, Berlin, Heidelberg, and Vienna: Springer, 2007.

Schiavone, Aldo. *The Invention of the Law in the West*. Translated by Jeremy Carden and Anthony Shugaar. Cambridge, MA, and London: The Belknap Press of Harvard University Press, 2012.

Schiller, Arthur. *Roman Law. Mechanisms of Development*. The Hague, Paris, and New York: Mounton Publishers, 1978.

Schulz, Fritz. *A History of Roman Legal Science*. Oxford: Clarendon Press, 1946.

Stein, Peter G. "Labeo, Marcus Antistius." In *The Oxford International Encyclopedia of Legal History*, edited by Stanley N. Katz. Oxford and New York: Oxford University Press, 2009.

Stein, Peter G. "The Two Schools of Jurists in the Early Roman Principate." *Cambridge Law Journal* 31 (1972): 8–31.

Tuori, Kaius. *The Emperor of Law. The Emergence of Roman Imperial Adjudication*. Oxford: Oxford University Press, 2017.

Watson, Alan. *Law Making in the Later Roman Republic*. Oxford: Clarendon Press, 1974.

Wieacker, Franz. *Römische Rechtsgeschichte*. I. *Einleitung, Quellenkunde, Frühzeit und Republik*. Munich: Beck Verlag, 1988.

Wieacker, Franz. *Römische Rechtsgeschichte*. II *Die Jurisprudenz vom frühen Prinzipat bis zum Ausgang der Antike im weströmischen Reich und die oströmische Rechtswissenschaft bis zur justinianischen Gesetzgebung*. Munich: Beck Verlag, 2006.

Wolff, Hans Julius. *Roman Law: An Historical Introduction*. Norman: University of Oklahoma Press, 1951.

5 Justinian and the *Corpus Iuris*

The most important legal undertaking of Antiquity was the compilation of what was later called *Corpus Iuris Civilis* promulgated by Emperor Justinian. It is rightly said that this body of laws and jurisprudence, along with Aristotelian writings and the Bible, constitutes one of the three pillars of Western culture. The *Corpus Iuris*, a true temple of justice, is both an endpoint and a starting point in world history. Histories of Rome usually end with Justinian's *Corpus Iuris*; Byzantine histories and Western legal histories, on the other hand, begin with the *Corpus Iuris*. Justinian's codification is the bridge that links Antiquity, the Byzantine Empire, and Europe. It is also the link between civil law and common law, and between canon law and civil law. To know about the *Corpus Iuris* is to know about something that was instrumental for the development of justice and law in the past, continues to operate in the present, and will probably have its impact in the future. The *Corpus Iuris*, especially the Digest, has not only a historic value but an intrinsic one because it embodied the creative spirit and permanent character of all of Roman jurisprudence.

Emperor Justinian

One of the most prominent legislators in human history, Justinian the Great was Eastern Roman emperor from August 1, 527 to his death on November 14, 565 in Constantinople. Flavius Iustinianus was born around 482 CE at Tauresium (in the current Republic of Macedonia). His father, Sabbatius, was the brother-in-law of the childless Emperor Justin I. Emperor Justin adopted his nephew Justinian and provided him with an excellent education in Constantinople, in both Latin (Justinian's original language) and Greek. Appointed to *magister militum* (high military command) in 520 and consul in 521, Justinian married the former actress Theodora, who died childless in 548.

In 527, Justinian became co-regent, and later that year, after Justin's death, he succeeded his uncle as sole emperor. A vigorous, hard-working, and energetic man, talented but unattractive in character, Justinian planned to restore and unify the old glory of the Roman Empire under one emperor, one religion, and one law. According to his ambitious project, he continued the wars with the Persians, and, in the West, he regained North Africa, Italy, and a part of southern Spain from the control of the barbarian invaders. Warfare occupied much of Justinian's efforts and attention. His military success was, however, ephemeral. His successors lost most of the West, and the empire was reduced to the East, both in territory and in culture. During the lengthy reign of Heraclius (610–41), the official language of the empire became Greek.

Justinian's ecclesiastical policy was based on the Eastern idea that church and state were inseparably linked as inherent elements of a single Christian empire. Justinian felt he had the duty of improving the governance of the church, of defending orthodox religious doctrine, and of fighting to end dogmatic divisions. He passed many religious laws against pagans and heretics, and he passionately loved religion and theology.

The most complex doctrinal religious issue during his reign was the struggle between the orthodox Christological doctrine accepted at the Council of Chalcedon (451 CE) and the Monophysite doctrine. According to the Council of Chalcedon, both divine and human natures coexist in the person of Christ. On the contrary, the Monophysite doctrine affirmed that Christ has only a divine nature. Monophysitism was strongly supported in Syria and Egypt. Moreover, Theodora, Justinian's wife, was also a strong supporter of Monophysitism. With little success, Justinian tried to resolve dogmatic divisions by subordinating the church to the emperor (caesaropapism). He was not able to develop a categorical distinction between church and state as it was later cultivated in Western Christianity. Justinian was a solid Chalcedonian, but at the end of his life, he came closer to the doctrine of Aphthartodocetism, deeply related to Monophysitism, which affirmed that the body of Christ was naturally incorruptible. His new approach led to the expulsion of some leading Chalcedonian bishops.

Justinian's compilation

The purpose of Justinian's compilation was to restate the whole of Roman law in a single legal source of law with binding force over the entire empire. Justinian's major legal work, often called a codification, was not a codification in the modern sense but rather an up-to-date and systematized compilation or collection of legislation and legal literature. Emperor Justinian himself gave no collective title to his compilation. He used only once the expression *corpus iuris* in the generic sense of body of law (C.J. 5.13.1pr.: *omne corpus iuris*). In the Middle Ages, the whole compilation was called *Corpus iuris* by the medieval glossators. From the end of the sixteenth century up to our own time, to distinguish Justinian's compilation from the compilation of canon law (*Corpus Iuris Canonici*), jurists have usually referred to Justinian's compilation as *Corpus Iuris Civilis*. That collective name was first used in the edition by Dionysius Gothofredus (Denis Godefroy) in 1583.

The Justinian compilation, composed in Latin, consists of three independent legal projects, all related by his single overriding intention for the whole: a body of imperial constitutions (the Code), a body of brief extracts of jurisprudence (the Digest or, in Greek, Pandects), and a textbook for the students of the whole empire (the Institutes). After the publication of the Code, Justinian also continued with his legislative efforts for more than thirty years by promulgating about 150 new constitutions (the Novels: *novae leges*). Some of these novels were to be applied throughout the empire, some of them in just part of it. They were written in Latin or Greek, based on their intended scope of application. The authoritative edition of Justinian's *Corpus Iuris Civilis* was produced at the end of the nineteenth century by Theodor Mommsen in collaboration with Paul Krüger (the Digest), and by Paul Krüger himself (the Institutes and the Code). Rudolf Schöll and Wilhelm Kroll produced the authoritative edition of the Novels in 1895. The standard edition of the *Corpus Iuris* contains the Institutes and the Digest in the first volume, the Code in the second volume, and the Novels in the third volume (Berlin: Weidmann, 1895).

Some of Justinian's constitutions usually referred to by their first words (e.g., *Imperatoriam, Tanta*) provide information about the plan for the codification. The main architect and inspiration for the codification was Tribonian. Born in Side, in Pamphylia, around 500 CE, Tribonian was a practicing lawyer and an erudite writer in both Latin and Greek. A man of great talent and capacities, in 529 he was appointed *quaestor sacri palatii* (senior legal official). He was a member of the commission in charge of the codification of imperial law (529) and of the commission in charge of the preparation of the body of classical legal literature. In 532 he was removed from his office of quaestor, but he continued working on the legal codification as a *magister officiorum*. In 533, he headed the commission that prepared the Institutes and, one year later, the commission of the second edition of Justinian's Code. He died around 542.

Justinian's Code

In February 528, just a few months after his accession, Justinian established a commission to prepare a comprehensive compilation of imperial enactments that were to bear his name: Justinian's Code (*Codex Iustinianus*). It would be a consolidation and update of existing codes (the Gregorian, the Hermogenian, and the Theodosian Codes) and the imperial constitutions enacted afterward. Members of the commission, headed by the politician John of Cappadocia, included Tribonian, Theophilus (a law professor in Constantinople), and two advocates of the court of Constantinople. The commissioners were explicitly authorized to edit texts: omitting what was obsolete, superficial, or contradictory; restating in clear language what was ambiguous; and changing or adding what was necessary. The commission worked hard and with notable speed to prepare the Code in fourteen months. The Code was enacted by the imperial constitution *Summa* on April 7, 529 and sent to all provinces. It came into force in the whole empire on April 16, 529.

After the promulgation of the Code, Justinian went on to issue so many imperial constitutions (many of them related to particular legal controversies) that the Code became outdated within five years. A revision was necessary. After the whole codification project was completed (533), the Code was revised again under the guidance of Tribonian. In November 534 the new edition of the Code (*Codex repetitae praelectionis*) came into force through the constitution *Cordi*. The first edition of the Code (529 CE) did not survive, but the second one (534) did. The only parts of the first edition preserved today are the two constitutions *Haec* and *Summa*, which also were published at the beginning of the second edition.

Justinian's Code consists of twelve books, divided into titles. Within the titles, the imperial constitutions (including the name[s] of the emperor[s], the addressee, and the date) are arranged in chronological order. The latest constitution published therein is of November 4, 534, and the earliest is by Emperor Hadrian (C.J. 6.23.1). The first book deals with ecclesiastical law, the sources of law, and the administration of the empire. Specifically, the Code begins with the imperial constitution of the emperors Gratian, Valentinian II, and Theodosius I of 380 that declared Christianity to be the state religion of the empire. Books 2 to 8 address topics of private law; book 9 deals with criminal law; and books 10 to 12 deal with administrative law and tax law. The Justinian Code followed the same pattern of composition as the Theodosian Code. They differ in the material contained, in their arrangement and structure, and in the degree of alterations made to earlier imperial constitutions.

The Digest

The Digest (also officially called Pandects) constitutes the main part of Justinian's compilation. On December 15, 530, Justinian addressed the constitution *Deo Auctore* to Tribonian. Tribonian had to select members for a commission to excerpt and compile the writings of the ancient jurists into a single work, which would be called Digest or Pandects (in Greek) (*Deo auctore* §12). Justinian reasoned that the writings of the ancient jurists were so voluminous and confusing that they had become unmanageable and beyond the reasonable comprehension of any human being.

The commission consisted of four law professors (Theophilus, Cratinus from Constantinople, and Dorotheus and Anatolius from Berytus) and some high officials and advocates of the court in Constantinople. The commissioners were able to complete their work in just three years because of their familiarity with legal writings. On December 16, 533, Justinian published the Digest (and the Institutes) through a constitution both in a Latin version (*Tanta*) and in a Greek version (*Dedoken*). The two versions were not entirely identical in content. Two weeks later, the Digest and the Institutes came into effect over the whole empire. In both versions of the constitution (*Tanta*/*Dedoken* §19), Justinian prohibited citing in court the original legal writings of ancient jurists. As a result, the Digest replaced altogether the study of original juristic writings in law schools.

The Digest is made up of fifty books and is divided into titles with title headings. It basically follows the arrangement of Justinian's Code and the praetorian edict (*Deo auctore* §5). Every excerpt is identified by the name of its author, the title of the original work, and the number of the book in which it can be found. This does not mean, however, that each fragment is completely faithful to the original; the compilers had the capacity to make changes and alterations to adapt the texts to Justinian law. The earliest jurist included was Quintus Mucius Scaevola, the pontifex (died 82 BCE); the latest jurists were Arcadius Charisius and Hermogenian, of the age of Diocletian (r. 284–305 CE). The majority of the excerpts came from jurists of the later classical period. Ulpian furnished about two-fifths of the whole, making him the leading author, followed by Paul (one-fifth of the whole). Papinian was the leading author on questions of adultery; Macer, on public trials; Menander, on military law; and Gaius, on mortgage.

In 1820, Friedrich Bluhme discovered that the compilers had divided the legal writings into three large bodies or groupings of authors and works, in order to distribute the commission's work among three committees. These three groupings were: the edictal (542 books), the Sabinian (556 books), and the Papinian (294 books). There were 110 books not included in any of the three portions.

The first book provides a general introduction on law and justice, legal history, legal sources, and the jurisdiction of the magistrates, among other topics. From book 2 to book 5, the Digest addresses topics related to legal procedures; books 6 to 46 cover topics of private law (property, inheritance, and civil obligations); book 47 addresses private offenses; book 48 deals with public criminal law; book 49 refers to appeals, referrals, and the imperial treasure. Finally, book 50 refers to various topics on municipalities. At the end of book 50 is an explanation of legal terminology (D. 50.16) and a large compilation of legal rules (D. 50.17).

An almost complete manuscript of the Digest (*codex Florentinus*), probably produced at the end of the sixth century in the East, perhaps in Constantinople, has survived. It is therefore close in time to the reign of Justinian. The manuscript is also called *littera Pisana* because we know that in the twelfth century it was in Pisa. The large manuscript, comprising 907 sheets, is kept in the Laurentian Library in Florence. Many other manuscripts of the work are incomplete and contain only one of the three parts into which the Digest was divided in the Middle Ages by the glossators: *Old Digest* (*Digestum vetus*: books 1–24.2); *Infortiatum* (reinforced) (books 24.3–38), and *New Digest* (*Digestum novum*: books 39–50).

The authoritative critical edition of the Digest (*editio maior*) was produced by Theodor Mommsen (1817–1903), the great historian and winner of the Nobel Prize in Literature. It was published in two volumes in Berlin, in 1868 and 1870. Some years later, a simplified edition was published (*editio minor*).

After Mommsen died, Paul Krüger, beginning in 1908, revised and edited the editio minor, incorporating valuable improvements. Italian professors Pietro Bonfante, Carlo Fadda, Contardo Ferrini, Salvatore Riccobono, and Vittorio Scialoja produced a useful pocket edition of the Digest, based mainly on the edition of Mommsen (1908; reprint 1949). The authoritative English translation of the Digest was produced by Alan Watson.

Interpolations

The constitution promulgating the Digest stated that "Many things, and matters of the highest importance, have been changed for reasons of utility" (*Tanta* §10). This statement provides a good starting point for understanding both Justinian's intentions and how the compilers worked in accordance with the spirit and mandate of this emperor. Justinian's intention was to convert classical jurisprudence (ius) into a statute (lex), the best way to modernize and improve the law. This explains why, to preserve the uniformity of the new legal system, Justinian forbade critical commentaries on these modifications. He allowed only explanatory writings and additional notes to the titles of the Digest. To guarantee consistency was, therefore, a secondary goal of his project.

Compilers acted accordingly. They made abundant adjustments and alterations (suppressions, additions, substitutions), traditionally called interpolations. That happened specifically in areas of the law that were subject to significant changes between the period of the classical jurists and Justinian. Many times, the compilers made systematic alterations to eliminate old institutions. For instance, they inserted *traditio* for *mancipatio* (old institution), or *actio dotis* (action for recovery of a dowry) for the classical *actio rei uxoriae* (action for recovery all that belongs to a wife). Where classical jurists had *sponsio* (old solemn promise), the compilers put *fideiussio* (new type of suretyship).

Frequently, compilers did not change the wording but did change the context. A famous example is the statement, "the emperor is not bound by statutes" (*princeps legibus solutus est*, D. 1.3.31). Ulpian had written the statement in the commentary to the *lex Iulia et Pappia*, to exempt the emperor from application of the limitations of these two statutes dealing with the rights of unmarried and childless people to inherit property. The statement was generalized by compilers, however, and thus was included in the first book of the Digest under the general title of statutes, senatorial resolutions, and costumes.

We have certainty about alterations and omissions only where the same text has been transmitted in the Digest and in a different legal source, for instance in private collections of the fourth century (*Fragmenta Vaticana, Collatio legum Mosaicarum et Romanarum*). Sometimes the lack of consistency within an argument, and structural or grammatical irregularities and gaps, can be explained as simple pre-Justinianic or post-Justinianic abridgements or even as results of a defect of the manuscript.

Since the sixteenth century, researchers have made efforts to find these interpolations in order to recover the value of Roman juristic writings in their pristine, unaltered condition. In the countries in which Justinian law was directly applied, the search for interpolations was not extensive. At the beginning of the twentieth century, coinciding with the promulgation of the German Civil Code (BGB) and the Digest's loss of practical relevance, researchers began to overestimate the number and importance of interpolations. There was a collective fascination with discovering new interpolations. This attitude was ironically called "interpolation hunting" (*Interpolationenjagd*). When a text was complex and not well understood, the natural inclination was to consider it nonclassical and interpolated, instead of trying to find more sophisticated solutions. After the Second World War, there was a well-justified reaction against the hunters of Justinian's interpolations. Recently, however, there has been a tendency to underestimate their relevance and extent. A good balance is required. On the one hand, the excesses of the past must be avoided; on the other hand, textual critical considerations have to be taken seriously in research. Interpolations are there and must be detected to preserve the value of classical writings in their original form.

The Institutes

After the final draft of the Digest was completed, a commission was appointed to prepare a brief introduction to the Digest, which could be used as a textbook for first-year law students instead of Gaius's *Institutes*. This introduction would be like a lecture by the emperor to law students, imbued with the same legal force as the imperial constitutions. The commission that created this introduction, or Institutes, consisted of law professors Theophilus and Dorotheus, working under the supervision of Tribonian.

Justinian's Institutes were mostly based on Gaius's *Institutes* and his *res cottidianae*. Many parts of Justinian's Institutes were taken almost verbatim from the works of Gaius. This is why the emperor referred to him fondly as "our Gaius" (Inst. Proemium §6, Inst. 4.18.5, and *Omnem* §1). The compilers also used institutes of Florentinus, Marcianus, Ulpian, and probably of Paul, as well as some new imperial constitutions incorporating Justinian reforms. Justinian's Institutes were published on November 21, 533 under the title *Imperatoris Iustiniani Institutiones*, and they came into force, along with the Digest, on December 30, 533.

The Institutes comprise four books, divided into titles, and the titles into paragraphs. Unlike the Digest, the Institutes do not mention the juristic writings from which the texts were taken. Like Gaius's *Institutes*, Justinian's Institutes deal first with people, second with things, and finally with actions. They also contain two titles on the duties of judges and on criminal law, which correspond to nothing within Gaius's *Institutes*. Based on their stylistic features, books 1 and 2 were probably written by a different author than books 3 and 4. It is possible, therefore, that the two law professors, members of the commission, distributed the work between them. We do not know, however, which part should be attributed to Theophilus and which to Dorotheus.

The Novels of Justinian

The *Novellae constitutiones*, or "new constitutions," are the new legislation (*novae leges*) that Justinian enacted after the publication of the second edition of the Code (534 CE). Novels might be applicable in a concrete province, in a group of provinces, or in the whole empire. The majority of them survived in Greek. Most of Justinian's Novels concerned public offices, administration of provinces, tax law, criminal law, and ecclesiastical law, and they survive in Greek. Novels in Latin were concerned with North Africa and Italy, the Latin-speaking parts of the empire. Sometimes there were two versions of the same Novel, one in Greek and another in Latin (see Novel 66, of 538 CE). For Illyricum, a bilingual province of the empire, we know of novels in both Latin and Greek. No official collection of the Novels was ever produced. The Novels have been transmitted in different collections. The most complete collection we know of is the so-called Greek Collection of 168 Novels, which was used by the compilers of the *Basilika* (see next section) Originally, the collection was bilingual, including both Latin and Greek Novels. The Collection of 168 was probably initiated in Constantinople in the time of Justinian and includes Novels until the reign of Emperor Tiberius II (578–82). Up to Novel 120, the order is chronological. The rest are not arranged according to any principle. The collection includes some constitutions dating from before the second edition of the Code but not included within it.

There are two private collections of the Novels for teaching purposes: the *Authenticum* and the *Epitome Juliani*. The *Authenticum* is a collection of 134 Novels enacted by Justinian from 535 to 556 and probably created in Constantinople. The collection consists of Novels in Greek and only a few in Latin. The fourteen Novels in Latin have survived in the original, while the Greek Novels were translated word for word (*kata poda*) into Latin. The *Epitome Juliani* is a summary of 122 Novels enacted by Justinian (two are duplicates) from 535 to 555 and produced by Julianus, a law professor in Constantinople. It also contains additional Latin Novels that are not attested to in any other legal collection. The *Epitome Juliani* was well known in the West. In the twelfth century, however, the *Authenticum* appeared in Bologna and generally took the place of the *Epitome Juliani*. Initially it was thought that the *Authenticum* was a falsification, but the law school of Bologna established its authenticity, hence the name *Authenticum*. The earliest edition of the Greek text of Justinian's Novels was produced in 1531 by Gregor Haloander.

The *Basilika*

Because the *Corpus Iuris* was written in Latin, it was incomprehensible to many Greek-speaking Byzantine lawyers. The compiler Theophilus produced, as a teaching book, a Greek version of the Justinian's Institutes called the *Paraphrasis* in order to disseminate the Institutes throughout the Greek-speaking world. (An English translation is available, edited by J. H. A. Lokin et al., and published in 2010). In the eighth century, the *Paraphrasis* was published as an official legal collection in Greek called *Ecloga*, which adapted Justinian's law to Byzantine practice. Around 890, Emperor Leo the Wise (r. 886–912) completed an extensive Greek restatement of all of Justinian's codification in sixty books. The collection is grounded on all four parts of Justinian's compilation, although there is little from the *Institutiones*. The labor of compilation, however, began under his predecessor Basil I (r. 867–86). From the eleventh century, the collection was called the *Basilika* (from *basilikos*, or "imperial" [laws]), and it is considered the most important legal compilation of post-Justinian times. The laws were supplemented with explanatory notes (*scholia*) on the manuscript based on law professors' teachings in Justinian's time (old *scholia*) or from the eleventh and twelfth centuries (new *scholia*). The best edition of the *Basilika* and the scholia was produced by Herman Jan Scheltema (1906–81) and other researchers between 1951 and 1988. In 1345, a short version of the *Basilika* was published in six books (the *Hexabiblos*), which was in force in Greece until the promulgation of the Greek Civil Code in 1840.

Further reading

Corbino, Alessandro, and Bernardo Santalucia, eds. *Justiniani Augusti Pandectarum codex Florentinus*. Florence: Olschki, 1988.

Corcoran, Simon. "Roman Law and the Two Languages in Justinian's Empire." *Bulletin of the Institute of Classical Studies* 61 (2017): 96–116.

Evans, J. A. S. *The Emperor Justinian and the Byzantine Empire*. Westport, CT: Greenwood Press, 2005.

Honoré, Tony. *Justinian Digest: Character and Compilation*. Oxford and New York: Oxford University Press, 2010.

Honoré, Tony. *Tribonian*. Ithaca, NY: Cornell University Press, 1978.

Johnston, David. "The Justinian's Digest. The Interpretation of Interpolations." *Oxford Journal of Legal Studies* 9. 2 (1989): 149–166.

Jolowicz, Herbert Felix, and Barry Nicholas. *Historical Introduction to the Study of Roman Law*. 3rd ed. Cambridge: Cambridge University Press, 1972.

Kaiser, Wolfgang. "Justinian and the Corpus Iuris Civilis." In *The Cambridge Companion to Roman Law*, edited by David Johnston, 119–148. Cambridge and New York: Cambridge University Press, 2015.

Kaiser, Wolfgang. *Die Epitome Iuliani. Beiträge zum römischen Recht im frühen Mittelalter und zum byzantinischen Rechtsunterricht*. Frankfurt: Klostermann, 2004.

Kaser, Max. *Zur Methodologie der römischen Rechtsquellenforschung*. Vienna, Cologne, and Graz: Bohlau, 1972.

Kunkel, Wolfgang. *An Introduction to Roman Legal and Constitutional History*. 2nd ed. Translated by J. M. Kelly. Oxford: Clarendon Press, 1973.

Lokin, J. H. A. *et al.* (eds.), *Theophili Antecessoris Paraphrasis Institutionum*, trans. A. F. Murison, Gronningen, 2010.

Maas, Michael. *The Cambridge Companion of the Age of Justinian*. Cambridge and New York: Cambridge University Press, 2005.

Mantovani, Dario. *Digesto e masse Bluhmiane*. Milan: Giuffrè, 1987.

Mantovani, Dario and Antonio Padoa Schioppa, eds. *Interpretare il Digesto. Storia e metodi*. Pavia: IUSS Press, 2014.

Mommsen, Theodor, ed. *Digesta Iustiniani Augusti*. 2 vols. Berlin: Weidmann, 1868–70.

Mommsen, Theodor, Paul Krüger, Wilhelm Kroll, and Rudolf Schöll, eds. *Corpus Iuris Civilis*. 3 vols. Hildeshaeim: Weidmann, 1989–93.

Mommsen, Theodor, Paul Krüger, and Alan Watson. *The Digest of Justinian*. 4 vols. Latin text edited by Theodor Mommsen with the aid of Paul Krüger, and English Translation edited by Alan Watson. Philadelphia: University of Pennsylvania Press, 1985.

Radding, Charles and Antonio Ciaralli. *The Corpus Iuris Civilis in the Middle Ages: Manuscripts and Transmissions from the Sixth Century to the Juristic Revival*. Leiden: Brill, 2006.

Thomas, J. A. C. *The Institutes of Justinian: Text, Translation, and Commentary*. Amsterdam: North-Holland Publishing Co., 1975.

Wieacker, Franz. *Textstufen klassischer Juristen*. Göttingen: Vandenhoeck & Ruprecht, 1960.

Wolff, Hans Julius. *Roman Law: An Historical Introduction*. Norman: University of Oklahoma Press, 1951.

6 The revival of Roman law

The development of Roman law from the eleventh century into the modern era has had a profound and lasting impact on legal systems throughout the West. Paradoxically, though Justinian's codification was developed in the East, it was in the West that Roman law flourished again as a result of the recovery of the Digest in the eleventh century. Before that happened, knowledge of Roman law existed only through the Germanic codifications, especially the *Lex Romana Visigothorum* and, in Italy, Justinian's Institutes and Code.

From the eleventh century onward, Justinian's Roman law permeated all European legal systems to different degrees and at different times. The development of Roman law in Europe was not uniform. It followed different courses, had different emphases, and took on different details in each of the major European countries. The fusion of Roman law, canon law, and feudal law produced the *ius commune,* a common legal system in Europe in force until the era of national codifications. At the end of the sixteenth century, almost all of continental Europe was ruled by ius commune, with significant local variants (*ius proprium*), and a body of common legal literature. Roman law infused both Catholic Europe and the Protestant culture of Northern Europe. Around 1700, Roman law was used to identify the basic moral principles of natural law and the law of nations. Around 1800, Roman law influenced the French Civil Code and many others in the so-called age of codification. With the German Civil Code (BGB) coming into force in 1900, Roman law lost its direct applicability in European legal practice. Yet the Roman law tradition itself has survived: civil law systems have been so influenced by Roman law that legal interpretation remains incomplete if it does not take into consideration Roman legal sources. In our own day, the study of Roman law has educational purposes and may prove instrumental in the development of a new global law.

The recovery of the Digest

Two manuscripts of the Digest seem to have been discovered in the eleventh century: one called *Littera Florentina* or *Codex Florentinus* (also known as *Littera Pisana*) and the other called *Codex Secundus*. The *Codex Florentinus* comprises 907 sheets and was written in Byzantine-Ravenna uncials. It was produced in the East, perhaps in Constantinople, in the middle of the sixth century. The *Codex Florentinus* might have been kept in Amalfi (then a part of the Byzantine territory in Italy). In any case, it eventually passed to Pisa and was thus known during the Middle Ages as *Littera Pisana*. The *Codex Florentinus* was transferred to Florence as a prize of war in 1406 and has been kept in the Laurentian Library in Florence since 1782. All surviving manuscripts of the Digest come from it. The *Codex Secundus* was the ancestor of all the copies of the Digest made in Bologna, the university city in which Roman law was first studied. Unfortunately, the *Codex Secundus* did not survive.

Although the major law school of the eleventh century was that of Pavia, the professors and jurists of that city gave special attention not to the Digest but to a collection known as the Book of Pavia (*Liber Papiensis*), which combines Lombard and Frankish laws. The University of Pavia, however, was the first to use the method of glosses (brief notations of the meaning of a word) to explain the law. This method was imported to Bologna to analyze and study the civil law, that is, the Roman law of Justinian's *Corpus Iuris*.

Bologna became the first academic center specifically focused on the study of Roman law, and by the end of the twelfth century the Bologna School of Law held a preeminent position. Thousands of students from around Europe attended lectures there, participated in legal discussions, and received a rigorous education based on the special legal techniques developed at the law school. Law students learned a legal method, a legal grammar, rather than the specific laws to be applied in concrete cases. From Bologna, the study of the Digest spread through France, northern Spain, and later England and Northern Europe. In European Mediterranean countries – Italy, France, and Spain – Roman law permeated legal practice without displacing customary law; even local laws were interpreted in the light of Roman law texts.

The rediscovery of the Digest is not historically isolated. It has to be understood in the context of a European cultural resurgence, closely related to the birth of the medieval universities, the rise of self-governing towns, the increase in maritime and overland trade, and a general economic revival. Prominent European law centers included Bologna (founded in 1088), Salamanca (1218), Paris (1219), Padua (1222), Naples (1224), Toulouse (1229), Oxford (about 1240), Orleans (about 1260), Coimbra (1290), Cambridge (1318), Prague (1348), Krakow (1364), Vienna (1365), and Heidelberg (1385), among others.

Western scholars were intellectually stimulated by the critical reading or discovery of important ancient works such as the Aristotelian canon or the writings of Plato, and many of them were to different degrees involved in the battle between imperialists (who affirmed the emperor's supremacy over the pope) and papalists (who affirmed the pope's supremacy). Meanwhile, the idea of the restoration of the Empire (*renovatio imperii*) and the conviction of the fundamental continuity of Roman law and heritage under the Holy Roman Empire was prevalent at the end of the eleventh century.

The civil law glossators

A gloss (from the Latin for "tongue" or "language") is a short comment or explanatory note for unfamiliar words or legal concepts that require clarification. It was the basic form of explanation. Originally glosses were inserted between the lines of the manuscript (interlinear glosses), but gradually they expanded into the margins of the text (marginal glosses). Civil law glossators were the scholars of the eleventh and twelfth centuries who specialized in the study and teaching of Roman law sources and used the explanatory technique of writing glosses in manuscripts of the *Corpus Iuris.* The canon law glossators of the same period were focused on canon law sources: the so-called *Decretum Gratiani* and the various compilations of the papal decretals letters.

The glossators' method and teaching style, based on logic and rhetoric, formed the foundation of European legal theory for centuries. It can be said that the glossators were the fathers of European jurisprudence. At the heart of European jurisprudence lies the idea, supported by the glossators, that the legal application of an intellectual rationale in the administration of justice, and not the use of force, is the best path for resolving conflicts between and among humans and nation-states.

Civil glossators regarded the Justinian Compilation as sacred, and they used their glosses to underscore the indisputable truth and authority of the legal text. For the civil glossators, the primary authority was the *Corpus Iuris,* as the Bible was for theologians and the writings of Aristotle were for philosophers. The two principles illuminating the method of the glossators were unconditional adherence to the text as it was revealed and logical formalism. The glossators considered the law more closely related to logic than to ethics. They did not use logic to test the validity of the argument provided by the text, but to harmonize divergences and clarify truths that they considered suprarational in character. The glossators did not develop a systematic approach by considering the consistent unity of the whole Compilation in its historical context. Instead, they originally focused on the exegesis of each particular legal text as an autonomous source of legal principles and rules. Synthesis was used only to integrate textual discrepancies into a common rule after a careful analysis and comparison of the purpose of each text. Civil glossators tried to discover the general principles (also called brocards) inherent to Justinian's *Corpus Iuris.*

Irnerius (also called Guarnerius or Werneius) was the founder of the school of glossators in Bologna, the first that applied the scholastic method of textual interpretation to the *Corpus Iuris,* especially to the recently rediscovered Digest. Irnerius can also be considered the first law professor in Western Europe. An expert in grammar and a legal practitioner, judge of the court of Emperor Henry V, Irnerius was supported by Margravine Mathilda of Tuscany and passed away sometime after 1125. After Irnerius, the oldest glossators at the University of Bologna were the so-called Four Doctors: Bulgarus, Martinus Gosia, Hugo de Porta Ravennate, and Jacobus. Like Irnerius, the Four

Doctors wrote apparatuses or collections of marginal glosses, as well as *quaestiones* (disputations), *distinctiones* (elaborated classifications), and other kinds of legal writings.

The most celebrated and brilliant lecturer of the Four Doctors was Bulgarus, who was called "mouth of gold" (*os aureum*). Bulgarus and Martinus were the leaders of two opposing schools at Bologna, corresponding in many respects to the schools of the Sabinians and Proculians during the Roman Principate. Bulgarus adhered more closely to the letter of the law than Martinus. According to Bulgarus, the interpreter should look for the purpose of the law (*ratio legis*), taking into consideration other texts related to the same topic as necessary. According to Martinus, by contrast, equity could modify the apparent meaning of a rule when considering the *Corpus Iuris* as a whole. Therefore, he thought, all texts that can illuminate the legal problem should be consulted and analyzed. Bulgarus's approach eventually prevailed. He was succeeded as a leader of the School of Bologna by his pupil Johannes Bassianus, who believed that the right analysis of a text required four steps: (1) fixing the problem; (2) finding contrary texts and analyzing the suggested solutions; (3) finding the general rules or brocards to be applied; and (4) holding final public discussion of the topic. The Italian jurists Matteo Gribaldi Moffa (c. 1505–64) summed up the method of the glossator in a famous Latin couplet: *praemitto, scindo, summo, casumque figuro / perlego, do causas, connoto, et obiicio* ("I introduce the problem, I analyze it, I summarize it, and I frame the case / I read through the text, I set my arguments, I remark on other points, and I discuss objections").

Bassianus's outstanding pupil was Azo. A professor at Bologna, where he had been born around 1150, Azo was famous for his *Summa Codicis, Summa Institutionum*, and *Summa Digestorum*, which became longstanding treatises of European common law. He also elaborated a collection of brocards. His most celebrated work, however, was his collection of legal glosses (technically called apparatus) to the first part of the Digest (*Digestum vetus*) and the Codex (books 1 to 9). The popularity Azo enjoyed was so great among Italian lawyers that it used to be said that without Azo on one's side, it was a waste of time go to court: *Chi non ha Azzo, no vada al Palazzo*. His *Summa Codicis* was translated into Old French and was consulted and often copied verbatim by Henry Bracton (c. 1210–c. 1268) in his famous work *On the Laws and Customs of England*.

Azo's best-known pupil was Franciscus Accursius (c. 1185–1263). Accursius compiled the so-called Great Gloss (*Magna Glossa* or *Glossa Ordinaria*), which is the consolidation of more than a hundred thousand glosses of his predecessors. We do not know the exact date of the completion of the Great Gloss, but by the middle of the thirteenth century the work was largely complete. The Accursian gloss was considered the pillar of European common law. Its importance is reflected in the maxim: "What the gloss does not recognize, the court does not recognize." After the publication of the Great Gloss of Accursius, the center of legal productivity and development switched from Bologna to Orleans, where two great jurists taught: Jacques de Révigny and Pierre de Belleperche. These two lawyers have been considered the precursors of the school of commentators.

The commentators

European jurists (predominantly Italians) from the fourteenth century until the new school of humanism appeared in the sixteenth century are usually called commentators. Their teaching methods were substantially similar to those of the glossators, but the commentators went beyond the glossators. The commentators were able to transform Justinian's law into a common law for the entire continental Europe (ius commune). They were the architects of a new European legal system based on the integration of the ius commune with local laws, ordinances, and customs (*iura propria*).

The commentators made important contributions to both legal science and legal practice, writing sophisticated lectures and commentaries on the texts of the Digest and giving legal opinions based on the social realities of the time. They felt free to disregard the original context as they applied the Roman texts, and they paid special attention to current law beyond Justinian's codification. The commentators approached Roman law as a universal law, timelessly valid and able to resolve all kinds of legal controversies. This universalization of Roman law opened the doors to its application to new situations and circumstances that were unknown to the Romans. The commentators were also able to harmonize Roman law and local law. For these reasons, commentators had enormous impact on political, social, and legal affairs. They developed new doctrines on criminal responsibility, conflict of laws, the legal personhood of institutions, ownership, and commercial law, among other things.

The most celebrated commentators were Bartolus of Sassoferrato, followed by his pupil Baldus de Ubaldis. Bartolus (1314–57) was born to a humble family in Venatura, Italy, near Sassoferrato, in the province of Ancona. A student of the famous commentator Cino da Pistoia (Cinus de Sighibuldis) in Perugia and of Jacobus Buttrigarius and Ranierus de Forlivio in Bologna, Bartolus became a doctor of civil law at the age of twenty. After serving as a judge in the small cities of Toldi and Pisa, he became a professor of civil law in Pisa and later in Perugia, where he died. During his short life, he had great impact on his time. He gave his name to the school that led the study of civil law during the fourteenth and fifteenth centuries: the Bartolists. In fact, people said that if one were not a Bartolist, one could not be a good lawyer (*nullus bonus jurista nisi sit bartolista*). Bartolus wrote comprehensive commentaries on all parts of the *Corpus Iuris*, exhaustive lectures (*repetitiones*), and disputations (*disputationes*), as well as important monographs both in public and private law. Some writings under Bartolus's name are of dubious authenticity or are inauthentic. For instance, the commentary on Justinian's Institutes in Bartolus's collected works was written by Jacques de Revigny. Bartolus developed practical solutions in case of a conflict of laws: between canon law and civil law; between civil law and local law; or between local laws. Along with the Great Gloss of Accursius, Bartolus's writings became the standard works of jurisprudence until the arrival of humanism in the sixteenth century.

Baldus de Ubaldis (1327–1400), doctor of both civil law and canon law (*doctor utriusque iuris*), led legal theory during the second half of the fourteenth century. Son of Franciscus de Ubaldis, a professor of medicine, Baldus was born in Perugia, where he studied civil law under Bartolus. He taught civil law in Perugia with Bartolus and then in Pisa, Florence, Padua, Perugia again, and Pavia. Among his students were Petrus Ancharanus, Franciscus Zabarella, Paulus de Castro, Petrus Belfortte (later Pope Gregory XI), and Johannes de Imola. Baldus also worked as a lawyer. His more than twenty-five hundred legal opinions (*consilia*) made him wealthy. A cultivated and imaginative jurist, Baldus wrote extensive commentaries on civil law, canon law, and feudal law, as well as many monographs. Baldus died on April 28, 1400 in Pavia, while writing a legal opinion.

Roman law and canon law

During the Middle Ages, the Church was the leading public institution with the greatest intellectual talent. The law of the Church, however, was not comparable to Justinian's Compilation. For this reason, civil lawyers considered canon law methods and techniques to be intellectually inferior in rank. Around 1140, however, the monk Gratian, a canon lawyer from Bologna, published the *Concordia discordantium canonum* [Harmonizing the divergent norms], known as Gratian's Decree (*Decretum Gratiani*), an authoritative collection of canon law material that tried to harmonize apparent textual contradictions. Gratian's sources were the Bible, Justinian's Code, the writings of the Church Fathers, papal decretals, and acts and decrees of the councils and synods. The *Decretum* marked the starting point of the development of canon law as a legal science, because of the systematic and critical way in which materials were arranged and analyzed. Medieval canon law was a well-balanced combination of ecclesiastical sources and medieval interpretation of Roman law.

Gratian's followers, the school of decretists, started to produce and collect the existing glosses while the civil glossators were doing their jobs. In the thirteenth and fourteenth centuries there was strong competition between civil commentators and canon lawyers. Although the law of the Church differed from civil law, and the work of civilists and canonists remained distinct in content and application, canon law and civil law were so intertwined than one could not understand either without the other. The civil law was concerned with justice in order to guarantee happiness and prosperity on earth; the canon law focused on justice to ensure the salvation of the souls (*salus animarum*).

Canon law and civil law constantly interacted by the principle of complementarity: on the one hand, in the absence of canon law norms, ecclesiastical courts used to apply civil law; on the other hand, secular courts regularly took into consideration general principles of canon law to resolve concrete civil legal issues. This explains why many lawyers were instructed in both civil and canon law (*utrumque ius*).

Papal legislation was vigorous after the publication of the Gratian's Decree, and, as a result, canon lawyers had to respond to it in different ways than Roman law experts did. In 1234 Pope Gregory IX promulgated a large collection of new papal decretals (called *Liber Extra*, edited by Saint Raymond of Penyafort). Pope Boniface VIII, in 1298, propagated a further collection (*Liber Sextus*). In 1582, after the Council of Trent (1545–63), Pope Gregory XIII disseminated a critical and official compilation of all canon law materials from the *Decretum Gratiani* to the later decretals of the fourteenth and fifteenth centuries. It was called *Corpus Iuris Canonici* (the body of canon law). The name was an evident allusion to Justinian's *Corpus Iuris*. *Legist* was the name churchmen gave in referring to an expert in Roman Justinian law.

Roman law and English law

Roman law cannot be considered an essential element of English law; however, since Roman law was known in England when Anglo-Norman law began to develop intellectually, medieval Roman law contributed to the formation and development of English common law during the twelfth and thirteenth centuries. Native English scholars knew and taught civil law in accordance with the literature that Bolognese scholars produced.

The first of these Bolognese scholars to teach in England was Magister Vacarius. Born about 1120, Vacarius studied civil law in Bologna and was called to England in about 1143 by Archbishop Theobald. Vacarius taught around 1150 at Oxford, where the main text in the school of civil law was his book on the subject, popularly called *Liber pauperum* [Book of the poor (students)]. Divided into nine books, the work is a collection of basic texts of the Digest and the Code, including the last three books (*Tres libri*). The teaching of Roman law spread from Oxford to Cambridge in the thirteenth century to train lawyers for practice in ecclesiastical courts.

Important books of the Anglo-Norman period, such as Ranulf de Glanvill's *Tractatus de legibus et consuetudinibus Regni Angliae* [Treatise on the laws and customs of the Kingdom of England] and, especially, Henry de Bracton's *De legibus et consuetudinibus Angliae* [On the laws and customs of England], show the knowledge and training of two English authors in medieval Roman law. The first part of Bracton's work contains references to about two hundred different sections of Justinian's Compilation. Bracton realized that the best foundation for an explanation of English law was the Roman legal structure of concepts articulated by Roman jurists. Roman law also penetrated English law through canon law, which was applied in English law in church courts, especially in relation to marriage and testaments. Since the members of the Court of Chancery (on equity) were clergymen, the canonical idea of equity, and indirectly the Roman one, influenced the development of English equity.

The English common law system and civil law system did not completely separate until after the Tudor period (1485–1603), when the Inns of Court had finally prevailed over academic legal institutions in relation to the education of barristers, sergeants-at-law, and judges. Nevertheless, the Court of Admiralty, the Court Star Chamber, as well as the ecclesiastical courts continued applying the principles and rules of Roman law in maritime, penal, and ecclesiastical matters.

A rebirth of interest in Roman law occurred in the sixteenth century and in the first half of the seventeenth century, when distinguished scholars such as Alberico Gentili (1552–1608) and Richard Zouche (1590–1661), among others, taught at Oxford. Although the revival was brief, the presence of Roman law continued, especially through William Blackstone's *Commentaries on the Law of England* (1766–70), whose structure is based on the Roman division of law into matters relating to persons, things, and actions. In the nineteenth century, English judges and legal practitioners were willing to borrow rules, ideas, and concepts from the civil law tradition or even directly from Roman law.

The French humanists

The historical and aesthetic interest in classical antiquity during the Renaissance provided a new intellectual context for the study of Roman law: the school of the French humanists. The method of this school was called *mos gallicus*, because the school was mainly developed in France as a reaction against the method of the Italian commentators (*mos italicus*). Legal humanists fostered a new critical attitude toward the ancient legal sources. They promoted the rediscovery and accurate reconstruction of the ancient texts, contextualizing and historicizing them. In doing so, they called into question the authority and practical validity of Roman law. The humanists considered the work of the commentators devastating because the need to apply the law in practice had led them to move away from the original text. According to the humanists, just as Roman law was a product of Roman society and changed with political circumstances, so French law should be a product of French society. In their view, there was no reason to apply Roman law to sixteenth-century France. At the same time, however, they believed that eternal rational principles underlay the *Corpus Iuris Civilis.*

Protestant reformers influenced legal humanism. It is no mere coincidence that many French humanists were in fact French Protestants (Huguenots). Moreover, they expanded legal humanism into the Netherlands. The so-called Dutch Elegant Jurisprudence grew out of the flight to Northern Europe of leading humanists like Hugues Doneau (1527–91) from persecution. The core idea illuminating the humanist method was similar to the core idea of the Reformation: to return to the original source. Just as the Protestant theologians disputed the authority of the Church Fathers and proposed a pure return to the original source of holy scripture, the legal humanists disputed the authority of glossators and commentators and proposed a return to the primary source, the *Corpus Iuris Civilis*, insofar as it revealed the writings of the classical Roman jurists. Prominent legal humanists included Lelio Torelli and Antonio Agustín, who produced an edition of the Digest in 1553 based on the Florentine manuscript.

The Italian jurist Andrea Alciato can be considered the leader and founder of legal humanism, and the French jurist Jacques Cujas was the preeminent humanist. Andrea Alciato (1492–1550) was born in Alzate, near Milan, studied law in Pavia, under the Bartolist Giasone del Maino and Filippo Decio, and taught at Avignon, Bourges, and Pavia. During his stay in Bourges, the law school became one of the most famous in Europe. He wrote, among other important works, a commentary on the three last books in Justinian's Code (*Annotationes in tres libros Codicis*), as well as some essays on law and interpretation (*Paradoxa, Parerga iuris*) that were considered leading representative works of the new legal humanism. Alciato's most famous work is *Emblemata* (1531), a collection of short Latin verses that attained great popularity in Europe and created a new literary genre.

Jacques Cujas (Cuiacius, 1522–90) was born in Toulouse, where he studied law. After teaching Roman law in Cahors, in 1555 he moved to Bourges to succeed François Baudoin (1520–73), who was forced to leave France for religious reasons. Cujas refused to take any part in the French religious wars between Catholics and Huguenots. "This has nothing to do with the praetorian edict" was Cujas's ordinary answer to those who asked him about religious matters. His great rivals at Bourges, the famous jurists Hugue Doneau (1527–91) and François Hotman (1524–90), left Bourges after the Massacre of Saint Bartholomew's Day in 1573.

Cujas's most important work was *Observationes et emendationes*, a commentary on the *Corpus Iuris Civilis*. His interest was far from limited to Justinian's Compilation, however. He recovered and published a part of the Theodosian Code, and he procured the manuscript of the *Basilika*. He also worked on feudal law and canon law. In his *Paratitla*, summaries of the *Corpus Iuris Civilis*, he condensed in maxims and rules the most relevant legal principles and provided precise and clear definitions. In 1577, Cujas's *Opera Omnia* were published in Paris, collected and edited by Cujas himself. He died in Bourges on October 4, 1590.

Sometimes, and paradoxically, the school of humanists fell into a dogmatic attitude, condemning as "Tribonianism" all kinds of historical development outside the classical sources. Humanists established a strict (and artificial) wall of separation between historical and practical interests. This explained why the humanist school remained a scholarly project in the hands of sophisticated and learned scholars without strong influence on legal practice. Neither in Italy nor in Germany was legal humanism a success. An Italian Protestant, Alberico Gentili (1552–1608), who moved from Italy to England for religious reasons, wrote six dialogues (*De iuris interpretibus dialogi sex*) against the high theoretical approach of the French humanists and in defense of a Bartolist and more practical approach.

The German "modern use" of the Digest

In Germany, unlike in France, jurists deeply influenced by Dutch jurists approached Roman law in a more practically oriented way, which is called *usus modernus Pandectarum* ("the modern use of the Digest"). The usus modernus held sway in the seventeenth century and the first half of the eighteenth century. This name of usus modernus, conventionally given by later historians, came from one of the main works of the new style, written by Samuel Stryk (*Specimen usus modernus Pandectarum*, 1690–92).

The usus modernus constituted a new step in the development of legal theory in Europe. In some sense, usus modernus refreshed the mos italicus of the Italian commentators while taking advantage of the quality of learning and style provided by the mos gallicus. The modern jurists were able to harmonize the positive law of Germany with the Roman texts. They applied Roman texts to legal problems that the Romans certainly did not consider and submitted Roman law texts to critical scrutiny. In some cases, the jurists who applied usus modernus concluded that rules of Roman law did not fit modern conditions and that, instead, the application of canonical rules or particular laws was preferable.

In addition to Samuel Stryk (1640–1710), notable jurists of the usus modernus included Benedict Carpzov (1595–1666), Hermann Conring (1606–81), David Mevius (1609–70), Georg Adam Struve (1619–92), Johannes Voet (1647–1713), Augustin Leyser (1683–1752), and Justus Henning Böhmer (1674–1749), among others.

The Dutch Elegant Jurisprudence

During the seventeenth and eighteenth centuries, humanism flourished so abundantly in the Netherlands that it was called the "most elegant jurisprudence" of Europe. Dutch jurists were able to merge the tradition of Roman law with Dutch feudal customary law, especially from the province of Holland, and to turn Roman–Dutch law into an autonomous legal system, predominantly Roman, which was applied in the Dutch colonies. Representative jurists of the School of Elegant Jurisprudence included Hugo Grotius (1583–1645), Ulrich Huber (1636–94), Johannes Voet (1647–1713), Gerhard Noodt (1647–1725), and Cornelis van Bijnkershoek (1673–1743). Of all of them, Hugo Grotius has a place of high honor in legal theory.

A child prodigy, Grotius was one of the leading theologians, jurists, and humanists of his time, and one of the most influential jurists of all ages. He is considered one of the founders of modern natural law and international law, as well as one of the founders of Dutch law. His reputation as a legal thinker rests basically on three works: a) *Mare liberum* [The freedom of the seas, 1609], in defense of the free use of the seas and against the Spanish and Portuguese monopolization of the colonial trade; b) *Introduction to the Jurisprudence of Holland* (written in Dutch in 1619), a short treatise that was the first explanation of the Roman–Dutch legal system; and c) *De iuri belli ac pacis* [On the law of war and peace, 1623], which presents an international legal system based on natural law and freed from traditional moral theology. Grotius was deeply familiar with Roman law and used it especially to find practical and ethical rules that were binding on nations. For him, Roman law was authoritative not because of any imperial authority, but because the standards of classical Europe reflected natural law as a logical necessity.

The school of natural law

A school of thought contemporary with the usus modernus was the so-called school of natural law. Founded by Hugo Grotius and influenced by Greek philosophy and Protestant rationalism, the school of modern natural law defended the existence of valid rational legal principles inherent in the nature of human beings. Natural law scholars tried to find these absolute legal principles, emancipated from faith and creeds and confessions, in the writings and statements of antiquity, especially in Roman law. They understood law as a sort of legal mathematics. While they drew on Roman law to support natural law, for them natural law was not Roman law. Rather, natural law scholars' interest in Roman law lay in the fact that it provided good materials to build their own abstract and logical system of natural law. They rejected Roman legal formalism, and they did not pay special attention to philological and historical developments. Although the new natural law was not really a product of Roman law, many principles of Roman law survived in European jurisprudence as natural-law principles. Major legal problems within international relations of that time provided the best occasion for applying natural law theory to the field of international law. The new international law became the most exquisite product of the natural law school.

Distinguished scholars of the school of natural law were Samuel Pufendorf (1632–94), Christian Thomasius (1655–1728), and Christian Wolf (1679–1754). Of these three natural law scholars, the most original was Pufendorf. He was the first to develop a general theory of natural law emphasizing natural duties more than natural rights. Although Pufendorf used Roman categories, he replaced the Roman systematization of persons, things, and actions by three categories of human duties: to God, to the agent himself, and to others. Pufendorf always maintained the Christian character of natural law: although natural, it is deduced from the Christian principle of loving God and others as oneself. Pufendorf's significance in the development of European private law is enormous. The structures of later codifications, especially the "general part" (Allgemeiner Teil) of the codes and systematizations of contracts, were inspired by the doctrines of Pufendorf. His most important works are:

Elementa jurisprudentia universalis [Elements of a universal jurisprudence, 1660], *De jure naturae et gentium* [On the law of nature and nations, 1672], and *De officio hominis et civis iuxta legem naturalem* [On the duty of man and citizen according to natural law, 1673].

The school of natural law triggered and thoroughly influenced the codification movement of the eighteenth century. Even in England and Scotland, where there was no substantial codification, the school of natural law influenced the modern law of contracts and negligence.

The age of codification

The legal phenomenon of codification, a term coined by Jeremy Bentham (1748–1832), was a product of natural-law theories applied to particular legal systems. The codification movement was founded on a belief in the human capacity to establish an all-inclusive legal system based on pure natural reason. Natural law was a means of inquiring about the value and quality of the positive law of each country. It was also a way of finding the criteria and standards of substantive rights law. The phenomenon of codification opened the door to the possibility of rethinking and reworking all the fundamental principles, premises, and pillars of the European legal systems. Each code was meant to offer a coherent and complete statement of the principles and rules that should be applied to a particular area of the law (civil law, criminal law, procedural law).

The phenomenon of codification was particularly significant in France in the years following the Revolution of 1789, but it was also important in Prussia, Bavaria, and Austria, and it spread to all civil-law countries to different degrees during the nineteenth century and the first part of the twentieth century. The French Civil Code of 1804 (still in force, although amended in many details) was the most prominent achievement of the natural-law codification movement and the intellectual legal articulation of national sovereignty. It was considered a monument to the perfection of reason. France, as one undivided nation, was to have a common law for all French citizens based on reason, not on customary law. Because the Civil Code had to be supported by reason, it had to be clear, concise, simple, and well structured. The commission in charge of the preparation of the Civil Code, led by Jean-Étienne-Marie Portalis (1746–1807), relied on the works of Robert Joseph Pothier (1699–1772). A legal expert of international repute, Pothier was able to join Roman law and French customary law on a rational basis. His *Treatise on the Law of Obligations or Contracts*, firmly articulated in accordance with Roman law, was instrumental for both the elaboration of the French Civil Code and for the expansion of Roman law principles around the world.

The Civil Code followed Napoleonic invasions and was the model for many other codes both in France and beyond. It had extraordinary success not only in Europe (Belgium, Luxembourg, the Netherlands, Italy, Spain, Portugal, Hungary, Romania, and Greece) but also in Latin America, Turkey, Egypt,

China, and Japan. Louisiana represents a remarkable case of civil law codification in the United States. American law has produced digests, restatements (without formal legal status), subject-specific codes, and statutory compilations, but the American tradition did not embrace intensely the idea of codification, which is more characteristic of the civil law tradition.

The German historical school

The codification movement seemed to put an end to the history of the tradition of Roman law in Europe, but it did not. The reawakening of Roman law in the nineteenth century was directly related to the powerful reaction against the idea of codification and the rationalist passion of the Enlightenment. In France, Montesquieu had opposed the concept of the natural law of reason, pointing out the irrational element of the law as well as the strong connections between the legal institutions, culture, and circumstances of each particular period of history. In England, Edward Gibbon, in his famous *History of the Decline and Fall of the Roman Empire* (1776–89), demonstrated how the laws of a nation constitute a significant part of its history. In Germany, Gustav Hugo (1764–1844) emphasized the inherent historical nature of the law, which could not be reduced to legislation. According to Hugo, the development of Roman law was a product of the creativity of the classical jurists, not of the Roman emperors. Codification, insofar as it demanded legislation, weakened the creativity of the real legal actors and practitioners.

The ideas of Hugo influenced Friedrich Carl von Savigny (1779–1861), one of the most important legal thinkers of the civil law tradition and founder of the German historical school of jurisprudence. Born in Frankfurt, graduated from Marburg, professor of law in Berlin beginning in 1810, and minister for legislation (1842–48), Savigny argued that law could not be reduced to a pure construction of reason because the law was a product of the culture and ethos of each society. The symbolic starting point of the historical school was Savigny's famous pamphlet *Vom Beruf unserer Zeit für Gesetzgebung und Rechtswissenschaft* [On the vocation on our age for legislation and legal science, 1814], which was directed against the essay *Über die Nothwendigkeit eines allgemeinen bürgerlichen Rechts für Deutschland* [On the necessity of a general civil code for Germany, 1814] written by Anton Thibaut (1772–1840), professor of law at Heidelberg. Inspired deeply by the French codification experience, Thibaut had proposed a civil code for Germany, arguing that a law based on reason could be applied to all the states of the new German Confederation (*Deutscher Bund*), established by the Congress of Vienna (1814). The response of Savigny was that it was impossible to codify without first understanding the laws and institutions of the different parts of Germany, because law is fundamentally a product of history. According to Savigny, history is the path to understanding national conditions and circumstances. Each people has its individual character, its own consciousness, what was later called "national spirit" (*Volksgeist*), and this spirit left its mark upon all legal institutions and laws.

According to Savigny, what Germany needed was not to create a rationalistic code but to dive into its own history, to understand its own laws. Only after fulfilling this essential task could a codification make sense. This theory of the Volksgeist fit accurately with the general trends of German nationalism, a natural product of the democratic ideas developed by the French Revolution, and the sense of German unity derived from the French Wars and Napoleonic oppression. Only the founding of the German Empire in 1871, and with it the founding of the German nation, provided the political and constitutional framework for the codification of the law.

The historical school of jurisprudence was divided into two branches: the Romanists (including Savigny, Georg Friedrich Puchta, and Adolf Friedrich Rudorff, among others) and the Germanists (including Karl Friedrich Eichborn, Jacob Grimm, and Georg Beseler). The Romanists focused on Roman law and its reception in Germany as a constitutive part of the Volksgeist, while the Germanists focused on medieval German law as an expression of the German soul. Both branches engaged in historical research into the evolution of the law, and according to Savigny, both Roman law and German law were to constitute the two pillars of the new German legal science. By the middle of the nineteenth century, however, the school had split because some Germanists did not accept the reception of Roman law as a portion of the German national soul. They regarded Roman law not as a national product but as a bug inside the purest Germanic law.

Savigny wrote three exemplary works besides the famous pamphlet against Thibaut: the dogmatic monograph *Das Recht des Besitzes* [The law of possession, 1803], the masterful *Geschichte des römischen Recht im Mittelalter* [History of the Roman law during the Middle Ages, 1815–31], and the brilliant *System des heutigen römischen Rechts* [System of modern Roman law, 1840–49]. In *The Law of Possession*, written when Savigny was only twenty-four years old, Savigny tried to expound the institution of possession as it had been according to the original Roman sources. *The Law of Possession* is a masterpiece that ended up taking the old uncritical approach to Roman Law. In *History of the Roman Law during the Middle Ages*, the best of all his works, Savigny purified the idea of Roman law of all alterations derived from the Middle Ages and the practice of the usus modernus. He was convinced of the unity of the European legal tradition and the important role of scholars to transmit this tradition. Finally, the seminal eight-volume *System of Modern Roman Law* made Savigny a foremost pioneer of the school of pandectists.

The school of pandectists and the German Civil Code

An offshoot of the historical school was the school of pandectists (from the Pandects, i.e., the Digest), founded by Savigny's pupil Georg Friedrich Puchta (1798–1846). Born in Cadolzburg in Bavaria, Puchta attended the

Gymnasium of Nuremberg, where he came under the personal influence of Hegel. Professor of law at Munich (1828), Marburg (1835), and Leipzig (1837), in 1842 Puchta occupied the chair in the University of Berlin (1842) that Savigny had vacated on becoming minister for legislation. Puchta is the father of strict conceptual formalism. His methodological influence on legal science was even greater than that of Savigny himself.

The lack of a national civil code in Germany until 1900 was the ultimate justification for the existence of the school, which was instrumental in drafting the German Civil Code. Pandectists were concerned about the scientific application of Roman law to current legal questions and, therefore, about systematization. Although pandectists built on classical Roman law sources, predominantly the Digest, they were able to create an autonomous theoretical system of legal principles, institutions, and legal dogmas. The method Puchta developed, called "jurisprudence of concepts" (*Begriffsjurisprudenz*), aimed at establishing a logical and systematic hierarchy of legal concepts that permeated the whole legal system. Law was a positive legal science with an independent existence – isolated from ethics, politics, and economic aspects of social life. These domains were not the business of legal theory, but of legislation. Rules and procedures were drawn exclusively from their own integrated system and doctrinal concepts. The legal validity of each rule would depend on its position inside the hierarchical system, and it would be an expression of the internal harmony of its own legal system. Potential gaps inside the legal system would be filled with creative construction. Legal imagination and innovative creativity contributed to purifying the system.

Pandectism produced many distinguished legal scholars, including Aloys Brinz (1820–87), Heinrich Dernburg (1829–1907), Ludwig Enneccerus (1843–1928), Andres von Tuhr (1864–1925), and Paul Oertmann (1865–1938). The most important among them was Bernhard Windscheid (1817–92), who is considered a pioneer of modern German civil law. Born in Düsseldorf, Windscheid taught in Basel, Greifswald (where he was friendly with Rudolph Jhering), Munich, Heidelberg, and Leipzig. He declined a tenured position in Berlin. From 1873 to 1886, he served with the First Commission in charge of drafting the German Civil Code, to which his contribution was significant. Windscheid developed the modern German legal concept of *Anspruch* (claim), distinguishing it from the classic Roman idea of *actio* (action). Windscheid's most important work is the *Lehrbuch des Pandektenrechts* (Textbook of Pandect Law, 1862–70), which quickly became the leading scholarly authority. Because of its objectivity, elegance, and practical function, this textbook dominated German legal science until the German Civil Code came into force.

The jurisprudence of interests

If Savigny was the most eminent German jurist of the first part of the nineteenth century, Rudolph von Jhering (or Ihering, 1818–92) was probably the most eminent jurist of the second part of the nineteenth century. Although originally a pandectist, Jhering moved away from pandectism to provide a sociological explanation of the evolution of Roman law.

A native of Aurich in Frisia and professor of Roman law in Giessen (1852), Vienna (1868) – where the emperor knighted him – and Gottingen (1872–92), among others – Jhering represents a radical and innovative methodological turning point from conceptual imagination to social realism, especially in relation to the doctrines of Savigny and Puchta. An energetic man with great intuition and a deep sense for the practical role of the law, Jhering attracted the general public with enthusiastic lectures and provocative contributions in journals on legal current issues. In one of his masterpieces, *Der Geist des römischen Recht* [The spirit of Roman law, 1852–65], Jhering rejected the notion of the Volksgeist as the only explanation of the origin of the law, as well as the jurisprudence of concepts, which had become pointless and unrealistic. The Roman elements coexisting in German law were incompatible with the idea of a law derived only from a national consciousness. According to Jhering, a well-balanced legal system should be able to assimilate ideas from outside, as Roman law did. On the other hand, Jhering also argued that the desire for logic so characteristic in the jurisprudence of concepts arises from a misunderstanding of the law. Concepts should be subordinate to life, and not life to concepts. Law is a result of social relations, not of concepts. For this reason, legal concepts have no meaning outside of the social relations they regulate. Roman law was not just based on moral principles but on a social and economic reality, which supported a jurisprudence of interests but not a jurisprudence of concepts.

In *Der Kampf ums Recht* [Struggle for law, 1872], Jhering argued that rights and laws are a product of the reality of society and should be considered the means of experiencing power and fulfilling the satisfaction of interests. For this reason, law should be explained in terms of human purposes, interests, and desires, not concepts, and the judges, in their decisions, should be concerned with the social purpose of the legislation and the competing interests of the parties. According to Jhering, it is not possible to establish a clear wall of separation between the public and the private because the state should be interested in all activities that contribute to the development of the political community. Jhering is considered the founder of the jurisprudence of interests, as well as one of the founders of the sociology of law. Jhering was widely read in the United States by leading American legal scholars: Oliver Wendell Holmes Jr. (1841–1935); Roscoe Pound (1870–1964); Karl Llewellyn (1893–1962), and Jerome Frank (1889–1957), among others.

Roman law in the United States

Roman constitutional history had a practical impact on the American constitutional experience. Because the founders of the American republic were steeped in classical literature, Roman constitutional principles and values illuminated the decision of the framers who drafted the US Constitution of

1787, as did the common law tradition or Protestant theology. The framing generation emphasized classical ideals of republican government, public honor, and civic responsibility. Both Federalists and Antifederalists often used ancient Roman history and Roman precedents to support their arguments. The ancient theory of the mixed constitution, extensively developed in the Roman experience, came to be manifested in the American structure of separation of powers. Bicameralism in Congress, the idea of checks and balances, and the provision of a vigorous presidency represent some of the US constitutional elements influenced by the Romans. Roman constitutional history is everywhere in the literature of the American Revolution.

Roman law, both private and public, constituted a constant reference point, as well as a source of inspiration and systematization, for later distinguished American lawyers and thinkers (James Kent, Josef Story, Oliver Wendell Holmes, and Roscoe Pound, among them), especially, although not exclusively, until the First World War (1914–18). The US Supreme Court, however, has used Roman law and Roman legal thought only occasionally, mostly for ornamental purposes and without really furnishing the basis of precedent. Since American law has remained steadily within the English common law tradition, Roman law has been mostly considered a foreign element in the American legal system without practical applications and value.

Originally, American law adopted some aspects of Roman law via English law. William Blackstone's *Commentaries on the Law of England*, one of the most influential treatises in early American jurisprudence, derived its structure from Roman law. This treatise served as a bridge between Roman law and US law since it had prevailed as the principal source for colonial precedent. American law also adopted some aspects of the civil law tradition via Spanish law (*Las Partidas*) and French law (Napoleonic Code). The example of Louisiana, where state law is still based on civil law, is unique. The reason for this distinction is that Louisiana was a Spanish and French territory prior to its American purchase from France in 1803. In some of the southwestern states, traces of the civil law tradition also remain. California, for instance, has a civil code (first adopted in 1872) based on a civil code that David Dudley Field (1805–94) originally prepared for the state of New York, organized in accordance with the civil law tradition.

Roman law in the twentieth century

With the enactment of the German Civil Code on January 1, 1990, Roman law ceased to be directly applicable as a legal source in any European legal system. As result, following in the footsteps of Theodor Mommsen (1817–1903), the dean of classical studies in the nineteenth century, and Otto Lenel (1849–1935), Roman law research became more a historical matter, separate from legal practice. Roman scholars were focused on the reconstruction of the classical Roman legal sources. In this context, they developed a method of identifying interpolations (the "hunt for interpolations") coming from post classical editors or Justinian's compilers. Today, the approach to interpolations is more cautious.

The study of Roman law was also located as a part of the wider context provided by ancient legal history (*Antike Rechtsgeschichte*) within the province of the sciences of antiquity (*Altertumswissenschaften*). Scholars studied the relation between Roman law and other laws of antiquity, especially Greek law and Mesopotamian law. Roman law scholars were also focused on the interdisciplinary study of epigraphy and papyrology as long as the discovery of new inscriptions and papyri provided significant new information on Roman law. Leading this approach was Ludwig Mitteis, who was the teacher and mentor of a new generation of great German Roman scholars, such as Leopold Wenger (1874–1953), Paul Koschaker (1879–1951), Fritz Pringsheim (1882–1967), and Ernst Rabel (1874–1955), one of the founders of modern comparative law.

In Italy, Vittorio Scialoja (1856–1933), greatly influenced by Windscheid, led a new generation of distinguished Roman scholars. Prominent representatives of the Italian school were: Pietro Bonfante (1864–1932), Salvatore Riccobono (1864–1958), and Vincenzo Arangio-Ruiz (1884–1964). From the end of the Second World War to the end of the twentieth century, three great scholars led research of Roman law: Max Kaser (1906–97), Franz Wieacker (1908–94), and Wolfgang Kunkel (1902–81). Rooted in the German neohumanism of the late nineteenth century, Kaser represents the systematic approach to Roman law, while Wieacker and Kunkel represent the historical approach. Some contemporary scholars are expanding the social context of Roman law and developing a new social approach for the study of law in the Roman world.

Recently, the European Union has produced a revival in the study of Roman law, and specifically, in the European ius commune and the civil law tradition. According to a new approach, Roman law, as an icon of unity that goes beyond national boundaries, offers the background and the theoretical method for building up a European private law.

Roman law and global law

The most important function of Roman law in the twenty-first century will be its instrumental value in the development of the new global law. The transformation of the law that governs our international community of nation-states (international law) into a law that is capable of properly ordering the whole human community (global law) requires the creation of a new legal paradigm. Following the Roman classification of persons, things, and actions, this new paradigm should substitute humanity as a whole for the "person," downgrade the generic concept of "things" to global issues that affect humanity, and shift the focus of the concept of "action" to that of a global rule of law. In the construction of this new global paradigm, Roman law can play a key role.

Additionally, Roman law can help develop a global legal education. Globalization has connected all the world's legal systems. This increasing legal interdependence demands a universal legal terminology recognized and accepted by all countries and peoples, no matter the legal tradition they belong to. This terminology can be based on Roman law, which is the most influential and far-reaching legal system in history. Roman law may well be termed the *lingua franca* of global law.

Further reading

Ando, Clifford, Paul J. du Plessis, and Kaius Tuori, eds. *The Oxford Handbook of Roman Law and Society*. Oxford and New York: Oxford University Press, 2016.

Astorino, Samuel. "Roman Law in American Law: Twentieth Century Cases of the Supreme Court." *Duquesne Law Review* 40 (2002): 627–654.

Bederman, David J. *The Classical Foundation of the American Constitution*. Cambridge and New York: Cambridge University Press, 2008.

Bellomo, Manlio. *The Common Legal Past of Europe*. Translated by Lydia G. Cochrane. Washington, DC: The Catholic University of America, 1995.

Calasso, Francesco. *Medio Evo del diritto*. Milan: Giuffrè, 1954.

Caenegem, Raoul C. van. *The Birth of the English Common Law*. Cambridge and New York: Cambridge University Press, 1988.

Caenegem, Raoul C. van. *European Law in the Past and the Future: Unity and Diversity Over Two Millennia*. Cambridge and New York: Cambridge University Press, 2002.

Cortese, Ennio. *Le grandi linee della storia giuridica medievale*. Rome: Il Cigno Galileo Galilei, 2001.

Domingo, Rafael, ed. *Juristas universales*. 4 vols. Madrid: Marcial Pons, 2004.

Domingo, Rafael. *The New Global Law*. Cambridge, New York: Cambridge University Press, 2010

Grossi, Paolo. *A History of European Law*. Translated by Laurence Hooper. Malden, MA: Wiley-Blackwell, 2010.

Hoeflich, Michael H. *Roman and Civil Law and the Development of Anglo-American Jurisprudence in the Nineteenth Century*. Athens, GA and London: The University of Georgia Press, 1997.

Ibbetson, David J. *Common Law and Ius Commune: Selden Society Lecture Delivered in the Old Hall of Lincoln's Inn, July 20th, 2000*. London: Selden Society, 2001.

Jhering, Rudolph von. *The Struggle for Law*. 2nd ed. Translated by John J. Lalor. Chicago: Callaghan and Company, 1915.

Koschaker, Paul. *Europa und das römische Recht*. 4th ed. Munich: Beck Verlag, 1966.

Lange, Hermann. *Römisches Recht im Mittelalter I. Die Glossatoren*. Munich: Beck Verlag, 1997.

Lange, Hermann, and Maximiliane Kriechbaum. *Römisches Recht im Mittelalter I. Die Kommentatoren*. Munich: Beck Verlag, 2007.

Radding, Charles, and Antonio Ciaralli. *The Corpus Iuris Civilis in the Middle Ages: Manuscripts and Transmissions from the Sixth Century to the Juristic Revival*. Leiden: Brill, 2006.

Robinson, Olivia F., T. D. Fergus, and William N. Gordon. *European Legal History*. 3rd ed. London, Edinburgh, and Dublin: Butterworths, 2000.

Savigny, Friedrich Carl von. *System des heutigen römischen Recht*. 8 vols. Aalen: Scientia Verlag, 1981.

Stein, Peter. *Roman Law in European History*. Cambridge and New York: Cambridge University Press, 1999.

Straumann, Benjamin. *Roman Law in the State of Nature: The Classical Foundations of Hugo Grotius' Natural Law*. Cambridge and New York: Cambridge University Press, 2015.

Waelkens, Laurent. *Amne Adverso: Roman Legal Heritage in European Culture*. Leuven: Leuven University Press, 2015.

Whitman, James Q. *The Legacy of Roman Law in the German Romantic Era: Historical Vision and Legal Change*. Princeton, NJ: Princeton University Press, 1990.

Wieacker, Franz. *A History of Private Law in Europe*. Translated by Tony Weir. Oxford: Clarendon Press, 1995.

Winkel, Laurens. "Roman Law in Its Intellectual Context." In *The Cambridge Companion to Roman Law*, edited by David Johnston, 9–22. Cambridge and New York: Cambridge University Press, 2015.

Wolff, Hans Julius. *Roman Law. An Historical Introduction*. Norman: University of Oklahoma Press, 1951, esp. pgs. 186–225.

Zimmermann, Reinhard. *Roman Law, Contemporary Law, European Law: The Civilian Tradition Today*. Clarendon Law Lectures. Oxford and New York: Oxford University Press, 2001.

Part II

Roman law in action

7 Civil litigation

The history of legal procedures is hardly less than the history of the legal system itself. Roman law is no exception. Legal remedies so influenced the structure and evolution of Roman law that substantive law can be understood only from this procedural perspective. Roman jurists were more concerned about specific legal remedies than abstract rights. For this reason, Roman law is by nature and character a law of actions. Action (*actio*) is the right of suing before a judge for what is due to one (Celsus, D. 45.1.51; Inst. 4.6pr.). Actions are at the heart of Roman law, as writs are at the heart of medieval English law, rights are at the heart of American law, and *Ansprüche* ("claims") are at the heart of German law. According to Roman lawyers, we can say that *ubi actio, ibi ius*: where there is an acting legal remedy, there is a right, and not vice versa.

Three different systems of procedure conducted Roman civil trials over the course of Roman legal history: the system of legal actions (*legis actiones*), the formulary system (*ordo iudiciorum*), and the extraordinary cognition (*cognitio extraordinaria* or *cognitio extra ordinem*). The three systems succeeded one another in time but with some overlap. The system of *legis actiones* was the oldest. It existed at the time of the Twelve Tables (Gaius 4.17a), and it constituted the only civil procedure until the *lex Aebutia* (around 130 BCE) abolished it (with some exceptions) and introduced the formulary system. The formulary system was the standard procedure that dominated the classical period. The new procedure bestowed a new relevance on the position of the praetor and prescribed written forms. The formulary system was completed by two statutes in Augustus's time, the controversial *duae leges Iuliae* (Gaius 4.30). Augustus's laws abolished oral proceedings and declared written proceedings to be mandatory.

A new procedure, *cognitio extra ordinem*, or extraordinary cognition, was administrative in nature. Begun during the Principate, it developed gradually and ultimately superseded the formulary system during the Late Empire. This system prevailed in the postclassical period. The cognitio rested on the idea that the administration of justice should be provided by the emperor, and therefore all proceedings should be under the control of public imperial officers. The cognitio was closer to modern procedures than the formulary system was.

This chapter will mainly address the formulary procedure, since it was the procedural system that enabled and fostered the development of Roman jurisprudence. Major jurists of the classical period wrote their works in connection with it. References to the other systems will be made only to enable a full understanding of the formulary system.

The best source of information about the Roman civil procedures is probably book four of the *Institutes* of Gaius, which provides unique material about the system of the legis actiones. New inscriptions like the *lex Irnitana*, six bronze tablets containing fragments of municipal laws found in 1981 in Spain, or the collection of first-century tablets from Herculaneum and Puteoli, revealed new data and details on Roman legal proceedings. Cicero also provided important information, as he placed Roman procedure at the center of speeches like *Pro Caecina* and *Pro Quinctio*. Quintilian and Aulus Gellius, among others, are also valuable sources for understanding procedure.

Legis actiones

Older than the Twelve Tables and marked by unreasonable archaism and enormous formalism, the system of the legis actiones ("actions based on law") was the earliest form of Roman legal procedure. Its origin is obscure. Its remarkable feature was the use of prescribed oral formularies of claims framed by the pontifical, or priestly, jurisprudence in accordance with the wording of new statutes or adapting the wording of new formularies to existing statutes.

There were five formularies. Three of them served to initiate a claim (*legis actio sacramento, legis actio per iudicis arbitrive postulationem*, and *legis actio per condictionem*), and two were for execution of claims (*manus iniectio* and *pignoris capio*). The *legis actio sacramento* consisted of a formal wager between the plaintiff and the defendant, and the deposit of a sum of money (*sacramentum*). The procedure was different when it referred to the claim of ownership (*sacramentum in rem* or *vindicatio*) versus the enforcement of an obligation (*sacramentum in personam*). According to Gaius (4.13), the *legis actio sacramento* was of general application in the sense that it could be used in disputes in which another legal action was not available. The *postulatio iudicis arbitrive* was available only for cases specifically authorized by statutes. It was used for claims founded on a solemn promise (*sponsio* or *stipulatio*) and for the division of an inheritance or joint property, among other uses. The *lex Silia* and *lex Calpurnia* introduced the *legis actio per condictionem*, probably in the third century BCE. The *lex Silia* established the procedure for suing for a fixed sum of money (*certa pecunia*); the *lex Calpurnia* set up the procedure for suing for specific things (*certa res*).

The two legal actions to enforce the execution of a previous judgment were different from these first three. The *manus iniectio* was a form of personal execution on a debtor for specific claims when the debtor did not fulfill the monetary judgment within thirty days. Unlike the *manus iniectio*, the *pignoris capio* allowed a creditor to take a pledge for the debtor's property. It could be applied even in the absence of the debtor because it was extra-judicial.

The procedure of the legis actiones was divided into two stages: one before the magistrate (initially a consul and, after 367 BCE, a praetor), and the other before a citizen appointed as judge. In the first stage, called *in iure*, the magistrate formulated the issue by establishing the limits of the dispute. The first stage ended with the joinder of issue (*litis contestatio*). During the second stage, *apud iudicem*, the judge conducted the trial in accordance with the framing that the magistrate had established. Few rules governed this second stage, which ended with the judge pronouncing the judicial decision orally in the presence of both parties after observing the parties' pleas, hearing the witnesses and lawyers, and investigating the matter.

Gaius (4.30) writes that the procedure of the legis actiones fell into popular disfavor owing to a rigid formalism and lack of flexibility. To illustrate this inflexibility, Gaius (4.11) reports the case of a man who raised an action over the cutting down of vines. He lost his case because he used the word "vines" (*vites*) instead of "trees" (*arbores*) as was prescribed in the very general terms of the Twelve Tables (8.11). Another important disadvantage to this system was that the magistrate could neither establish new forms of legal actions nor extend the application of existing legal actions to new claims not provided by the law. The need to accommodate legal procedures to new economic and social developments demanded the vesting of more jurisdictional power in the hands of the magistrate.

The formulary procedure

The formulary procedure encompassed the ordinary civil proceedings (*ordo iudiciorum privatorum*) during the classical period. The main features of the legis actiones procedure remained. The formulary procedure, however, developed as a procedure built upon the initiative of the plaintiff and the collaboration of the defendant. In a certain sense, the litigants had the power to decide what the next step in proceedings should be. The plaintiff was responsible for bringing the controversy to the joinder of issue, although he could not compel the defendant to submit to it without praetorian support. Like the legis actiones, this procedure was also divided into two stages: the first before the praetor magistrate (*in iure*), in which the issue was defined and a judge appointed; and the second before the judge (*apud iudicem*), in which the final judgment was pronounced. Neither the praetor nor the judge was an expert in law as a matter of course, but both were expected to act with the collaboration of the jurists.

Unlike the procedure of the legis actiones, the formulary procedure incorporated written formalities. The key role of the written formula gave the whole formulary system its name. In formulary procedure, the parties no longer had to use the ritual words established by the civil law. Instead, the plaintiff had the freedom to plead the event, which could bring an action with the support of the praetor, based in civil law or praetorian law. Thus, formulary procedure gave great power and relevance to the praetor. He could grant (*dare actionem*) or refuse to grant an action (*denegare actionem*); he could introduce new actions or modify old ones, formulate praetorian remedies, and admit defenses. By setting out model clauses of actions (about two hundred) or other remedies in his yearly edict, the praetor controlled the proceedings because the issues must ultimately be embodied in a formula the praetor approved.

The praetor was the jurisdictional magistrate par excellence. If both parties were Roman citizens, the magistrate with jurisdiction inside the limits of Rome was the urban praetor. If one or both litigants were not Roman citizens, the jurisdictional magistrate was the praetor peregrinus. The aediles curules had jurisdictional power over sales concluded in the market of Rome. In the provinces, the governor had the jurisdictional power and played the role of the praetor. Local magistrates were to display and administer justice according to the edict of the provincial governor (chapter 85 *lex Irnitana*). In Italian municipia, the local magistrates had a limited jurisdiction, and it was possible for the parties to demand transfer of the procedure to Rome (*vadimonium Romam*). The plaintiff, however, should appear before the praetor of Rome or before the provincial governor, but not both successively.

The final judicial decision of the trial was entrusted to a private citizen without public office, the judge (*iudex*). Both parties freely chose him from a list of potential candidates (*album iudicum*), and the praetor authorized him to rule on the case. When the judge was able to make some judgments at his discretion, he was called arbitrator (*arbiter*). For certain claims, especially when a public interest was at stake, three or five judges were chosen (*recuperatores*). Recuperatores were always selected by lot (chapter 84 *lex Irnitana*).

According to Gaius (4.104), trials that took place within a mile of Rome between Roman citizens and before one Roman judge were called legitimate (*iudicia legitima*). They rested on statutory law. All others, in which one of these conditions was not satisfied, depended on the imperium of the praetor (*iudicia imperia continentia*). The distinction was important: a) the legitimate trial expired eighteen months from the joinder of the issue, but all others expired with the end of the imperium of the magistrate; b) the legitimate trial was extinguished by the loss of a person's civil status (*capitis deminutio*); and c) in these trials, women needed the cooperation of a guardian (*auctoritas tutoris*) to become a litigant. Additionally, in the legitimate trial, personal actions could be extinguished by operation of the law itself (*ipso iure*) when the defendant had already been sued for the same issue by the same plaintiff in a previous trial. In all other trials, however, the extinction of the action was effective not automatically, but only when the praetor granted the defendant an exception.

Preliminary proceedings

In the formulary procedure, a summons before the praetor (*in ius vocatio*) was a private affair managed directly by the plaintiff. The plaintiff, not the praetor, had to inform the opponent either orally or in writing about the nature of the lawsuit (*editio actionis*), and to compel the defendant's attendance before the praetor. Summons of consuls, praetors, and other high magistrates were banned. Roman citizens were also exempt in some circumstances (funeral, wedding, trial, and so on). Children and freedmen could not summon parents or patrons, respectively.

After being notified, the defendant could not offer resistance and had to immediately accompany the plaintiff into the praetor's court, according to provision of the Twelve Tables (1.1: *si in ius vocat, ito*). It is hard to imagine this abruptly imposed duty occurring in the classical period, however. For one thing, the defendant could avoid this immediate obligation by appointing an appropriate guarantor (*vindex*), who was charged with bringing the defendant before the praetor on a fixed day. The figure of the vindex is obscure, and it disappeared in later Roman law after its role merged with that of the procurator. Moreover, the defendant could promise the plaintiff to appear in a specific place at a later time to meet and go together to the court to initiate the procedure under penalty of forfeiting a sum of money. This promise (sometimes called extrajudicial *vadimonium*) was the general means for initiating the formulary procedure at the end of the Republic.

The praetor backed up the private summons with certain formal legal sanctions and remedies to prevent the plaintiff from having to bring the defendant to court by force. The praetor used to grant some actions against a defendant who, after having been summoned into court, failed to appear or to send a guarantor. The praetor could also grant action against someone who used force to take away a litigant who had been summoned to appear (Gaius 4.46).

Litigants before the praetor

During the preliminary hearings, the praetor exercised a conciliatory function. He tried to settle the litigants' controversy in a friendly way. The plaintiff explained again, now in the presence of the praetor, the nature of the claim (*editio actionis*), indicating the specific legal remedy by which he wanted to sue (*postulatio actionis*). Sometimes, instead of defending himself, the defendant acknowledged the plaintiff's claim (*confessio in iure*). In this case, the defendant was condemned by his own judgment (Paul, D. 42.2.1). In some cases, the praetor authorized the plaintiff to question the defendant about some significant circumstances that could affect his personal liability. For instance, in a suit against the heir of a debtor, the plaintiff could ask the defendant whether the defendant was an heir and for what share, and in a suit against the owner for the wrongdoings of his slave, the plaintiff could ask the defendant if the slave was in his power.

When the debt was a fixed sum of money, the plaintiff might request an oath from the defendant denying the existence of that debt. If the defendant took an oath swearing that there was no debt, the action concluded (Ulpian,

D. 12.2.7). If the defendant refused to swear, the praetor would order an immediate execution on the defendant's property (*missio in possessionem*). This coercive measure, which the praetor applied by virtue of his imperium, was the general sanction the praetor authorized when a defendant refused the required cooperation for the proper development of the proceedings (*indefensus*).

Under the supervision of the praetor, the parties would determine the exact formulation of the issue (formula), including the name of the appointed judge by a consensual selection procedure. Names of potential judges were displayed on an annual list (*album iudicum*). The candidate was chosen by a process of alternating rejection by the parties. Persons not listed in the album could be appointed by agreement of the parties. If the defendant refused to participate in the selection of the judge, the plaintiff had the right of unilaterally choosing the candidate. When a tribunal of three or five judges, the recuperatores, was required, the panel was chosen by lot from a pool of judges listed in the album. Senators removed from the Senate, women, people under legal age, and deaf people, among others, could not serve as a judge.

If some interruptions or adjournments were necessary before the joining of the issue, or the praetor's business had concluded for the day, the plaintiff, with the praetor's backing, could demand that the defendant promise to appear at the next hearing (*vadimonium*). Since this promise was a praetorian stipulation, it was a mandatory promise for the defendant. In case of the justified absence or unavailability of the magistrate, or when parties needed more time to prepare for the next procedural steps, the praetor could order a three-day postponement of the proceedings (*intertium*).

Representation in litigation

Litigants could appoint representatives, usually friends or relatives. Besides a guardian (*tutor*) or an administrator (*curator*), specific representatives in litigation were the *cognitor* and the *procurator*. The cognitor was appointed by authorization (*iussum*) according to prescribed and solemn words in the presence of the other litigant, but not necessarily in the presence of the cognitor: "Since I am claiming the land from you, I give you L. Titius as my cognitor in this matter" (Gaius 4.83). The cognitor fully represented the principal and was essentially a procedural alter ego of the real party. When the cognitor assumed the representation, the plaintiff gave up his principal's right of action. He could not later sue the same defendant for the same issue (*non bis in idem*). The judgment, however, was enforced either for or against the principal; as a result, it was the principal who had to give security to pay the judgment debt (*cautio iudicatum solvi*).

The procurator, by contrast, was appointed informally, merely by mandate (Gaius 3.84). He was an indirect representative. For this reason, the procurator of the plaintiff had to give security that the principal would ratify and would not sue again with the same action (*cautio de rato*), and the procurator of the defendant had to give security to guarantee the payment of the judgment debt (*cautio iudicatum solvi*). As a result, the name of the procurator was inserted in the *condemnatio* of the formula, and the execution after a judgment was only for or against him. Full representation was gradually extended to the procurator so that, in Late Antiquity, the difference between procurator and cognitor lost its relevance. Under Justinian, there were no cognitors for legal representation.

The formula of the action

Each legal action was based on a proper and precise written formal statement (formula) in which the issue was exactly defined and pleaded. The formula informed the judge of what the case was strictly about and required the judge either to condemn the defendant or to absolve him, as the case might be. The plaintiff or his legal advisers first proposed the formula, but the defendant could modify it with the authorization of the praetor. The formula, although solemn, was flexible, consisting of several clauses. Some of these were mandatory (the appointment of the judge, the statement of the claim, and the judgment debt), and some were required by the praetor to give the case more detailed specification (demonstration or prescription) or to protect the defendant (exceptions).

The appointment of the judge (*nominatio iudicis*) appeared at the head of each formula ("Let Titius be judge"). After the nomination came the most important part of the formula: the *intentio* or exact definition of the claim directed to the judge in hypothetical terms: "If it appears that Numerius Negidius ought to give Aulus Agerius three thousand sesterces …" Aulus Agerius and Numerius Negidius were imaginary names used in the formulae and were expressions of the Roman sense of humor. Aulus Agerius referred to the plaintiff (the person who sues: *is qui agit*, hence Agerius). Numerius Negidius referred to the defendant because it was he who might have to pay (*numerare*, hence Numerius) the judgment debt and who normally rejected (*negare*, hence Negidius) the plaintiff's claims.

If the plaintiff claimed in the intentio more than he was entitled to, he lost the case as an overclaim (*pluris petitio*). Overclaim also occurred when the plaintiff claimed in a city other than that in which the payment had to be performed, or before the payment was due. In personal actions in which the claim was uncertain (*intentio incerta*), a demonstration would be inserted at the beginning of the formula (prior to the statement of intention) to identify more accurately the subject of the controversy. The demonstration constituted an integral complement to the intention, and it was relevant in case of new trials on the same subject. The demonstration usually began with the Latin word *quod* (because, or inasmuch): "Because Aulus Agerius sold to Numerius Negigius the slave Clitus, whose sale is the matter involved in this case …"

The defense that the defendant was proposing against the plaintiff's claim was inserted into the formula through a clause called exception (*exceptio*).

The exception did not deny the plaintiff's claim. It only added a counter-hypothesis in favor of the defendant for the judge to consider. The structure of the exception was a conditional clause with a negative: "unless something else is also true." The defendant, for instance, could object that, although he indeed had to pay a thousand sesterces to the plaintiff (*intentio*), it was also true that the time to pay had not yet elapsed (*exceptio pacti*). The defendant could also allege that the plaintiff had acted fraudulently (*exceptio doli*: "unless some fraud had been committed by the plaintiff") or that the defendant was the owner of the claimed object according to civil law ("unless the defendant had proved civil ownership"). Examples abound.

The insertion of an exception in the formula required the praetor's approval. If the plaintiff rejected this insertion, the praetor could threaten him with refusal of the action. The plaintiff, however, could oppose the defendant's exception with a *replicatio*. That happened when a further set of relevant facts was also true that the judge needed to consider to reach the right conclusion. For instance, when the defendant alleged that the plaintiff had agreed not to sue him in court for a certain time (*exceptio pacti*), the plaintiff could allege that, although that was true, a new agreement had annulled or modified the limit of time (*replicatio pacti*). Replicatio was not the last word. The praetor might insert in the formula a *triplicatio* or even further.

Different from the exception, but close to it, was the prescription (*praescriptio*), a preliminary formula clause limiting the scope of the claim. It was a necessary limitation, a reservation that the judge should consider. That happened, for instance, when the claim consisted of an installment. Without prescription, the defendant could allege that the action was extinguished when the plaintiff sued him for a second partial payment. Prescription, however, allowed later actions derived from the same transaction. To avoid the effects of the joinder of the issue (*non bis in idem*), the plaintiff asked the praetor to insert a prescription in the formula that allowed him to bring an action for the remaining partial payments when they became payable (Gaius 4.131).

The *condemnation* (*condemnatio*) was the clause in which the judge was given the power of condemning or absolving the defendant in accordance with the instruction of the formula (Gaius 4.43). According to the formula, the judge had only the choice to condemn for a sum of money (judgment debt). His final judgment was always monetary. He had no power to condemn the defendant to perform some activity or service, to hand over an item to the plaintiff, and so on. A basic condemnation would be: "You, judge, condemn Numerius Negidius to pay Aulus Agerius three thousand sesterces; but if it (the intention) does not appear, absolve him." In those actions in which the condemnation was not directed at a fixed sum (*certa pecunia*), the judge would also establish the amount the defendant had to pay to the plaintiff.

A discretionary clause (*clausula arbitraria*) could be incorporated in the formula of some actions in which the restitution of the claimed object implied a more valuable benefit to the plaintiff than a monetary judgment. The clause stated: "and the claimed object (*res litigiosa*) has not been restored to Aulus

Agerius according to the opinion of the judge." In these cases, the praetor authorized the judge to delay his judgment and to condemn the defendant only if there had been no restitution of the claimed object to the plaintiff. To encourage the defendant to return the claimed object, the judge fixed the judgment debt according to the subjective value established by the plaintiff's oath (*iusiurandum in litem*). The judge, however, had the choice to condemn the defendant to an amount less than that established by the plaintiff's oath when the judge considered the plaintiff's claim exorbitant. Finally, the judgment debt could be limited by establishing a maximum to which the defendant could be condemned, for instance, to the extent of the actual profit or to the extent of the *peculium*. In those formulas of divisory actions (*actiones divisoriae*), a clause called adjudication could be inserted, entitling the judge to assign the whole or part of the claimed object to one party as his whole property. Adjudication was considered a mode of acquisition of ownership. Suppose that Titius, Caius, and Sempronius decided to divide some common property. The judge could adjudicate a part of the land to each one. Even in these cases, however, a monetary condemnation could make sense in order to adjust differing reciprocal liabilities among the co-owners.

For an overall view of the formula, consider two different formulae of actions: the *condictio*, which is the basic action for payment of a due sum of money, and the *rei vindicatio*, which is the action for recovery of property. The formula for the condictio is: "Let Titius be judge. If it appears that Numerius Negidius must pay two thousand sesterces to Aulus Agerius, you, judge, condemn Numerius Negidius to pay two thousand sesterces to Aulus Agerius; if it does not appear, let him be absolved." A little more complicated was the formula of the action for recovery of property: "Let Titius be judge. If it appears that the slave Nicia that is at issue belongs to Aulus Agerius under civil law, and has not been restored to Aulus Agerius according to the opinion of the judge, whatever the slave's value shall be, you, judge, condemn Numerius Negidius to pay three thousand sesterces to Aulus Agerius; if it does not appear, let him be absolved."

Classifications of actions

For the Romans, the primary distinction of formulae, and therefore of actions, was that of actions *in rem* and actions *in personam*. In actions in rem, the plaintiff alleged a special relation with the concrete thing he claimed. In a certain sense, the position of the defendant was secondary, and therefore the name of the defendant did not appear in the intention. His name was not required to fix the claim but was required only in the condemnation. A common case was the action for recovery of property (vindication; see formula above), which entitled the owner of an item to sue any possessor of the thing for its recovery. By contrast, in actions in personam, the plaintiff alleged that some other person was under obligation (contractual or delictual) toward him. Without the name of the defendant, it was not possible to determine the claim precisely, and therefore in the formula of personal actions, the name of the defendant had to be inserted in the intentio. A typical example was the action for a payment (condictio: see formula above).

A second important classification of actions was the division into civil actions and praetorian actions. In civil actions, the praetor granted an action whose formula already existed in civil law (*rei vindicatio, condictio*). Praetorian actions, in contrast, were partial or complete creations of the magistrates; therefore, they were outside the realm of civil law. There were three kinds of formulae in praetorian actions.

a Formulae with a fiction were formulae the praetor adapted by the insertion of a "presumed understanding" or fiction to expand the application of the civil formulae to new situations. For instance, when the praetor wanted to protect a person who was not the civil heir, he could insert the fiction, "as if he were civil heir." The praetor could also apply civil law to foreigners under the fiction, "as if he were a Roman citizen."
b Formulae in which the name inserted in the condemnation was different from the name inserted in the intentio occurred, for instance, in Rutilian action, created by the praetor Publius Rutilius Rufus around 118 BCE. In the formula for this action, the name of a bankrupt debtor appeared in the intentio to fix the claim, but it was the name of the purchaser of the property of the bankrupt debtor (*bonorum emptor*) that appeared in the condemnation, since he sued in the name of the person to whom the bankrupt debtor was in debt.
c Formulae called *in factum conceptae* in which there was no similarity with the formula of any action existing in civil law. The praetor could create a new formula condemning the defendant if the plaintiff proved certain factual elements described in the intentio. An example was the action for fraud (*actio de dolo*), introduced by the praetor Aquilius Galus in 66 BCE. Actions *in factum* abounded and were applied in a variety of legal relations.

Finally, an important distinction existed between actions in good faith (*actiones bonae fidei*) and actions of strict law (*actiones stricti iuris*). Actions in good faith were those personal actions in whose intentio was added the expression *ex fide bona* (based on good faith). In those cases, the judge had the power to determine the final judgment on principles of good faith by estimating the condemnation, incorporating the possibility of offsets, taking into consideration some formless pacts made by the parties, considering exceptions after the joinder of the issue, and so on. Actions in good faith included, among other things, all actions derived from consensual or real contracts. All actions that were not established according to good faith were regarded as based on strict law (*actiones stricti iuris*). This name seems to have come from Justinian (Inst. 4.6.28). Closely related to actions in good faith were actions *in bonum et aequum conceptae* (Gaius, D. 4.5.8), in which the praetor authorized the judge to establish the judgment debt in the condemnation of the formula at his discretion. The nature of the claim was related to a behavior of the defendant that caused some harm to the plaintiff. Unlike the actions in good faith, these actions did not have contractual character. An example was the action against wrongful acts (*actio iniuriarum*).

Praetorian remedies

As a bearer of supreme power, or imperium, the praetor could grant some remedies other than actions, with the aim of administering justice. Four of these remedies were the praetorian stipulations, the interdicts, the *missiones in possessionem*, and the *restitutiones in integrum*.

a Praetorian stipulations were verbal promises required by the praetor of one or both of the litigants to ensure the successful development of the proceedings or to protect the interest of the parties. A promise in the form of a stipulation provided the promisee a legal remedy (a security) that did not exist in civil law. A stipulation, for instance, could insure against potential damage to a house in dangerous condition (*cautio damni infecti*) or against certain abuses by the usufructuary (*cautio usufructuaria*). It could also ensure the restitution of the dowry in case of divorce (*cautio rei uxoriae*).

b Interdicts were one of the oldest and most important creations of praetorian law. They were administrative praetorian orders, made at the request of a claimant imposing a certain form of behavior on the addressee: to do something or to abstain from doing something. Many interdicts were provisory in nature, with the purpose of protecting concrete existing situations and rights. Interdicts were numerous and of great variety. A large appendix of the praetorian Edict included all of them. They protected all kinds of public and private interests that the praetor thought were in need of protection. There were interdicts to protect the use of public roads, navigation on public rivers, the good condition of sewers, and public places against damage from construction – but also private possessions, servitudes, inheritances, and more. The most important interdicts in practice were those dealing with possession. Justinian's law removed the distinction between actions and interdicts.

c *Missiones in possessionem* were decrees of the praetor authorizing the claimant to take over the property of his adversary in whole or in part. Missiones were provisional in nature, but in the long term they might have had the effect of destroying rights in civil law. The purposes of these coercive measures varied. For instance, the praetor decreed the *missio* when the defendant was absent in court, or against an insolvent debtor, or to protect the rights of an unborn heir (*ventris nomine*) or the rights of a legatee against the heir who refused to give a promise for the payment of a legacy. The legal consequences also varied greatly: such decrees might result in a right of the claimant to sell the whole property of the adversary, to sell only a portion, or just to possess it.

d The last coercive means was the *restitutio in integrum*. It was, in some respects, the most important of all praetorian remedies since it extinguished civil law rights. The purpose of this extraordinary coercive means, established for reasons of equity, was the restoration or reinstatement of a former legal position to the claimant against a wrongdoer or against the immediate beneficiary of a transaction. For example, after an investigation by the praetor at the request of a claimant, the praetor could declare nonexistent and ineffective a transaction that was valid according to civil law but that had prejudiced the claimant's legal position. This could occur, for instance, to protect against transactions concluded by minors (under twenty-five years old), transactions concluded under duress, some fraudulent transactions, and others.

Litis contestatio

The joinder of the issue (*litis contestatio*) was the final step of the proceedings at the praetor's court. It was the point of no return in a lawsuit. Once the judge was appointed and the formula was drawn up, the parties would strike an agreement in the presence of the praetor, in which they accepted the legal remedies as well as the final judgment debt (*sententia*). Through the joinder of the issue, the original claims of the parties were transformed into a new claim of fulfilling the final judgment debt. All original obligations brought into the issue were destroyed. After the *litis contestatio*, a second lawsuit for the same claim and by the same parties was excluded; the plaintiff's rights to sue the defendant for the same issue (*eadem res*) were consumed (*actio consumitur*). If the plaintiff tried to sue again, the praetor would reject the new action immediately or, at least, grant the defendant a formal exception when some conditions and circumstances needed to be examined (Gaius 4.106–07: *exceptio rei iudicatae vel in iudicium deductae*). After the joinder of the issue, any action was transmissible to the heirs, and the attempt to alienate the object of the pending suit (*res litigiosa*) was to be of no effect (Ulpian, D. 44.6.1). The defendant holding the claimed object was defended by the praetor through an exception against a third person claim.

Apud iudicem

The proceedings before the judge were oral and public. The parties were present but did not formally participate in the proceedings. If the plaintiff was absent (that is, if he did not appear after a long waiting period), the defendant was absolved by the judge. If the defendant was away without an excuse, proceedings continued, giving the plaintiff the opportunity to prove his case. The proceedings started with the advocates' speeches, followed by the taking of evidence. After some discussions with the judge, he pronounced the final judgment. Hearings could be repeated until the judge was prepared to make his final decision.

Each party had to assure the attendance of witnesses that the judge should hear. Neither the parties nor persons closely connected to the parties could act as witnesses. Slaves could be witnesses in cases in which evidence did not exist. (Usually slaves were examined by torture.) There were no strict rules of evidence. A judge was bound only by the instructions given in the formula, not by a concrete piece of evidence or by previous decisions (precedents). Nor was the judge bound by the council of legal experts who advised him during the proceedings. The final judgment, given orally and publicly, in the presence of the parties, was most likely written down. According to the formula, the judge had to either condemn or absolve; conditional judgment was not allowed. If the judge concluded that he was not able to make a decision according to justice because of the ambiguity of the case, he could make an oath declaring that he was not yet clear about the case (*res sibi non liquere*). If that happened, the parties would nominate another judge or try to obtain more evidence (Ulpian, D. 4.8.13.4). There was no appeal, although during the Principate an appeal directed to the emperor against judicial decisions was finally recognized.

Execution of the judgment

In classical times, execution of the judgment was mainly against the property of the debtor and not against the debtor himself (personal execution). If the judge accepted the plaintiff's claim, the defendant had to comply with the condemnatory judgment debt (*iudicatum*). If the defendant did not pay the judgment within thirty days, the plaintiff could sue the defendant in a special action called *actio iudicati*. This action was introduced following the standards and procedural rules of any other action. It usually concluded, however, before the praetor, in the stage *in iure*, by a decree in which the praetor ordered the fulfillment of the judgment debt and authorized execution against the goods of the debtor (*missio in bona*). Only under certain exceptions – for instance, when the defendant affirmed that he had already paid the judgment or that the judgment constituted a flagrant violation of the law – would the suit go before a judge again. If the defendant did not prove his allegations, he would be condemned to pay double.

The decree of missio in bona implied that the creditor could administer the whole insolvent debtor's property (not just goods sufficient to meet the debt) on behalf of all creditors of the debtor. The decree was followed by a public auction managed by a magister appointed by the creditors under the supervision of the praetor. The praetor issued an interdict to protect the buyer when obtaining the goods belonging to the debtor. The debtor was declared infamous, a condition that produced not only harm to his reputation but also certain legal disabilities (ineligibility for being a judge, among others). Augustus mitigated the bluntness of this procedure by introducing the possibility that the debtor's goods would be sold up to the extent of the debt but not beyond that.

Arbitration

By voluntary and formal agreement (*compromissum*), the parties could submit the decision of a dispute to arbitration. The enforcement of the award came from the reciprocal stipulations given by the litigants and was strengthened by penalties as an additional part of the agreement. The advantage of arbitration was that the arbitrator had more freedom to determine an award than did the judge of the formulary procedure, who was always bound by the praetor's instructions inserted in the formula. Even the arbitrator, however, was under the supervision of the praetor, insofar as the arbitrator was bound by a unilateral acceptance of his authority (*receptum arbitri*), enforceable under praetorian law. The arbitrator assumed his duties by using the words "I accept" (*recipio*). The praetor could compel the arbitrator to pronounce his award with administrative measures (a fine, a seizure of pledges, and so on). The arbitrator was not to be compelled, however, to make an award if the parties did not properly submit to arbitration (Ulpian, D. 4.8.11.1). Legal capacity for submitting to arbitration was broader than legal capacity for litigation under the formulary procedure. The general rule was that anyone who could make a valid contract could make a formal agreement to arbitration. The death of a party terminated the arbitral agreement, unless there was an express provision that the obligations would survive to the heirs.

Cognitio extra ordinem

As mentioned, extraordinary cognition was the procedure that gradually replaced the formulary procedure, especially in the third century CE. The medieval romano-canonical procedure and many modern procedural systems derived from it. Extraordinary cognition was adopted first in the provinces, until it became exclusive when Constantine II officially abolished the formulary procedure in 342 CE (C.J. 2.57.1). The new cognition was administrative in character. Based on the idea that administration of justice was an imperial function, in the new cognition the centrality of the proceedings resided in the magistrate-judge rather than in the parties. As a result, the contractual structure of the proceedings was gone. Lawsuits no longer depended on the parties' private initiative.

The magistrate began to be involved not only in the trial but also in the summons. The plaintiff could still summon the defendant privately to appear before the judge (*denuntiatio*). However, the plaintiff could also address to the magistrate a written statement of claim (*libellus*) and ask him to summon the defendant. The magistrate sent a copy of the claim to the defendant, ordering him to enter a defense and to appear in court on a fixed date. The magistrate could also summon a defendant or third party on his own initiative (*evocatio*). If the plaintiff did not appear on the appointed day, the case concluded.

The *litis contestatio* remained as a name, as did much of the old procedural terminology, but legislation modified most of its effects. The *litis contestatio* exactly defined the conflict, but the procedure no longer included an agreement to accept the judgment, nor was the action consumed. Exceptions could be admitted even right before the final judgment. The extraordinary cognition contained more rules for the formulary procedure about the burden of proof, the proof of documents, the capacity to give evidence, and other items. The court summoned witnesses and could force them to give surety for their appearance. The judgment was written, but it was recited publicly at a formal sitting of the court. Condemnation was not necessarily monetary.

As result of the tendency toward bureaucratization, an organized appeal system to a higher court (and even to the emperor in important matters) was developed for the first time in Roman law. In the provinces, the governor heard appeals of the cases decided by his subordinates in the first instance. Under Justinian's law, there could not be more than two appeals on any one judicial decision (C.J. 7.70.1), and no case was to continue for more than three years after joinder of issue. The establishment of an official fee system made litigation more expensive than before.

Further reading

Berger, Adolf. *Encyclopedic Dictionary of Roman Law*. Philadelphia, PA: The American Philosophical Society, 1953; reprint 1980.

Buckland, William Warwick. *A Text-Book of Roman Law*. 3rd ed., revised by Peter Stein, 604–744. Cambridge: Cambridge University Press, 1963.

Camodeca, Giuseppe. *Tabulae Pompeianae Sulpiciorum (TPSulp.): Edizione critica dell' Archivio Puteolano dei Sulpicii.1.*Rome: Quasar, 1999.

Cannata, Carlo Augusto. *Profilo istituzionale del proceso privato romano: I. Les legis actiones. II. Il proceso formulare i.* 2 vols. Turin: Giappichelli, 1980–82.

De Angelis, Francesco, ed. *Spaces of Justice in the Roman World*. Leiden: Brill, 2010.

Domingo, Rafael. *Estudios sobre el primer título del edicto del pretor*, 3 vols. Santiago de Compostela: Universidad de Dantiago de Compostela, 1991–95.

d'Ors, Álvaro. *Derecho privado romano*. 10th ed., §§68–130. Pamplona: Eunsa, 2004.

Fiori, Roberto. *Ea res agatur: I due modelli del processo formulare repubblicano*. Milan: Giuffrè, 2003.

Jolowicz, Herbert Felix, and Barry Nicholas. *Historical Introduction to the Study of Roman Law*. 3rd ed., 175–232, 395–420, 439–50. Cambridge: Cambridge University Press, 1972.

Johnston, David, "Vadimonium, the Lex Irnitana, and the Edictal Commentaries." In *Quaestiones iuris. Festschrift für Joseph Georg Wolf zum 70. Geburtstag*, edited by Ulrich Manthe and Christoph Krampe, 111–123. Berlin: Duncker and Humblot, 2000.

Kaser, Max, and Karl Hackl. *Das römische Zivilprozessrecht*. 2nd ed. Munich: Beck Verlag, 1996.

Kelly, John M. *Roman Litigation*. Oxford: Clarendon Press, 1966.

Kelly, John M. *Studies in the Civil Judicature of the Roman Republic*. Oxford: Oxford University Press, 1976.

Liebs, Detlef. *Summoned to the Roman Courts. Famous Trials from Antiquity*. Los Angeles, Berkeley, and London: University of California Press, 2012.

Metzger, Ernest. "Litigation." In *The Cambridge Companion to Roman Law*, edited by David Johnston, 272–298. Cambridge and New York: Cambridge University Press, 2015.

Metzger, Ernest. *Litigation in Roman Law*. Oxford and New York: Oxford University Press, 2005.

Metzger, Ernest. *A New Outline of Roman Trial*. Oxford and New York: Oxford University Press, 1997.

Meyer, Elizabeth A. *Legitimacy and Law in the Roman World. Tabulae in Roman Belief and Practice*. Cambridge: Cambridge University Press, 2004.

Murga, José Luis. *El proceso clásico*. Zaragoza: Universidad de Zaragoza, 1980.

Pugliese, Giovanni. *Il proceso civile romano*. II. *Il proceso formulare*. Milan: Giufrè, 1963.

Roebuck, Derek, and Bruno de Loynes de Fumichon. *Roman Arbitration*. Oxford: Holo Books, The Arbitration Press, 2004.

Schulz, Fritz. *Classical Roman Law*, 11–70. Oxford: Clarendon Press, 1951.

Thomas, J. A. C. *Textbook of Roman Law*, 69–122. Amsterdam, New York, and Oxford: North-Holland Publishing Company, 1976.

Waelkens, Laurent. *Amne adverso. Roman Legal Heritage in European Culture*, 141–192. Leuven: Leuven University Press, 2015.

Wenger, Leopold. *Institutes of Roman Law of Civil Procedure*. Rev. ed., translated by Otis Harrison Fisk. Littleton, CO: Fred B. Rothman & Co., 1986.

Wenger, Leopold. "The Roman Law of Civil Procedure." Translated by Arthur Schiller. *Tulane Law Review* 5 (1930): 353–395.

Zulueta, Francis de. *The Institutes of Gaius. Part II. Commentary*, 221–302. Oxford: Clarendon Press, 1953.

8 Family law

The Roman family constituted the basic structural framework of Roman society. The Latin *familia* means, essentially, "household" and can refer to both persons and things (see Ulpian, D. 50.16.195.1). The concept included all persons under the power of a single head (the paterfamilias) and, in a broader sense, all relatives connected by blood or marriage. In a still broader sense, the Roman family encompassed all personal property, including slaves and physical objects. Social stratification, sexual inequality, and legal subordination were defining features of the Roman family.

The family was the Roman legal unit par excellence, and its head, the father, the only person with full recognition under Roman law. The power of the head of the family over his descendants lasted not until his children married and developed their own households, but until the father himself died. In the typical case, the Roman family consisted of a legitimately married adult male Roman citizen along with his wife, children, grandchildren, and slaves. The Roman family was traced exclusively through the father's lineage (patrilineal) and was founded on his absolute control over the other family members: his wife (*manus*), children (*patria potestas*), and slaves (*mancipium*). According to the Romans, the condition of women was below that of men (Papinian, D. 1.5.9). Women were considered weaker than men (Twelve Tables V.1), so the law created more extensive protections for women in legal and business matters. In early stages of Roman family law, moreover, there was little difference between sons and slaves.

The family began with marriage, and marriage was basically a matter of intention: the intention to live together as husband and wife. Beyond that condition, the partners had to have the legal capacity to marry and fall outside of certain statutory prohibitions. People unable to achieve marital status together could live together in other kinds of sexual partnership. Although inferior in dignity, concubinage was socially accepted and very common among the Romans. Emperor Marcus Aurelius, for instance, lived with a concubine after his wife's death so "as not to introduce a stepmother over all his children" (*Vita Marci Antonini philosophi* 29.10).

The Romans established a genuine slave society, i.e., a political community one part of which prevailed and lorded over the other. Freedom was more of a privilege for some citizens than a general right for everyone. According to the Romans, slavery was a social institution of the law of nations that generated great social and economic value. It was regarded as a social need, a prerogative of the wealthy, and an appropriate penalty for enemies captured in war. Slaves performed domestic services and worked on farms, in mines, and at mills. They were teachers, physicians, accountants, but also barbers, gladiators, and mule drivers. By the late first century BCE, about 20 to 30 percent of the population in Roman Italy consisted of slaves: more than a million slaves out of a population of about five to six million.

Persona, caput, and status

The Roman idea of person (*persona*) was distinct from the idea of an individual (or entity) with legal capacity. Originally, persona meant a mask, i.e., a character in a theatrical performance. By extension, it referred to the role played in life by an individual, and by metonymy to the human being as such playing his or her role in society. Persons (*personae*) included all individuals, whether or not they were rights-bearers. So slaves were persons (see Gaius 1.121; 2.187; 3.189), even though legally they were considered objects (*res corporales*).

Synonymous with the person was the head, *caput* – caput thus being used as synecdoche, as a part representing the whole person. But caput also was a technical term, especially in the expression *capitis deminutio*. Originally, *capitis deminutio* meant a reduction in the size of a group by the loss of one of its members. Thus, when a Roman citizen lost citizenship, the Roman People was diminished; or when a son was adopted, the biological family was diminished. Later, the term came to signify a lowering of personal status owing to a change in family identity (*capitis deminutio minima*), loss of citizenship (*capitis deminutio media*), or loss of freedom (*capitis deminitio maxima*). In general, a person's status denoted his or her legal position with respect to the household (familia) and the people of Rome. The main factors determining an individual's legal status were citizenship and social rank.

The most fundamental division in the law of persons was that between free persons and slaves (Gaius 1.9). Next came the divide between Roman citizens and foreigners or strangers (*peregrini*), which made room for the intermediate and particularly favorable legal status of *Latini*. Finally, there was the divide between those who were independent (*sui iuris*) and those who were submitted to a paterfamilias (*alieni iuris*). The social distinction between the upper classes of Roman society (*honestiores*: the more honorable) and the lower classes (*humiliores*: the more lowly) acquired legal relevance during the Principate. Honestiores included members of the Senate and their families, equestrians (*equites*), local magistrates (*decuriones*), and military veterans. All others were humiliores – a category that included freeborn persons below the status of local magistrates and freed people (*libertini*). Although never defined technically, some legal differences between honestiores and humiliores appeared in private law and, especially, in criminal law. The most humiliating and degrading punishments (capital punishment by crucifixion or by exposure to wild beasts, torture, and corporal punishment, among others) were applicable only to lower classes. Where humiliores were punished by capital death, honestiores were only sent into exile; where humiliores were punished with forced labor (*deportatio*) or even death for a certain crime, honestiores were only punished with temporary expulsion to an island along with confiscation of their property (*relegatio*).

Paternal power (*patria potestas*)

Paternal power was the comprehensive power of the oldest male ascendant, commonly the father or grandfather (paterfamilias), over male and female legitimate descendants (*liberi*) and adopted children. A woman's children remained under the paternal power of her husband or father-in-law, even if her own paterfamilias was still alive. Every Roman male citizen (with or without children) who was not under paternal power, whatever his age, was himself a paterfamilias. In other words, every independent (*sui iuris*) male was a paterfamilias. Women could be independent but not paterfamilias because they could not have paternal power. The term materfamilias had different meanings. Originally, a materfamilias was a wife under her husband's legal power (*manus*). Once the institution of manus disappeared, materfamilias referred to the respectable female sui iuris (see Ulpian, D. 1.6.4). The term, however, had no legal relevance.

Agnation was the relationship among persons who were under the same paternal power (e.g., brothers and sisters, adopted children), or who would have been if the head of the family were still alive (e.g., among brothers after the death of their father and grandfather). The bond of agnation obtained among offspring in the male line from a common ancestor. Cognation, by contrast, referred more generally to all blood relations. It included the female line and biological children of a family even after they had been given up for adoption or emancipated. Typically, persons tied by agnation were also blood relatives (brothers, for instance), but not always (adopted siblings). Between mother and son, between mother and daughter, or between emancipated brothers, there was a bond of cognation but not agnation.

Patria potestas was strictly private. It had nothing to do with public affairs. A son, for instance, could vote or even hold office without paternal restrictions of any kind (Pomponius, D. 1.6.9). When Quintus Fabius Maximus, consul in 213 BCE, arrived at the Roman camp in Apulia, he met his father, the famous Fabius Maximus Cunctator, consul in 214 BCE and then proconsul. Following the orders of his son, Cunctator had to dismount his horse, acknowledging the supremacy of his son's consular imperium over his paternal power (Gellius, *Noctes Atticae* 2.2.13).

The peculiar institution of Roman patria potestas was as unique as it was severe. Originally, paternal power was unrestricted and lifelong, except in case of emancipation. As head of the family, the father even had the power of life and death over his family members (*ius vitae et necis*). This inhumane right, undoubtedly exercised in Republican times, was strictly limited, however, under imperial legislation, and it was extinguished under Justinian's laws. The father also had the right to veto family members' proposed marriages and to require or forbid them to divorce; the right to all acquisitions deriving from their transactions; the right to hand children who had wronged someone over to the injured party, instead of paying the debt himself; the power to appoint guardians or heirs for his children; and so on. The lives of all submitted to paternal power were completely controlled by the father or paterfamilias.

Limitations of the rights and powers of the father were followed by the gradual recognition of some personal and property rights for other members of the family. Although they could not have property of their own, sons were able to administer a father's property (*peculium*) and to develop business in the family's interest. Paternal power persisted as an institution throughout the classical and postclassical periods, and it was still relevant under Justinian's laws (see, for instance, Inst. 2.9).

Manus

Similar to patria potestas was a husband's marital power (*manus*, literally "hand"). In Republican times, when women married, they normally fell under their husband's marital power. The most common form for establishing the manus was the so-called *coemptio*, a sort of solemn purchase of the woman by the husband. Manus could also be created by the religious ceremony of *confarreatio* in the presence of a high priest and ten witnesses. Finally, manus could be established by prescription through cohabitation for one year (*usus*).

A wife under the power of her husband had the legal position of his daughter. She was freed from any previous parental power and entered her husband's family. All possessions she had before marriage belonged to her husband (or her new paterfamilias). As a result, she gained succession rights similar to those of his children. Manus was not as comprehensive as paternal power, however. For instance, a husband lacked the power of life and death over his wife. By the beginning of the Principate, marriages *in manu* had essentially disappeared, and a wife under marital power could remove herself from it by divorce. She remained under paternal power while living with her husband until the death of her paterfamilias.

Guardianship (*tutela*)

Independent persons (sui iuris) – that is, those not submitted to paternal or marital power – could be under guardianship, depending on their age and sex. Guardianship was available for children under puberty (boys under fourteen and girls under twelve) and women. Originally, its purpose was more to conserve the family's property than to protect the ward's interests. Guardianship was considered a prolongation of paternal power, so the position of guardian (technically called tutor) was closed to women. Nonetheless, a tutor's power was not as extensive as a father's. For instance, a tutor had no power of life and death, and he could not give a ward up for adoption. His power implied duties regarding education, maintenance, and administration of the ward's property. Legal acts of the tutor affected and bound the tutor, not the ward. If a tutor sold something belonging to the ward, it was the tutor and not the ward who was bound by the contract (indirect agency). In the late Republic, guardianship shifted from a privilege to a burden, from a right to a duty, and the interest and protection of the ward prevailed over the tutor's rights and powers. Under later Principate, guardianship was regarded as a public service (*munus publicum*), and tutors came ever more under the control of public authorities.

According to the earliest law consolidated in the Twelve Tables (V.6), the father had the right to appoint a tutor by will for his children (*tutor testamentarius*). The tutor had to be a male citizen and must have attained puberty. The appointment was effective from the moment in which the will came into effect, but the tutor had the right to reject the guardianship (*abdicatio tutelae*); accordingly, he could also be dismissed by public denunciation and the filing of a charge against him (*accusatio suspecti tutoris*). At the beginning of the Principate, the tutor was bound to discharge his functions (*ius excusandi*). If no tutor had been appointed by testament or the appointed tutor had been excused, the Twelve Tables (V.6) entrusted guardianship to the nearest male agnate of the ward (*tutor legitimus*). Unlike the tutor appointed by will, a legitimate tutor had no right to abdicate or excuse, and he could not be removed. The ward, however, might demand of the legitimate tutor a rendering of accounts with an action to control accounts (*actio de rationibus distrahendis*). Legitimate guardianship over women was abolished by Emperor Claudius, in the first century CE.

When boys and girls had neither a testamentary nor a legitimate tutor, the *lex Atilia* (before 186 BCE) allowed the urban praetor to appoint a tutor by decree. The measure was extended to the provinces by *lex Julia et Titia* (31 BCE), authorizing each provincial governor to appoint tutors in his territory. Under the Principate, consuls and praetors usually appointed tutors. From the time of Marcus Aurelius, a special praetor was charged with overseeing guardianship. A tutor appointed by a magistrate could be dismissed at any time by the magistrate who appointed him. The ward could bring action against a tutor appointed by a magistrate or against a testamentary tutor for the restitution of the ward's property or to collect damages for the fraudulent or negligent administration of it (*actio tutelae*).

Curatorship (*cura* or *curatio*)

Curatorship is a technical term referring to the administrative duties of both public officials and private citizens under a great variety of circumstances and situations. In the public realm, for instance, this category included care of the grain supply (*cura annonae*), which aediles provided, and care of public morals (*cura morum*), which censors provided. Augustus also appointed curators (*curatores*) to oversee public roads, public buildings, and aqueducts. In the private realm, curators were appointed to care for the interests of an unborn child (*curator ventris*), for example, or for the estate of an insolvent debtor (*curator bonorum*) – or even, in some cases (e.g., if the tutor was absent or ill), for the interests of pupils under curatorship (*cura pupilli*).

The most important curatorships of individuals were over lunatics or insane people (*cura furiosi*), spendthrifts (*cura prodigum*), and individuals sui iuris under age twenty-five (*cura minoris).* Since women were ordinarily submitted to ongoing guardianship, the curatorship of minors applied basically to males between the ages of fourteen and twenty-five. The curatorship of lunatics and spendthrifts was established by the Twelve Tables (V.7). Usually the curator, like the tutor, was the closest agnate. If there was no suitable agnate, the magistrate could appoint a curator himself (Gaius, D. 27.10.13).

The development of the curatorship of minors seems to have begun with the *lex Laetoria* (erroneously called Plaetoria) around 191 BCE. According to an edict of the praetor developing that statute, when someone had taken advantage of a minor's lack of experience, the praetor would grant a remedy to revoke the transaction and restore the minor's original condition (*restitutio in integrum*). Because of the ever-present risk of exploiting minors' lack of experience, transactions with them were substantially reduced. Thus, to preserve these kinds of transactions, the Romans introduced the practice of calling in a curator to approve them. During the Principate, this practice led to the institution of a curator appointed by a magistrate at the minor's request. Emperor Justinian largely assimilated tutelage to curatorship of minors.

Women and guardianship over women

Women were subject to stringent legal restrictions under Roman law. As Papinian clearly acknowledged, "in many parts of our laws, the condition of women is inferior to that of men" (D. 1.5.9). Nor could women generally undertake actions on behalf of others. They could act only on their own behalf, and even then with some limitations. This explains why some prominent public and private roles were considered the business of men alone. For instance, women could not hold a magistracy or public office, be judges, bring lawsuits, act as procurators, or speak in court as advocates (see Ulpian, D. 50.17.2pr.). They could not be paterfamilias, adopt children, or, until late antiquity, serve as their children's guardian after their husband's death. As for actions on their own behalf, women needed the consent (at least tacit) of their father to form a legitimate marriage and to divorce. And they were unable to make wills until the time of Hadrian, and then only with a tutor's consent.

Sui iuris girls under the age of twelve were subject to guardianship for children below puberty (*tutela impuberum*), but women aged twelve or older who were not under paternal power (or *manus*) were also required to have a tutor (*tutela mulierum*), except for vestal virgins (Twelve Tables V.1). In the eastern provinces, husbands were commonly their wives' tutors, although Roman husbands usually preferred not to be tutors for their wives, in order to protect marital affection (*affectio maritalis*) and avoid conflicts of interest. Women's tutors were not personal custodians and did not control women's personal lives or their property. Women required the authorization of their tutor (*auctoritas tutoris*) to make a will, to alienate property by formal conveyance (*res mancipi*), to emancipate a slave, and to constitute a dowry, among other acts. But in practice, independent (sui iuris) women were able to conduct most of their own affairs (see Gaius 1.190). The requirement of consent was very often a formality because the woman's tutor incurred no liability by giving or refusing it. A woman was not granted any action against her tutor on account of the guardianship (Gaius 1.191), and the praetor could compel the tutor to give his consent when there were good reasons (Gaius, 1.190).

In order to promote marriage and procreation, Emperor Augustus's marriage laws (18 BCE and 9 CE) benefited motherhood (*ius liberorum*). Women could qualify for exemption from having a tutor by giving birth to three children (four for freed slaves) in Rome, or four in Italy, or five in the provinces. The institution of female guardianship survived at least as late as Diocletian (293 CE; see *F. V.* 325) and was abrogated probably in the fourth or fifth century. There is no trace of guardianship over women in Justinian's Compilation. The compilers deleted the expression *tutela mulierum* or replaced it with *tutela impuberum*.

Slaves

Florentinus defined slavery as an "institution of the law of nations by which someone, contrary to nature, is submitted to the ownership of another" (D. 1.5.4.1). Roman slavery was an institution essentially based on capture of enemies in war, not racially grounded as slavery in the New World would be. Prisoners of war lost their previous status and were usually sold to private owners as slaves. This rule of the law of nations was also applied to Romans captured by enemies, although captured Romans recovered their former status and rights when they returned to Roman territory (*postliminium*). Enslavement also resulted when a female slave gave birth, even if the father was free. But if the mother was free at any time from the child's conception to its birth, the child was born free (P.S. 2.24.2–3). Finally, enslavement could be imposed as punishment for some offenses (Ulpian, D. 48.19.2pr.).

Under Roman law, slaves were considered both human persons and things. Their legal position, therefore, was complex, as is shown by the abundant legal literature discussing issues in relation to slaves. As humans, slaves lacked all personal rights and responsibilities and had no legal capacity. They were able, however, to have quasi-marital relations (*contubernium*) (see implications in Ulpian, D. 21.1.35), and their tombs were considered religious places. Slaves could own nothing but could only acquire things for their owners.

Slaves could be neither plaintiff nor defendant in a lawsuit, but they were able to act on behalf of their master, doing business or managing his property. They often worked as financial or commercial agents in charge of a shop or a ship. They were also able to administer some assets (see section: *peculium*). Many slaves of both sexes provided sexual services at the request of their masters.

As property, slaves and their positions were subject to the master's absolute power (*dominica potestas*). Slaves were a type of property called *res mancipi*, which also included land, houses, and beasts, among other things. As property, slaves could be bought and sold, given, lent, donated, and bequeathed by will, like other goods and commodities. They could also be mistreated at will. For humanitarian reasons, some imperial legislation restricted the power of the owner to kill slaves or to inflict severe harm on them. Domitian, for instance, prohibited the castration of male slaves, and Hadrian imposed the capital penalty to the physician who performed the operation (Ulpian, D. 48.8.4.2). Hadrian also prohibited masters from killing slaves without the consent of a magistrate, and Antoninus Pius established that the gratuitous killing of a slave by a master constituted criminal homicide (Gaius 1.53; Inst. 1.8.2).

Manumission

From the Latin words *manus* (hand) and *missio* (release), manumission was the act of freeing a slave. It could occur in many ways (Gaius 3.56). For example, a slave might be released from the owner's power by a claim before the magistrate and in the presence of the master, in which a free man (called *adsertor libertatis*) would affirm that the slave was a free man (*manumissio vindicta*); by presentation of the slave to the censor for registration as a Roman citizen (*manumissio censu*); and by testamentary disposition of the slave's master (*manumissio testamento*). The last form of manumission was the most common. Testamentary manumissions were conditional on the slave's paying a sum of money to the heir. During the period between the opening of the will and the fulfillment of the condition, the slave remained enslaved (*statuliber*). The child of a female slave born during that period was also considered a slave.

More informally, however, manumission could occur by a letter from the master to the slave (*manumissio per epistulam*), by a declaration of the master before witnesses (*manumissio inter amicos*) or simply by an invitation to the slave to join the master's table (*manumissio per mensam*). A slave manumitted by informal procedures lacked many rights, including those of full citizenship. Such a slave was protected by praetorian law but not civil law. Slaves freed by praetorian law were called Junian Latins, because they had the same legal status as the existing Latins (*lex Iunia [Norbana]*, c. 19 CE). Emperor Constantine added another procedure for manumission: the master's giving consent in a church before a Christian congregation (*manumissio in ecclesia*).

Emperor Augustus transformed the law of slavery by the *lex Fufia Caninia* (2 BCE) and especially the *lex Aelia Sentia* (4 CE). The *lex Fufia Caninia* imposed a limit on manumissions by will: an owner of no more than two slaves could use this procedure to free the one or two slaves that he had; an owner of three to ten could use it to free half of his slaves. Owners of eleven to thirty slaves could manumit up to one-third of their slaves by will; owners of thirty-one to 100, one-fourth; of 101 to 500, one-fifth; and no one could so manumit more than 100 slaves (Gaius 1.42–43). The *lex Aelia Sentia* (D. 40.9) also stipulated three provisions. First, the owner had to be twenty years old for the manumission to be valid. Second, to become a citizen, the freed slave had to be thirty years old, unless the manumission was made before a praetor (*vindicta*). Freed slaves under age thirty were protected only by praetorian law (and were considered Latins after the promulgation of the aforementioned *lex Iunia*). Third, some freed slaves punished by their masters or condemned to fight with beasts, or tortured and convicted of crime, could never become citizens. They would remain as *dediticii*. Finally, manumission that defrauded creditors was void.

Justinian significantly changed the law of manumission. The new law abolished the status of Iuniani latini and dediticii, and it established that all manumissions whether formal or informal, should confer citizenship. The new law also required a document attested by five witnesses to validate informal manumissions (*per epistolam* and *inter amicos*). Restrictions on numbers of testamentary manumission were also abolished.

Patrons and freedmen

Some kinds of relation between the former master (*patronus*) and the freedman (*libertus*) survived manumission as patronage. A freedman always had to regard the person of the patron as honorable and inviolable (Ulpian, D. 39.15.19). Paradigmatic was the relation between Cicero and Marcus Tullius Tiro (died 4 BCE) his slave, personal secretary, and friend, whom Cicero manumitted in 53 BCE, perhaps on Tiro's fiftieth birthday. His frequent illness worried Cicero greatly (*Ad familiares* 16.8, 16.9, 10, 16.11, 16.13, 16.15). Tiro edited some of Cicero's speeches and letters as well as authoring a grammar and a *Life of Cicero*, unfortunately now lost. He may have developed an early form of shorthand.

A freedman was forbidden to marry his patroness or his patron's daughter. In case of poverty, both patron and freedman had the duty of reciprocal maintenance. Freedmen needed the permission of the praetor to sue their patrons, and in no case could they instigate criminal proceedings against the patron or be a witness in the trial. The patron could also require the continuation of some reasonable services (*operae*) and gifts (*munera*). These duties, however, were considered natural (*obligationes naturales*), so that the patron could not sue to enforce them unless the freedman had made an oath or a special stipulation to fulfill them (*stipulatio operarum*). Patrons had some rights of succession to the inheritance of their freedmen, although these varied based on whether the freedmen had made a will and had any children.

Unlimited liability of the *paterfamilias*

When a father owned a business (e.g., in agriculture, crafts, or manufacturing), he had unlimited liability (*in solidum*) for actions taken by his subordinates. When he appointed a son, a slave, or another employee to manage his business, he remained liable for contracts made by the business manager (*institor*) in connection with the business. The legal agreement between the father or principal and the business manager or agent rested on status or contract. Sons-in-power and slaves acted within the power of the principal (*patria potestas* or *dominica potestas*), while business managers not submitted to the *patria* or *dominica potestas* worked under contract.

The praetor introduced two actions in his edict to allow creditors to directly sue the owner or principal of a business: the *actio institoria* and the *actio exercitoria*. The former allowed a general claim against the paterfamilias or owner of the business for acts committed by the business manager in the development of the business. The *actio exercitoria*, however, allowed a specific claim against the pater if he was a shipper (*exercitor navis*) or appointed a captain (*magister navis*). In the latter case, the father was liable for commercial transactions entered into by the ship's captain.

The paterfamilias also had unlimited liability for actions taken by his sons-in-power or slaves when he had given them authorization (*iussum*) ahead of time or subsequent ratification (*ratihabitio*). Authorization could be revoked at any time before a transaction was concluded (Ulpian, D. 14.4.1.2). The paterfamilias could be sued directly in a praetorian action called *actio quod iussu* when he had authorized a transaction, in which case he could be liable for full damages to the plaintiff.

Peculium

The *peculium* was the institution that allowed sons and slaves to develop independent commercial activity. According to Roman law, all things acquired by a son or a slave were acquired for his father or master. A father, however, could allow his son (and a master his slave) to administer certain assets (peculium), including land, money, goods, commercial businesses, and even (other) slaves. Although technically this peculium remained the property of the father or master, in practice the assets were regarded as belonging to the son or slave as a sort of separated private property. The father or master, however, could take the peculium away at any time, and when the son or slave died, the peculium reverted to the father or master.

Under Augustus, anything acquired by sons in the course of their military service became part of their military assets (*peculium castrense*). The sons had full capacity to dispose of such assets as they pleased, even by will (E. P. 20.10). Emperor Constantine extended this category to include all of a son's earnings from any branch of public service. Around the same period, sons were permitted a limited interest in what they received from their mother or her relatives (*bona materna*). This interest was eventually extended to anything they received from someone other than their father (*bona adventitia*).

Where a son or slave entered into a transaction, the father or master was liable to the extent of the peculium, after deducting anything that was due to himself – or to the extent to which the father or master's estate had profited from the transaction (*actio de peculio et de in rem verso*, Gaius 4.72a). But where the father or master knew of the commercial business that his son or slave was entering with his peculium (Ulpian, D. 14.4.1pr.), the father or master, precisely because of his foreknowledge, was treated like an ordinary creditor, without having the privilege of deduction. If a creditor considered that he had been unfairly treated in the distribution process, he could bring the *actio tributoria* against the father or master to have his own share increased to the proper amount. All these actions (*institoria, exercitoria, quod iussu, de in rem verso, de peculio*, and *tributoria*) belonged to the category of *actiones adiecticiae qualitatis* ("added actions") – a term that medieval glossators applied based on Paul, D. 14.1.5.1.

Noxal liability

A father or master was also liable for offenses or delicts committed by a son or a slave. The father or master had options against this liability, however. He could either pay the damages caused by the son or slave, or surrender the offender to the person injured, for the latter to exact vengeance. Noxal liability, it was said, followed the wrongdoer (Ulpian, D. 9.1.1.12: *noxa caput sequitur*). Thus, if a son who committed a wrong was adopted, or a slave who committed a wrong came under the power of another master, liability was transferred to the new father or master. On the other hand, if the son became independent (sui iuris) or the slave was freed, there was no longer noxal liability, but only the possibility of a direct action against the wrongdoer. When action (e.g., *actio furti*, or *actio legis Aquiliae*) was directed against the father or master for offenses committed by his son or slave, it was called a noxal action (*actio noxalis*).

Marriage

The Roman jurist Modestinus defined marriage as "a union between a man and a woman, and partnership for the whole life, a community of human and divine law" (D. 23.2.1). Roman marriage (*matrimonium* or *iustae nuptiae*) was essentially monogamous, heterosexual, and intended to be lasting. It was seen more as a social fact or institution than a strictly legal act or contract. Within the Roman value system, it was considered inhumane to apply legal regulations, rituals, and duties to such an intimate and affectionate relation as marriage.

As a social fact, marriage had almost no effect on the legal status of the parties or on their property. No ceremony was legally necessary for contracting a marriage. No symbolic acts were legally required, no formalities, no cooperation of a magistrate, not even official registration. It was customary, however, for a marriage to begin with a solemn bringing of the bride to the bridegroom's house, accompanied by religious ceremonies (*deductio in domum mariti*).

Marriage was very often preceded by betrothal, especially among the Roman elite. Bare consent, even by proxy, sufficed to constitute betrothal (Ulpian, D. 23.1.4). Like betrothal, marriage was also concluded by the consent of the spouses, by the free and informal agreement of the parties: "consent, not consummation, constitutes marriage," as Ulpian affirmed (D. 50.17.30). If the would-be spouses were under paternal power, the consent of their fathers was also necessary. All that was legally required for a man and a woman to marry was the agreement to live together with the intention of establishing an enduring union as husband and wife (*affectio maritalis*).

The procreation of legitimate children was the main social aim of marriage. For this reason, the minimum age for contracting marriage became fixed at twelve for women and fourteen for men – i.e., the age of sexual maturation. However, women usually married in their mid- to late-teens, and men in their mid- to late-twenties. The capacity to contract a valid marriage according to civil law was called *conubium*. All Roman citizens (except those punished in certain ways) had conubium, but it was also granted to some groups (e.g., Latins) or individuals. Marriages between relatives within the third degree (brother and sister; uncle and niece, aunt and nephew) were generally prohibited, including those within three degrees by adoption. Serving soldiers were not permitted to marry until the time of Septimius Severus. Provincial magistrates were forbidden to marry women of the province during their term, and guardians were forbidden to marry their wards.

Probably in order to avoid mixing properties, Roman law banned the giving of gifts between spouses (Ulpian, D. 24.1.1.). This rule persisted until Justinian's law, with some exceptions (e.g., living for free in the other's house; Pomponius, D. 24.1.18). Prenuptial gifts were permitted, however, as were gifts intended to be transferred upon the donor's death (*mortis causa*).

Dowry

The dowry (in Latin *dos*) was property – possibly including land, goods, and movable property – commonly transferred to the bridegroom or his family by the bride or her family as her contribution to maintaining the marital household. Romans considered dowries a social practice and a moral duty but not a legal requirement for a valid marriage. Contributing to a relative's dowry was a gesture of family piety and an expression of wealth. Dowries were also, however, a clear way to distinguish marriage from concubinage, since "there can be no dowry without marriage" (Ulpian, D. 23.3.3). The dowry must be distinguished from both the peculium and the inheritance a daughter could expect to receive from her father. It was also distinct from the wife's property, over which she retained control during marriage.

A dowry could be constituted before, at the time of, or after a wedding (Javolenus, D. 23.4.1pr.), but always in connection with a marriage. Dowry agreements were usually signed by the groom's father and the bride's father before the wedding took place. If the groom was independent, he could himself be a party to the contract. If the bride was independent, she needed the consent of her guardian to make the agreement, since it involved a transfer of property. There were general rules about restitution of a dowry in case of death or divorce, but the parties could also include other arrangements in the agreement. Paul (D. 23.4.12.1) wrote that the dowry agreement often included the obligation to use the promised dowry to support the woman, as well as clauses regarding restitution.

While the husband was legal owner and administrator of the dowry, it was considered separate from his own property, and in some sense, as the jurist Tryphoninus affirmed, it still belonged to the wife (D. 23.3.75: *mulieris tamen est*). A dowry was the wife's business (*res uxoria*). The husband's control over the dowry was very limited. Without his wife's consent, the husband could not alienate dowry land or free dowry slaves. If he died or the marriage ended by divorce, the dowry reverted to his wife. If the wife died, the dowry constituted by the bride's father or grandfather (*dos profecticia*) fell to her family or her children. A *dos adventicia*, however – i.e., a dowry with a different origin – remained in the hands of the husband. A specific action for the restitution of a dowry to a wife (the so-called *actio rei uxoriae*) lay against the husband.

Divorce and remarriage

As the creation of a marriage was a social fact, so was its termination by divorce. The intentional and permanent (not merely temporary) interruption of conjugal life together accomplished a divorce (see Paul, D. 24.2.3). A marriage could be ended at any time by mutual and informal agreement or simply by the declaration of one of the spouses. Originally, divorce was reserved for serious marital faults or problems: in case of infertility, adultery, or drunkenness, or if one spouse had made copies of the household keys, for instance. The husband, however, could divorce his wife at any time. This complete freedom to divorce, extended in the classical period also to wives, did not in the Republican period require any legal formalities. The formulas of repudiation known from legal sources were neither imperative nor essential for a unilateral divorce. Indeed, prenuptial agreements or penal stipulations limiting or excluding the possibility of divorce were considered void. In practice, the spouse who wanted to divorce usually just informed the other spouse orally or in writing or by messenger. When spouses were under patria potestas, their fathers had the right to dissolve their marriage. The wife under legal marital power could also end a marriage by repudiation of her husband. In that case, however, she would remain under his manus, but no longer as his wife.

Christian emperors regarded frivolous divorce as an expression of Roman moral decadence, so they rejected the liberal idea of completely unrestricted divorce. They allowed divorce only on certain grounds. After divorce (or termination of marriage by death), each spouse was entitled to remarry. No prohibitions on legal marriage existed for widowers. Wives, however, had to wait for a period of mourning (ten months, and later one year) before marrying again. This rule existed, among other reasons, to avoid confusion about the paternity of any child born after the husband's death (*turbatio sanguinis*). After divorce, children born within a legitimate marriage remained under the father's power. The ex-wife could bring an action to retrieve her dowry, but the husband could retain part of it when divorce was due to the wife's fault or her father's instigation, or if the dowry was needed as maintenance for legitimate children.

Concubinage

An alternative to legitimate marriage under Roman law was concubinage (*concubinatus*), i.e., a permanent, monogamous sexual union between a man and a woman without *affectio maritalis*. A man could have either a wife or a concubine, but not two wives or concubines simultaneously (P.S. 2.20.1; C.J. 5.26.1). Polygamous relations were forbidden. The concubine was usually of lower status (for instance, a freedwoman or former prostitute) than the concubinator, and she did not take his rank (Ulpian, D. 32.49.4). Prohibitions on marriage between senators (and their descendants) and freedwomen, as well as rules forbidding soldiers in service to marry and restricting the marriage of provincial magistrates, all served to foster and dignify concubinage. As a matter of fact, it was often hard to distinguish concubinage from marriage. The presence or absence of a dowry was one of the best indicators, since (again) there was no dowry in concubinage. Another signal was gift-giving between the partners, since giving gifts was forbidden between spouses but not within concubinage. But many rules that applied to marriage were extended to concubinage as well. For instance, no concubine could be younger than twelve (Ulpian, D. 25.7.1.4), and children were forbidden to take as wives the concubines of their parents (C.J. 5.4.4. of 228).

Nevertheless, while it was not prohibited by law (Marcianus, D. 25.7.3.1), concubinage did not carry the legal rights and implications of a valid marriage. For instance, it did not produce legitimate children or, therefore, automatic heirs. Still, a concubinator could appoint guardians for his children, leave property for them, and (until Constantine) leave property for his concubine (C.Th. 4.6.2.4). Moreover, late imperial legislation allowed for the legitimation of children from concubinage by subsequent marriage.

Augustan legislation on marriage

With the aim of promoting marriage and procreation among Roman citizens and repressing adultery and nonmarital sex, Emperor Augustus enacted three relevant laws: the *lex Julia de maritandis ordinibus* (18 BCE), which prohibited intermarriage between senatorial families and ex-slaves, and between all citizens and disreputable persons such as prostitutes; the *lex Iulia de adulteriis coercendis* (17 BCE), which punished adultery as a criminal offense; and the *lex Papia Poppaea* (9 CE), which supplemented and complemented the other two laws. Tacitus (*Annales* 3.25–28) presents the *lex Papia Poppaea* as the summit of state intrusion into the private household. Augustan legislation on marriage and adultery was in force, with some modifications, for several centuries. It exasperated the upper classes of the Roman Empire. Nevertheless, the effects and scope of application of this legislation has frequently been exaggerated.

To encourage marriage and childbearing, Augustus ordered all male citizens between the ages of twenty-five and sixty, and all female citizens between the ages of twenty and fifty, to be married. He punished those who disobeyed by disabling them from receiving inheritances or legacies from those beyond the sixth degree of kinship. Widows were also required to remarry within two years of their husbands' death, and divorcees within eighteen months of divorce. Those who had not married by that time were punished with inheritance penalties and restrictions. Married couples without children could receive only half of any such legacies. Those married with three children, and especially the wife in such marriages, were rewarded with certain privileges (*ius liberorum*).

The *lex Iulia de adulteriis* made it a public crime to commit certain sexual offenses, especially adultery, i.e., sexual relations between a married woman and a man other than her husband. Illicit sexual intercourse with a nonmarried woman or a widow of honorable status was called *stuprum*. A father could kill his daughter and her lover if he caught them in the act of adultery. Guilty adulterous parties were banished to various islands, and part of their property was confiscated. Husbands were required to divorce adulterous wives.

Constantine's legislation on family and marriage

Constantine probably influenced Roman family law more than any other emperor after Augustus. Some of his laws on marriage and family matters were probably based on Christian motivations and values, such as the new laws removing penalties for celibacy and childlessness (C.Th. 8.16.1), drastically restricting unilateral divorce (C.Th. 3.16.1), rejecting the sale and abandonment of children (C.Th. 5.9.1), and regulating alimentary law (C.Th. 11.27.1–2). Even so, Constantinian legislation on family and marriage tried to preserve the traditional distinction between the freeborn and those born as slaves. For instance, Constantine extended the Augustan prohibition on marriage between senators and freedwomen, to exclude as well the marriages of local and provincial magistrates with former female slaves or other women of low status.

Justinian's legislation on marriage

Emperor Justinian adapted the traditional Roman institution of marriage to the Christian moral teachings on marital indissolubility. In his far-reaching Novel 22 of 536 CE, the emperor imposed additional penalties on those who divorced without a legitimate ground. In Novel 117 of 542 CE, serious penalties were introduced for those who decided to dissolve a marriage by mutual consent. In order to promote sexual continence, Justinian legislation discouraged the marriage of widows and allowed the dissolution of marriage without any penalty when either of the spouses decided to enter religious life (see Nov. 22). To establish a clear distinction between marriage and other kinds of sexual union, Justinian legislation emphasized formalities. In Novel 74 of 538 CE, for example, the emperor ordered that dowries and premarital gifts were obligatory for those of senatorial status.

Justinian's legislation protected the permanence of monogamous marital union and promoted the equality of the spouses within marriage. It also showed greater concern for the interests of wives and children (Nov. 98). With respect to freedmen, Justinian rejected the distinction between free and freed: women who had been slaves but were formally emancipated could thus marry whomever they wished (Nov. 78). The medieval Christian legislation on marriage was firmly founded on the laws of Emperor Justinian.

Further reading

Aubert, Jean-Jacques. *Business Managers in Ancient Rome: A Social and Economic History of Institores, 200 BCE–AD 250*. Leiden: Brill, 1994.

Buckland, William Warwick. *The Roman Law of Slavery: The Condition of the Slave in Private Law from Augustus to Justinian*. Cambridge: Cambridge University Press, 1908.

Domingo, Rafael. *La legislación matrimonial de Constantino*. Pamplona: Servicio de Publicaciones de la Universidad de Navarra, 1989.

du Plessis, Paul. *Borkowski's Textbook on Roman Law*. 5th ed., 113–151, Oxford: Oxford University Press, 2015.

Evans Grubbs, Judith. *Law and Family in Late Antiquity: The Emperor Constantine's Marriage Legislation*. Oxford and New York: Oxford University Press, 1995.

Evans Grubbs, Judith. *Women and the Law in the Roman Empire: A Sourcebook on Marriage, Divorce and Widowhood*. London and New York: Routledge, 2002.

Evans Grubbs, Judith, and Tim Parkin, eds. *The Oxford Handbook of Childhood and Education in the Classical World*. Oxford and New York: Oxford University Press, 2013.

Frier, Bruce W., and Thomas A. J. McGinn. *A Casebook on Roman Family Law*. Oxford: Oxford University Press, 2001.

Gamauf, Richard. "Slavery. Social Position and Legal Capacity." In *The Oxford Handbook of Roman Law and Society*, edited by Paul J. du Plessis, Clifford Ando, and Kaius Tuori, 386–401. Oxford: Oxford University Press, 2016.

Gardner, Jane F. *Being a Roman Citizen*. London and New York: Routledge, 1993.

Gardner, Jane F. *Family and "Familia" in Roman Law and Life*. Oxford and New York: Oxford University Press, 1998.

Halbwachs, Verena. "Women as Legal Actors." In *The Oxford Handbook of Roman Law and Society*, edited by Paul J. du Plessis, Clifford Ando, and Kaius Tuori, 443–455. Oxford: Oxford University Press, 2016.

Joshel, Sandra R. *Slavery in the Roman World*. Cambridge and New York: Cambridge University Press, 2010.

Joshel, Sandra R., and Lauren Hackworth Petersen. *The Material Life of Roman Slaves*. Cambridge and New York: Cambridge University Press, 2015.

Kaser, Max. *Das römische Privatrecht I. Das altrömische, das vorklassische und klassische Recht*. 2nd ed., 268–372. Munich: Beck Verlag, 1971.

Laes, Christian. *Children in the Roman Empire: Outsiders Within*. Cambridge and New York: Cambridge University Press, 2011.

Lindsay, Hugh. *Adoption in the Roman World*. Cambridge and New York: Cambridge University Press, 2009.

McAuley, Mairéad. *Reproducing Rome: Motherhood in Virgil, Ovid, Seneca, and Statius*. Oxford and New York: Oxford University Press, 2016.

Mette-Dittmann, Angelika. *Die Ehegesetze des Augustus: eine Untersuchung im Rahmen der Gesellschaftspolitik des Princeps*. Stuttgart: F. Steiner, 1991.

Phang, Sara Elise. *The Marriage of Roman Soldiers (13 B.C. – A.D. 235). Law and Family in the Imperial Army*. Leiden: Brill, 2001.

Rawson, Beryl, ed. *A Companion to Families in the Greek and Roman Worlds*. Malden, MA: Wiley-Blackwell, 2011.

Schulz, Fritz. *Classical Roman Law*, 71–202. Oxford: Clarendon Press, 1951.

Treggiari, Susan. *Roman Marriage: Iusti Coniuges from the Time of Cicero to the Time of Ulpian*. Oxford: Clarendon Press, 1991.

Watson, Alan. *The Law of Persons in the Later Roman Republic*. Oxford: Clarendon Press, 1967.

Watson, Alan. *Roman Slave Law*. Baltimore and London: The John Hopkins University Press, 1987.

Witte, Jr., John, and Gary S. Hauk, eds. *Christianity and Family Law: An Introduction*. Cambridge and New York: Cambridge University Press, 2017.

9 Property law

This chapter addresses the Roman law of ownership and the rights that modified it, including, for instance, the rights of predial servitude and usufruct. Classic Roman jurists focused on private property over other kinds, such as sacred property and public property. Their doctrine of ownership was so influential that it has prevailed for centuries and even now, although very much re-elaborated, maintains a substantial presence in the legal systems of the civil law tradition and in the realm of international law. There are even similarities to English property law, although English common law developed separately, based largely on feudal law.

The law of things (*res*)

The second and largest division of Gaius's classification (2.1), preserved by Justinian in his Institutes (Inst. 2.1pr.), concerned the law dealing with things (*res*). "Thing" is of course a very vague and ambiguous term, used by Roman jurists with many different senses. The most general refers to everything that exists in the universe, from physical objects (wine, a table) to intangible concepts (rights, obligations). Ulpian says that res comprises both legal relations and rights (D. 50.16.23). Even freedom could be considered a thing, but a thing without a price (Ulpian, D. 50.17.106: *res inaestimabilis*). Most of all, res refers to any economic asset. All objects and contents of a person's estate are things. In the law of contracts, res refers not only to the object, but to its physical delivery (*re contrahere*) to the other party. The Romans did not consider the human body a thing, because the human person was not the "owner of her own limbs" (Ulpian, 9.2.13pr.). They did consider animals as things inasmuch as animals could be owned and have a cash value.

Classification of things

According to their physical nature or legal conditions, things could be classified in many different ways (see Gaius 2.1-18).

First, things could be owned privately, i.e., belong to some private individual (*res in patrimonio*; e.g., wine, a house), or they could be expressly excluded from private ownership and all related legal transactions between private individuals (*res extra patrimonium*; e.g., air, rivers, the sea). Things excluded from private ownership could be open to the use of everybody (*res communes*; e.g., the sea, the air); or they could belong to the Roman People (*res publicae*: e.g., rivers, harbors); or they could be under divine law (*res divini iuris*: e.g., tombs and burial grounds; city gates and walls). Some things, though not actually belonging to anyone, were likely to be owned (*res nullius*: e.g., wild animals and abandoned property).

Second, in accord with the formalities required for the validity of a conveyance, things could be considered *res mancipi* or *res nec mancipi*. The former were things relevant to households in an agricultural society. This category was limited to slaves, beasts of draught and burden (oxen, mules, and horses), the land of Italy (or provincial land with the status of Italic land), and rustic predial servitudes. *Res mancipi* could be conveyed only by a solemn and prescribed ritual form called *mancipatio* (from *manu capere*: to grasp with the hand), which required the presence of five Roman citizens as witnesses and of a man who held a scale. All other things were *res nec mancipi*. With the development of commerce, the importance of this distinction declined.

Third, things could be physical or intangible. Physical things could be touched (land, gold, clothes), while intangible things, of course, could not be (rights and obligations, for example). The distinction was important because, in general, only physical things could be possessed (possession required a physical holding), and only they could be acquired by informal conveyance (*traditio*) or usucaption (acquiring title to property by uninterrupted possession).

Fourth, things could be movable (*res mobiles*) or immovable (*res immobiles*). The distinction was relevant to categorizing theft (there could be no theft of immovable things), protecting possession, calculating the period required for usucaption, and even resolving questions of procedure. Movable property roughly corresponded to personal property, while immovable property corresponded to real property or real estate. Notably, the distinction between movable and immovable things never occupied in Roman law the importance that the distinction between real property and personal property came to have in the common law tradition.

Finally, there were fungible and nonfungible things. Fungibles were "those things that are estimated by weight, number, or measure, for instance, wine, oil, corn, coined money, copper, silver, or gold" (Inst. 3.14pr.). Nonfungible things were those identified and valued in and for themselves: e.g., a particular horse or piece of land or slave. The difference had legal relevance with respect to some legal relations, and specifically when it came to rules regarding risk: for such purposes, fungible things were completely interchangeable, since one instance was as good as another; not so for nonfungible things. In general, only nonfungible things could be used without being consumed. For this reason, there could be no usufruct of fungibles.

Ownership

No Roman text offers a definition of ownership (*dominium*). The word *dominium* emerged at the very end of the Roman Republic. It was still unknown at the time of Cicero, though the word for owner (*dominus*) was in use. Under Roman law, ownership meant full power over physical things with no more limitations than those established by legislation or imposed by the nature of the thing itself (which made ownership of some things – a bit of breath, for example – inherently ephemeral).

Ownership encompassed the right to have, hold, use, enjoy, and alienate a thing, as well as to bring an action to recover it when necessary. The owner could give up or lose some of these rights, however (e.g., the right to use the thing or to take up the fruits of its use) while still maintaining the title of owner. In this sense, ownership, while it was the strongest legal title bestowed by Roman law, was not absolute. It was not heavily restricted, but public order and the interests of the community did justify some limits to private ownership. Special restrictions on the use of immovable property were also accepted, and expropriations were largely carried out, notably during the later Empire.

The main form of ownership was that recognized by Roman civil law (*ex iure Quiritium*). All Roman citizens, as well as non-Roman citizens with the right to commerce (*ius commercii*), were capable of acquiring quiritary or civil ownership over movable things and over land located in Italy. Provincial land without the status of Italic land was held by individuals in accordance with the rules of the law of nations for transferring property. After the Antonine Constitution provided citizenship to all free inhabitants of the Empire (212 CE) and Emperor Diocletian subjected even the land of Italy to the tribute (292 CE), the distinction between kinds of ownership lost any practical import.

Co-ownership (*communio*)

Co-ownership implied ownership of the same thing by two or more owners at the same time. The earliest form of co-ownership was that of the undivided estate of goods among co-heirs after the death of the paterfamilias (Gaius 3.154a: *consortium ercto non cito*). Each co-owner was considered the full owner of the whole common property, so that he could act for the whole group, limited only by the veto (*ius prohibendi*) of any other co-owners. Each co-owner could also demand the division of the common property by means of a partition action (*actio familiae erciscundae*). This kind of ownership disappeared in the early classical period.

Increasing commercial activity and business partnership fostered the development of a new form of joint ownership known as *communio pro indiviso*, later called by medieval jurists *condominium*. This kind of common ownership could arise by common purchase, inheritance, or legacy. Each co-owner had a share in the common property with the right of using, enjoying, or alienating it to the extent of his or her share, which did not need to be equal among the co-owners. It was not affected by the death of one of the co-owners, whose heirs would simply assume his or her position. All profits and expenses had to be shared by co-owners in proportion to their shares.

Each co-owner had the inalienable right to ask for partition. An agreement among co-owners never to divide was void. For the partition of the common property, each co-owner could bring a partition action: the *actio communi dividundo*, when common ownership was originated by purchase or legacy, and the *actio familiae erciscundae*, in the case of an inheritance. These actions empowered the judge to assign all or part of the common property to one or more of the co-owners. In addition to their primordial partition function, these actions served to resolve all other controversial issues that arose from common ownership (e.g., proportional distribution of expenses, indemnity, and compensation among co-owners).

Possession

The most important distinction in the law of property was that between ownership (*dominium*) and possession (*possessio*). While ownership was the supreme and most unrestricted right over a thing, possession was the actual holding of the thing, the state of having effective control over it. Ownership was a matter of entitlement; possession was a matter of fact. The owner of a thing could be its actual possessor (e.g., Titius might wear a toga that his mother had given him). Very often, however, the possessor was not the owner: a pedestrian finding a ring on the ground, a homeless person taking temporary shelter in an abandoned house, and a thief holding a stolen tunic all would be possessors without ownership. Possession and ownership were very much related, though, since possession was a key factor in the most common methods of acquiring ownership: delivery (*traditio*) and usucaption.

Roman law does not provide a unified doctrine of possession, and the terminology in the sources remains vague and ambiguous. Roman sources distinguished three kinds of possessions: natural, civil, and praetorian. Natural possession was the mere holding of a thing without any kind of specific legal protection. This was the sort of possession thieves had over stolen items, but also the kind had by anyone who held things as result of a contract with their owner: e.g., the bailee of an item loaned for use, the lessee of a piece of land, and so on.

Civil possession was possession *ad usucapionem* – the kind of possession that would enable the holder to acquire ownership based on continuous possession for a prescribed period of time (i.e., by usucaption). Civil possession required both the effective taking of control of a thing (*corpus*) and the intention to hold it as one's own (*animus*). The depositee, the borrower, and the hirer were not civil possessors because they did not have this intention. The owner who held an object was always also a civil possessor, as was the buyer of a thing once he had received it by delivery from the seller. It was possible to obtain civil possession through a procurator, tutor, or curator when they did not take possession in their own name (Paul, D. 42.1.20). The civil possessor ordinarily was also a praetorian possessor.

Praetorian possession (also called interdictal possession) was protected by means of possessory interdicts – quick provisory remedies granted by the praetor to protect the status quo (see next section). The praetor protected the praetorian possessor because the latter had a specific relation to an item that demanded protection separate from the protection given the owner. For example, a pledgee needed protection from the pledger in order to secure repayment. And a sequester – someone responsible for holding an item until a dispute over its ownership was resolved – needed his own protection, different from that given the litigants claiming ownership over the item.

These three kinds of possession, though related, constituted three independent legal concepts. Thus, one individual could have natural possession of an object, another praetorian possession, and still another civil possession. Suppose Titius threw out his wedding ring after divorce, and it was found by Caius, who then gave the ring to Sempronius as a pledge, while Sempronius lent it to his daughter Servia to wear to a party. In this case, Caius would be a civil possessor, Sempronius a praetorian possessor, and Servia the natural possessor.

Interdictal protection of possession

Thanks to the interdictal protection provided by the praetor, a possessor could assert or recover possession. Such possession, to be protrected by praetorian interdict, must not have been obtained by force (*vi*) or "viciously" (*possessio vitiosa*), clandestinely (*clam*), or by bailment at will (*precarium*) from the dispossessor.

Because "ownership has nothing in common with possession" (Ulpian, D. 41.2.12.1), interdictal protection could be used even against owners who had lost possession justly but then recovered it unjustly. On the other hand, the fact of owning did not exclude the owner from interdictal protection when he had been dispossessed. Thus, suppose the owner Titius had been dispossessed by Caius. Titius could bring a *rei vindicatio* to recover property, but it would also be possible for him simply to bring an interdict to recover possession, which would also allow him to avoid the inconvenience of having to prove ownership. Then, if he was unable to recover possession with the interdict, he could initiate the vindication procedure.

Interdictal proceedings were simple and rapid since they only required examination of the position of each litigant in relation to the other. The praetor would end by ordering maintenance or recovery of possession for the litigant who had the superior claim to possess. For cases concerning immovable property, the praetor would assign possession to the litigant who already had it, unless he had obtained it by force, clandestinely, or by bailment at will. For cases concerning movable property, the praetor would grant possession to the litigant who had the thing for the longer period during the preceding year. Book 43 of the Digest sums up the interdicts as elaborated by Justinian.

Acquisition of ownership

There are many possible criteria for classifying the various ways of acquiring ownership under Roman law. Some means of acquiring ownership (like *occupatio*) were recognized by the law of nations, and others were regulated by civil law (like *mancipatio, in iure cessio*, or usucaption). Some required a certain ceremonial form to take legal effect (e.g., mancipatio), while others did not (e.g., *traditio* or usucaption). Some were original, in the sense that the new ownership did not depend on the previous one (as with occupatio of an item never owned before), while others were derivative, depending on the condition of the previous owner (e.g., mancipatio, traditio).

The most common way of acquiring ownership was by acquisition from the former owner. Valuable and more permanent things were conveyed by formal appropriation (mancipatio); other things were conveyed by mere delivery (traditio). To fix defects in the mode of transference, the Romans also established usucaption, which allowed individuals to gain civil property by continuous and uninterrupted possession of it.

Mancipatio and *in iure cessio*

The mancipatio constituted the means par excellence for transferring civil ownership of *res mancipi*. Gaius's account of mancipatio is detailed (1.119–122). The solemn ceremony of mancipatio took place in the presence of the alienator and the acquirer, as well as no fewer than five Roman citizens who acted as witnesses, and another Roman tasked with holding a scale. The things to be mancipated also had to be present at the ceremony, although lands could be mancipated at a distance. Taking hold of the mancipated thing, as a sign of control over it, the acquirer would say: "I declare this thing to be mine by civil law, and be it purchased to me by this bronze ingot and bronze scale." He would then strike the scale with the ingot and pay a symbolic price to the alienator. Gaius (1.122) explained that the bronze ingot and the scale were used because formerly only bronze money was in use, and its value, before coinage was introduced, was measured by weighing. By Gaius's time, however, the weighing was largely a mere formality.

A guarantee in case of eviction (*auctoritas*), inherent to sale by mancipatio, was mentioned in the Twelve Tables (6.3). Over a period of one year for movable things and two years for immovable things, the transferee could bring an *actio auctoritatis* against the transferor (*auctor*) to compel payment of double the purchase price whenever a third party gained a claim of ownership (*rei vindicatio*) against the transferee resulting in eviction. Originally, therefore, mancipatio was a real sale, but over time it became a formal act used for performances besides sales. It was used, for example, to make testaments and donations and to constitute servitudes, dowries, and trusts, among other things. The legal transaction established by mancipatio appeared in additional declarations of the transferor (*nuncupatio*). Specific duties were also assumed by promises and mutual stipulations. Mancipatio was soon adapted for establishing, transferring, and extinguishing family powers by adoption or emancipation of children, noxal surrender, and so on. It disappeared gradually as the distinction between *res mancipi* and *res nec mancipi* lost significance, and written documents became more important. The word mancipatio does not appear in the *Corpus Iuris* of Emperor Justinian, and the concept was replaced by that of mere delivery (traditio).

Like mancipatio, transfer before the praetor – *in iure cessio* – was also a formal way of transferring civil property, but by fictitious litigation taking advantage of procedural formalities. Gaius (2.24) described the form: in the presence of the praetor, the acquirer said, while holding the item: "I declare that this thing is mine by civil law." The praetor then asked the transferor to make a claim to the item and, based on the silence of the latter, formally attributed that item to the acquirer. Like mancipatio, the in iure cessio was used for many legal transactions such as the constitution of servitudes, the transfer of inheritances, and the establishment of adoption, tutelage, or curatorship. In Justinian's *Corpus Iuris*, the expression in iure cessio was replaced with cessio.

Occupatio, accession, specification

Occupatio was an original and informal way of acquiring civil ownership that was recognized under the law of nations. It was the simplest way to become an owner: one only had to take an item that belonged to no one else (*res nullius*). Occupatio was the ordinary way to acquire wild animals captured by hunting or fishing, for example; after some disputes, Roman jurists agreed that wounded animals had to be seized to be acquired by occupatio (Gaius D. 41.1.5.1). Occupatio was also the way to acquire movable things that the owner had intentionally abandoned without intending to recover them. Immovable things required usucaption to be acquired.

Accessio was the way of acquiring property by uniting, merging, or mixing one's property with another's in a way that formed an indissoluble whole. It was what occurred, for example, when Titius would paint on Caius's canvas; or when Titia's wool was woven into Sempronius's toga; or when Titius's corn was sown on Caius's land; or when Titius built on his own land with Caius's materials. If the union of items was dissoluble, by contrast, there was no real acquisition by accession: for instance, if Titius could easily separate a jewel he had embedded in Sempronia's ring. Neither was there acquisition by accession when the owners had previously agreed to mix things of equal quality; e.g., a mixture of different juices.

The general rule of accession was that the whole unit belonged to the owner of the principal thing, such that the owner of the incorporated accessory thing lost property (Inst. 2.1.26). That happened regardless of whether the incorporation was effected in good faith or with the former owner's consent. These latter circumstances were, however, relevant for determining the potential compensation to the owner who lost property.

It was often a matter of philosophical discussion what the principal thing was and what was accessory (see for instance Gaius, D. 41.1.9.2; Gaius 2.78; Paul, D. 6.1.23.3). For instance, if Titius wrote on a piece of parchment (*membranae*) belonging to Caius, the parchment was considered the principal thing, and thus the writing belonged to Caius. If, however, Titius painted a picture on Caius's canvas, the painting was considered to be the principal item. If someone built on soil owned by another, the building belonged to the owner of the soil, since the structure (the accessory) was considered part of the plot of land (the principal thing) on which it stood: "the superstructure goes with the land" (Gaius 2.73: *superficies solo cedit*). Today, however, this rule has been overturned in many contexts, with "structure prevailing over land."

Slightly different from accession was specification: the acquisition of a new thing (*nova species*) made out of materials belonging to another person: e.g., if Titius turned Caius's bronze into a statue. The Sabinians ascribed ownership to the owner of the underlying materials, on the ground that a thing cannot exist without that of which it is made, while the Proculians gave ownership to the maker because the newly fashioned item as such had no previous owner. Emperor Justinian finally gave ownership to the maker, but only if the materials could not be restored to their former state (Gaius, D. 41.1.7.7).

Acquisition of fruits

The owner of a thing was, in general, also the owner of the fruits the thing produced, whether they were natural fruits (e.g., offspring of animals, products of fields) or civil fruits (the rent from a lease, the earnings of a slave). He owned them on the ground that the accessory – in this case, the fruits themselves – followed the principal (see Julianus, D. 22.1.25pr). In some cases, however, a person other than the owner had the rights to the fruits. For instance, the possessor in good faith, the long-term lessee (emphyteuta), the tenant of agricultural land (*colonus*), the usufructuary, or the ordinary tenant with permission of the owner were entitled to fruits. Because they were possessors, the possessor in good faith and the emphyteuta owned the fruits from the moment the latter were separated from the principal, fruit-bearing thing. The usufructuary and the tenant, however, were not technically possessors, so they only acquired the fruits after gaining actual control of them (*perceptio*). Their acquisition required the acquiescence (tacit or explicit) of the owner.

Traditio

Traditio was the voluntary and derivative way of transferring civil ownership of res nec mancipi and praetorian or bonitary ownership of res mancipi. This method of acquisition was based on natural law and was recognized by the civil law and the law of nations. It was the only form of conveyance that survived in the *Corpus Iuris.* Traditio consisted of the simple delivery of the thing to the transferee by the owner of the thing or by a person authorized by him. But Paul was emphatic: "Bare delivery of itself never transfers ownership" (D. 41.1.31pr.). For the delivery to transfer ownership, and not only possession, it had to be based on a valid ground or cause (*iusta causa*), such as a prior sale. Therefore, the bare common intention of the parties to transfer property was legally insufficient. If Titius sold his toga to Caius, the valid ground of the delivery was the fulfillment of the sale. There was consequently a transfer of ownership. Ownership would also have transferred if Titius had handed a necklace over to his friend Marca as a gift, since donation was recognized by Roman law as a valid ground for a transfer of ownership. No transfer would have occurred, however, if Titius had provided a toga to Caius while the latter was having his own repaired, or if Titius handed over a horse to Caius as security for a debt. Besides sales and donation, valid grounds for the transfer of ownership by delivery were the payment of a debt (*solvere*), the establishment of a dowry (*dotem dare*), or the making of a loan (*credere*) of money or fungible things (if I lent a loaf of bread I could not expect the same loaf back, but a different one of the same quality).

Although traditio required physical delivery, over time the physical element of delivery was reduced to a minimum, so long as effective control really transferred: for instance, a warehouse was considered to be transferred once the transferor had delivered the keys to the transferee, even when the latter had not yet opened the warehouse (Papinian, D. 18.1.74). A piece of land was transferred when both the transferor and the transferee were actually in sight of it, and not only when they had walked around its perimeter.

The increasing irrelevance of delivery led to two special cases: the *traditio brevi manu* and the *constitutum possessorium. Traditio brevi manu* took place when the transferee already held the thing but not as owner: e.g., if Titius lent Caius a toga and later agreed to sell it to him. In such a case, the handover of the toga would be superfluous. The delivery was temporally anticipated by the valid ground for transfer itself. *Constitutum possessorium* was the opposite case. It occurred whenever the owner transferred ownership but continued holding the thing under a different title – as when, for instance, Titius sold Caius a toga but they agreed that Titius would retain it on loan. In that case, there would be no anticipated physical delivery but a postposed one: when the loan ended, Titius would have to hand the toga over.

Donation

Donation was originally a valid cause for delivery but not a proper way of acquiring property. If Titius gave a ring to Caius, the latter became owner through delivery. The mere promise of Titius to deliver the ring did not transfer ownership. Gradually, by extension, donation meant any act of generosity – any disposition for the benefit of another person, for which recompense was not expected. Such a disposition could take different forms: transfer of ownership, constitution of a predial servitude or a usufruct over property belonging to the donor, or release of a debtor from his obligation toward the donor (*acceptilatio*), among other things.

The object of the donation could be anything of value, but the payment of a debt not enforceable by law (e.g., the fulfillment of a natural obligation) was not properly a donation. The law required that the donor had the intention to make a donation (*animus donandi*) and that the donee accepted it. Emperor Justinian eventually considered donation a way of acquiring property (Inst. 2.7pr.), probably since he considered the agreement to make a gift an autonomous, effective, and enforceable legal act (C.J. 8.53.25).

Donations could produce an immediate effect (*inter vivos*) or an effect only upon the death of the donor (*mortis causa*). The *lex Cincia* (204 BCE) imposed restrictions on the amount of donations inter vivos, except when the donor was closely related to the donee. The complicated system of the *lex Cincia* was replaced in the late Empire by a system of registrations of all donations. Unlike donations inter vivos, which were in principle irrevocable, donations on contemplation of death were unilaterally revocable by the donor until his death. They were also automatically revoked by the law where the donor became insolvent or the donee predeceased him. Later, donations mortis causa would be largely assimilated to legacies (Inst. 2.7.1)

Usucaption

Usucaption was a way of acquiring civil ownership of a thing through uninterrupted possession of it for a certain time: one year for movable things and two years for immovable things. As an institution of civil law, it could be used by Roman citizens and foreigners granted the right to have contractual relations (*ius commercii*). Usucaption was essentially used to consolidate defective ownerships, clarify titles, and prove ownership, thereby removing uncertainty. On the one hand, usucaption served to consolidate the ownership transferred by mancipatio after the period of liability to the actio auctoritatis, when the transferor was not the owner of the transferred thing. After an uninterrupted period of possession without disturbance, the law considered it inefficient or idle to keep the window open for new challenges to the transfer's validity. On the other hand, usucaption served to fix defective ownership – e.g., where a res mancipi was transferred without the required mancipatio, or a res nec mancipi was transferred by someone who was neither the owner nor someone authorized by him.

Besides the aforementioned period of time required by the law, the acquisition of civil ownership by usucaption required property subject to private ownership (*in commercio*); provincial land could not be acquired by usucaption, even by a Roman citizen. Furthermore, stolen things and things taken by force were excluded from usucaption, even when they were in the hands of a possessor in good faith. Thus, usucaption also required the possessor's good faith (or subjective honesty and truthfulness) when taking possession of the thing. (The loss of good faith during the process of usucaption, by a person's learning that he was not entitled to possess the thing, was legally irrelevant for acquisition by usucaption.) Also needed was a valid title (*iusta causa* or *iustus titulus*). It was not enough that the possessor believed in good faith that the title existed. Valid titles included, for example, the sale of a thing not belonging to the transferor, the donation of a thing not belonging to the donor, the vindicatory legacy of a thing that did not belong to the heir, and the abandonment of immovable things. What made for a valid title for acquisition by usucaption was a matter of controversy among the Roman jurists (Ulpian, D. 41.3.27). Finally, one thing clearly required was continuous and uninterrupted possession. If, however, the possessor died before the minimum period of possession required for usucaption, his heir could take advantage of the time elapsed during the life of his predecessor. The requirements of usucaption were summarized in the following medieval hexameter: *res habilis titulusque fides, possessio, tempus* (an object capable of private ownership and title, good faith, possession, and time).

Longi temporis praescriptio

This was an institution similar to usucaption and originated in the Eastern provinces to resolve questions surrounding the acquisition of provincial land, which could not be owned by Roman citizens. Originally, the praescriptio was a sort of defense, similar to the exception in the formulary procedure, i.e., a remedy to protect a person who possessed provincial land for at least ten years if both plaintiff and defendant lived in the same village (under Justinian, in the same province); or for a person who possessed the land for twenty, if the plaintiff and defendant lived in different villages (P.S. 5.2.3; C.J. 7.33.9.12). Subsequently, this protection was extended to cases involving movable items possessed by peregrines (foreigners) until the category of peregrines disappeared after the enactment of the Edict of Caracalla (212 CE). In order to be protected, the defendant had to have a valid title and good-faith possession at the beginning.

The longi temporis praescriptio evolved gradually from a form of extinctive prescription, i.e., one where the claim against the possessor was made permanently unenforceable, to a form of acquisitive prescription, like usucaption, by which the possessor could acquire ownership. Justinian (C.J. 7.31 of 531) consolidated the usucaption and the provincial prescription into one; however, he reserved the term usucaption for the acquisition of movable things (now through possession for three years) and used the term longi temporis praescriptio or similar expressions for the acquisition of land.

Rei vindicatio

The rei vindicatio was a real action (*actio in rem*) founded on civil law by means of which the owner of an item, who lost possession of it, sued the possessor for recovery. The plaintiff usually requested this remedy of rei vindicatio after losing in an interdictal procedure against the possessor protected by possessory interdicts. Under Justinian's law, however, the civil owner could bring action not only against the possessor protected by possessory interdicts but also against so-called fictitious possessors, that is, those who had fraudulently given up possession to prevent the rei vindicatio.

Proving ownership was very often a difficult task for the plaintiff. If the plaintiff had received the thing from another person, he had to prove that his predecessor was also the owner when he transferred that thing to him. But in order to prove the validity of this transfer of property, he also had to prove that the *previous* transferor was also the owner. This could lead to an endless series of impossible proofs of ownership, which the medieval jurists humorously called Devil's proof (*probatio diabolica*). The institution of usucaption lightened the owner's burden of proof. Gaius made a clear statement about this point (D. 6.1.24): "Anyone who has decided to sue for a thing ought to consider whether he can obtain possession by some interdict. For it is much more convenient to be in possession himself and put the burden of being plaintiff on his adversary than for him to sue with his adversary in possession."

The formula for an action rei vindicatio was the following: "Let Titius be judge. If it appears that the slave Nicia that is at issue belongs to Aulus Agerius at civil law, and the slave has not been restored to Aulus Agerius according to the opinion of the judge, whatever the slave's value shall be, you, judge, condemn Numerius Negidius to pay XXX sesterces to Aulus Agerius; if it does not appear so, let him be absolved." According to the formula, the purpose of the action was twofold. On the one hand, it served to determine ownership of the thing at issue. On the other hand, it served to compel the defendant to return the possession of the thing to the plaintiff, once the latter had proven his ownership, or to pay its value according to the plaintiff's estimation.

If the defendant refused to defend his claim in court, the praetor simply handed the item in question over to the plaintiff. The defeated defendant then had to return property with all the fruits and accessories which came into existence after the joinder of the issue (*litis contestatio*), but not with those that had existed before. The defendant would also be liable for intentional damages caused to the thing before the joinder of the issue as well as for intentional and negligent damages caused to the property after joinder. Roman law allowed possessors in good faith (but generally not possessors in bad faith) to seek compensation for improvements and reimbursement for expenses.

Interdictum quem fundum and *actio ad exhibendum*

Two complementary remedies served as a preparation of the action for recovery of property (rei vindicatio). The praetor protected the person who wished to recover an immovable thing with an *interdictum quem fundum*, a special interdict against the possessor of a piece of land who declined to defend against the rei vindicatio. The action *ad exhibendum* was correlative to the interdict but in the context of movable things. The purpose of the action was to force the defendant who refused to cooperate in the recovery procedure to show the praetor the item in dispute, which the plaintiff might take into his possession with the permission of the magistrate. The action lay against any kinds of possessors, including those who gave up possession simply to avoid the rei vindicatio. Sometimes, therefore, the action ad exhibendum was not only a preliminary action but a substitute for the rei vindicatio; sometimes, however, the action served to protect other rights short of ownership.

Actio Publiciana

The Publician action was created in the first century BCE, probably in 67 BCE, by praetor Quintus Publius. It protected the acquirer of a res mancipi by way of traditio rather than the required mancipatio or in iure cessio, when he lost possession before accomplishing the required usucaption. The action contained the legal fiction that the time of usucaption had already passed, and that the plaintiff therefore had become a civil owner. The plaintiff had to prove only that he had acquired the thing under conditions required for usucaption. His good faith was presumed, although this presumption could be rebutted.

The person protected by the Publician action was considered to be a praetorian or bonitary owner, since he was completely protected by the praetor not only against any holder but even against the true civil owner. If the bonitary owner was sued in a rei vindicatio action by the civil owner, the praetor protected the bonitary owner by granting the special defence that the thing had been sold and delivered to him (*exceptio rei venditae et traditae*). When the civil owner opposed the actio Publiciana by inserting in the procedural formula the defense called *exceptio iusti dominii*, the praetor protected the bonitary owner with a counter-defense called *replicatio rei venditae et traditae.* Suppose that Titius sold and delivered his horse to Caius. Later Caius lost possession when the horse made its way back to Titius's farm. Caius could sue Titius with the actio Publiciana. Titius could object that he was the civil owner pleading a defense (*exceptio iusti dominii*), but Caius might reply that Titius sold and delivered the horse to him (*exceptio rei venditae et traditae*). The defense (*exceptio*) could be adapted to similar cases (e.g., in case of donation of the horse without mancipation).

Predial servitudes or land easements

The ownership of land could be limited in favor of neighbors. Predial servitudes belonged to these so-called rights over another's property (*iura in re aliena*). They were real rights vested in a person as owner of a land (dominant land) over a neighboring land (servient land) in order to make a certain use of it. From the point of view of the neighboring servient land, servitudes constituted burdens or restrictions imposed by a private legal act, effective not only against the owner of the servient land but against all possessors of it. Although Romans never conceived of one plot of land having rights over another, servitudes were inherently predial in the sense that the owner (or sometimes the possessor) of a land could take advantage of an existing servitude as long as he maintained his condition of owner (or possessor) of the dominant land. Unlike the contractual relations which usually bound and entitled only the contracting parties, servitudes, once established, bound and entitled the existing owner or possessor, even when he had had no role in the creation of the servitude.

No servitude could force the owner of the servient property to perform some activity; it could not impose an active duty (*servitus in faciendo consitere nequit*). For instance, an obligation of the owner of the servient land to cut down some trees and furnish some wood could never be the object of servitude. The burdens imposed by servitudes had to consist of not doing something (e.g., preventing the owner of the servient land from raising a structure beyond a certain height) or of putting up with certain behavior by others (e.g., allowing the transportation of water across the land). However, the use of the servient land always had to be advantageous to the dominant property, and its use had to cause as little inconvenience as possible. Since ownership implied full rights of utilization over the owned thing, "no one can have servitude on a property of his own" (Paul, D. 8.2.26: *nulli res sus servit*). There could be two or more servitudes over the same land, but "the servitude of a servitude could not exist" (Paul, D. 33.2.1). Servitudes were perpetual and could not be created conditionally or with sunset clauses. Servitudes were also indivisible. Thus, if the dominant or servient lands, or both, were divided among common owners, the servitudes remained as one.

The main distinction among servitudes was made between rustic and urban servitudes. The distinction referred to the purpose and nature rather than the location of the servitude. Rustic servitudes served a prevailing agricultural purpose. They were considered to be res mancipi, and in the earliest regime they constituted a form of limited ownership. Later they were recognized as intangible things and thus could not be possessed. Examples of rustic servitudes were the right to cross another's land on foot or on horseback, and the right to draw water, to burn lime, and to dig sand. Urban servitudes included building rights in neighboring properties, such as rights to light, support, and a certain view, to drainage and encroachment, and so on.

Rustic and urban servitudes could be created by in iure cessio, by adiudicatio, by legacy, and in early Roman law by usucaption. In provincial land, servitudes were created by agreement (*pactiones et stipulationes*). Rustic servitudes could also be created by mancipatio. Servitudes could be extinguished by merger into a single ownership, by in iure cessio, by destruction of the landed property, or by the disappearance of their utility: e.g., the right to draw water across the servient land ceased if the stream of water permanently dried up (Paul, D. 8.3.35).

The owner of the dominant land was protected by the praetor with the *vindicatio servitutis* (later called *actio confessoria*) against the owner of the servient land who denied the existence of the servitude. The *actio negatoria* protected the owner of the servient land who denied the existence of any servitude attached to it. Many servitudes were protected by means of special interdicts.

Under the term servitude, Justinian's compilers included not only predial servitudes but also so-called personal servitudes, forming a unique legal concept. These personal servitudes include the right to use and take the fruits of another's property (*ususfructus*); the right simply to use another's property without taking its fruits (*usus*); and the right to use another's house (*habitatio*) or slaves (*operae servorum*). Classical jurists regarded the last two institutions as two different forms of usus, and usus as a limited usufruct. The personal servitude was inherently tied not to a piece of land but to the person of its holder. Classical lawyers called personal servitudes by their specific names: usufruct and use.

Usufruct

The jurist Paul defined usufruct as "the right to use and enjoy the things of another impairing their substance" (D. 7.1.1). The usufructuary, therefore, had the thing at his disposal and had the right to take the fruits without diminishing, deteriorating, or destroying it (*salva rerum substantia*). The owner of the thing, on the other hand, retained bare ownership (*nuda proprietas*), and he could dispose of the thing without violating the rights of the usufructuary. The rights of the usufructuary could be limited by the instrument of the usufruct's constitution, even by the application of a fixed term to the usufruct (Ulpian, D. 7.4.3pr.). The usufructuary was bound to promise to use the thing as an honest man and to restore it at the end of the usufruct (*cautio usufructuaria*). The owner of the thing was entitled to deny the delivery of the thing until this special promise (caution) was given to him as a guaranty.

In its origin, usufruct was basically alimentary. The main purpose of the usufruct was the desire of the owner to provide sustenance particularly to his wife and other members of the family after his death. A husband could often be reluctant to give property to his wife because, until the time of Hadrian, she could not herself make a will and so, after her own death, her property would pass to her next relative according to the intestacy rules of civil law (and not according to a will of her own design). The constitution of a usufruct provided a way to maintain a widow while assuring a good successor, usually from within one's own family.

The usufruct, although a real right (*ius in rem*), was so rigorously personal that the beneficiary could not alienate it. A transfer of the usufruct was allowable only from the usufructuary to the bare owner, for the sake of consolidating property. Another consequence of the personal character of the usufruct was its limitation to the life of the usufructuary. He could not transfer the usufruct to his heirs. The usufructuary acquired ownership of both natural and civil fruits by gathering them (*perceptio*).

Since the item in question had to be returned at the end, a usufruct could not be constituted over a fungible object, such as money or perishables. However, a decree of the Senate (*Ulpiani Regulae* 24.27; Papinian, D. 33.2.24) at the beginning of the Principate allowed the creation of a usufruct over perishables, according to which the beneficiary became the owner of the perishable goods, provided that he made a secured promise that a return of similar value would be made at the end of the usufruct. This special usufruct was called quasi-usufruct. Gaius, however, was unwilling to accept the usufructuary character of this legal invention of the Senate, since "natural reason cannot be altered by the authority of the Senate" (D. 7.5.2.1). Unlike the predial servitudes, the usufruct was divisible. There could be common ownership of the same usufruct. Although originally a usufruct could not be possessed, classical lawyers sometimes extended interdictal protection to the usufructuary. The usufructuary was protected with the *vindicatio usus fructus* (later called *actio confessoria*) against the owner or any possessor of the thing in question. The praetor also protected the usufructuary with a special interdict (*interdictum quem usum fructum*) against the possessor of a piece of land who declined to defend it against the *vindicatio usus fructus*.

The usufruct was basically constituted through a legacy. In general, the ways of constituting servitudes were also applicable to the usufruct, with some restrictions. Owing to its strictly personal character, however, the usufruct could not be acquired by acquisition of the ownership of the land linked to the usufruct, since the usufruct, unlike servitudes, was not inherently predial. The usufruct ended by the death of the holder (not, however, by the death of the owner of the land), by in iure cessio to the owner, by acquisition of the land property by the usufructuary (*consolidatio*), by the expiration of its term, and by disuse for the period prescribed for purposes of usucaption.

A limited usufruct was the usus, which was a usufruct without entitlement to the fruits (Gaius, D. 7.8.1). This exclusion was not absolute, however; over time the user was allowed to take fruits to meet his basic daily needs. The rules of acquisition, extinction, and remedies protecting the use were very similar to those of the usufruct.

Emphyteusis and *superficies*

Two further limited real rights were known in late Roman law: the long-term lease of state land (later known as *emphyteusis*), and the right to lease a building (*superficies*). Emphyteusis (in Greek, to implant) developed in Egypt and North Africa in the third century CE, and in the fifth century emperor Zenon recognized it as a specific contract, different from the sale and the lease, although having certain elements of both (C.J 4.66.1). Emphyteusis was a long-term or even in-perpetuity lease of agricultural land to an emphyteuta who had to pay a ground rent (called *canon*) to the owner. The emphyteuta was entitled to the use and enjoyment of the land, and could transfer his right to his heirs or alienate it, so long as the ground rent was paid. In case of sale, the owner had a right of preemptive purchase and was otherwise entitled to a payment equal to 2 percent of the purchase price. The emphyteuta was protected by a variant of the vindication to assert his rights. The dominus, however, remained the owner. The emphyteusis ended when rent was not paid for three years, or by agreement between the owner and the emphyteuta, or by death of the emphyteuta without heirs, or by destruction of the land.

Similar to the emphyteusis was the right to erect a building and lease it in public land against payment of a rent called *solarium*. Although the owner of the land acquired ownership of the building in accordance with the rule, "that which stands with the land goes with the land" (*superficies solo cedit*), the *superficiarius* was entitled to the use and enjoyment of the building for as long as he paid rent, and he could transfer his right to his heirs. The superficiarius was protected with a variant of the vindication as well as with a special interdict (*interdictum de superficiebus*).

Further reading

Baldus, Christian. "Possession in Roman Law." In *The Oxford Handbook of Roman Law and Society*, edited by Paul J. du Plessis, Clifford Ando, and Kaius Tuori, 537–552. Oxford: Oxford University Press, 2016.

Berger, Adolf. *Encyclopedic Dictionary of Roman Law*. Philadelphia, PA: The American Philosophical Society, 1953; reprint 1980.

Birks, Peter. "The Roman Law Concept of dominium and the Idea of Absolute Ownership." *Acta Juridica* 1 (1985): 1–38.

Birks, Peter, ed. *New Perspectives in the Roman Law of Property: Essays for Barry Nicholas*. Oxford: Clarendon Press, 1989.

Buckland, William Warwick. *A Text-Book of Roman Law*. 3rd rev. ed. Edited by Peter Stein, 180–281. Cambridge: Cambridge University Press, 1963.

Buckland, William Warwick, and Arnold D. McNair, eds. *Roman Law and Common Law*. 2nd ed. Revised by F. H. Lawson, 60–142. Cambridge: Cambridge University Press, 1952.

Capogrossi Colognesi, Luigi. *Proprietà e diritti reali*. Rome: Il Cigno Galileo Galilei, 1999.

du Plessis, Paul. "Property." In *The Cambridge Companion to Roman Law*, edited by David Johnston, 175–198. Cambridge and New York: Cambridge University Press, 2015.

Diósdi, György. *Ownership in Ancient and Preclassical Roman Law*. Budapest: Akadémiai Kiadó, 1970.

Hausmaninger, Herbert, and Richard Gamauf. *A Casebook on Roman Property Law*. Translated by George A. Sheets. Oxford and New York: Oxford University Press, 2003.

Johnston, David. *Roman Law in Context*, 53–73. Cambridge: Cambridge University Press, 1999.

Kaser, Max. *Eigentum und Besitz in älteren römischen Recht*. 2nd ed. Cologne: Böhlau, 1956.

Kaser, Max. *Das römische Privatrecht*. Volume I, *Das altrömische, das vorklassische und klassische Recht*. 2nd ed., 373–473. Munich: Beck Verlag, 1971.

Mousourakis, George. *Fundamentals of Roman Private Law*, 119–182. Berlin and Heidelberg: Springer, 2012.

Nicholas, Barry. *An Introduction to Roman Law*, 98–157. Oxford: Clarendon Press, 1975.

Rodger, Alan. *Owners and Neighbours in Roman Law*. Oxford: Clarendon Press, 1972.

Savigny, Friedrich Carl von. *Das Recht des Besitzes. Eine civilistische Abhandlung*. 6th ed. Giessen: G. F. Heyer, 1837.

Schulz, Fritz. *Classical Roman Law*, 334–454. Oxford: Clarendon Press, 1951.

Thomas, J. A. C. *Textbook of Roman Law*, 125–210. Amsterdam, New York, and Oxford: North-Holland Publishing Company, 1976.

Vacca, Letizia. *Possessio e tempo nell'acquisto della proprietà. Saggi romanistici*. Padua: CEDAM, 2012.

Waelkens, Laurent. *Amne Adverso. Roman Legal Heritage in European Culture*, 277–322. Leuven: Leuven University Press, 2015.

Watson, Alan. *The Law of Property in the Later Roman Republic*. Oxford: Clarendon Press, 1968; reprinted Aalen: Scientia Verlag, 1984.

Zulueta, Francis de. *The Institutes of Gaius. Part II. Commentary*. Oxford: Clarendon Press, 1953.

10 The law of succession

The law of succession addresses the legal destiny of a person's rights and duties after his death. Closely tied to the fundamental and peculiar features of Roman family and society, the law of succession presents vast difficulties for Roman lawyers because of its highly sophisticated nature and lack of systematic coherence. It is no coincidence that eleven out of fifty books in the Digest address the law of succession.

The development of the law of succession reflects important social changes in Roman economic structures and value systems. It echoes the progression from an old Roman agrarian society to a new commercial one. From a technical legal perspective, the law of succession reveals the tension between civil law and praetorian law. Without formally altering the civil law, the praetor introduced fundamental adjustments to protect emancipated persons, blood relatives in the female line, and surviving spouses, among others.

At the heart of the classic Roman inheritance system lay the idea that the last freely made will of a Roman citizen disposing of his property after death should prevail over any earlier will. The testament (or will) had an early and mature development in Roman law. That was probably because Romans considered it essential to make a testament before they died. According to Plutarch (*Cato* 9.6), Cato the Elder regretted only three things in his whole life: that he had entrusted a certain secret to his wife, that he had paid fare to get places by ship instead of walking when he might have walked, and that he had lived one whole day of his adult life intestate, i.e. without having made a will.

Practically speaking, the first thing to know in disposing of a deceased person's property was always whether he or she had left a valid will, because the provisions of a will would trump the principles laid down by the law of intestacy. Still, this chapter will address intestate succession first, because it is older than testamentary succession and thus provides a helpful framework for understanding the latter. We begin, however, with a few basic concepts common to both kinds of succession, to make the rest of the chapter's exposition intelligible.

Universal succession and *hereditas*

Succession (*successio*), in general, means taking the place or position previously occupied by another person. By far the most important case of succession was succession upon death, i.e., the succeeding of an heir in the legal position of the deceased, for which the Latin term was *hereditas* (inheritance).

The primitive law of succession reflected the cohesion of the patriarchal family. The father survived in his sons, who were also his heirs. The heir, therefore, perpetuated the father's personality and continued fulfilling the family duties (worship, administration of property, etc.). Roman jurists euphemistically called the deceased *de cuius*, an abbreviation of the Latin *de cuius bonis agitur* (he whose estate is concerned). This Latin expression continues to be used in many legal systems of the civil law tradition.

Succession was originally universal in the sense that it encompassed, as a unit, all the rights and duties of the deceased. Universality did not mean totality; it did not demand the appointment of just one heir. Much as the condition of son is not weakened by the fact of having siblings, the condition of heir was not diminished by the sharing of an inheritance with other heirs. The coheir, too, was universal in the sense of being entitled to a certain portion or quota of the entire estate, and not simply to particular items. Thus, according to this principle of universality, the share of a coheir increased when another coheir failed to take his share upon intestacy or under the will (*ius adscrescendi*). The later Roman jurists applied the term succession to refer also to the acquisition of individual items, e.g., by legacy or donation *mortis causa* (Ulpian, D. 39.2.24.1a). This general distinction in Roman law between universal and singular succession has prevailed in modern law.

In general, we could say that rights related to property law and the law of obligations (so-called patrimonial rights) usually survived death, but there were important exceptions. Strictly personal rights and duties were excluded: for instance, the *patria potestas* was extinguished with the death of the father. Marriage was evidently extinguished with the death of one of the spouses. Usufruct, too, as a strictly personal real right, was extinguished by the death of the usufructuary. Some contractual relations (partnership and mandate) were extinguished by the death of a party, and penal actions were extinguished by a debtor's death. Possession, as a de facto condition, passed to the heir only once he came to physically hold the thing belonging to the estate.

Types of succession

The law of the Twelve Tables recognized both intestate and testamentary succession. Testation prevailed over intestacy. However, the law of testamentary succession did sometimes limit the testator's freedom of disposal by providing for succession against the person's will. That happened, for instance, when the testator had passed in silence over a close relative neither instituted as an heir nor formally disinherited in accordance with the civil law. The two kinds of succession, testate and intestate, were mutually exclusive. "One cannot die partly testate and partly intestate" was merely the rule (Inst. 2.14.5: neque idem ex parte testatus ex parte intestatus decedere potest). That rule had many exceptions, and it has not been generally accepted in modern law.

Succession could be in accordance with civil law (civil succession), or in accordance with praetorian law (*bonorum possessio* or praetorian succession). Civil succession was determined by the Twelve Tables, statutes of the legislative assemblies, and juristic interpretations. Praetorian law, on the other hand, was basically made up of edicts in which the praetor introduced significant innovations in the interest of accommodating the law of succession to new contexts and circumstances. By granting, refusing, or adapting some remedies, the praetor mitigated the more severe principles of the civil law. Praetorian law generally promoted cognation against agnation, simplified legal formalities and constraints, and recognized the entitlement of the surviving spouse. More on each of these points below.

Heir (*heres*)

An heir was a universal successor upon death according to civil law. He succeeded to the whole legal position of the deceased and not only to the late person's individual rights of ownership (Pomponius, D. 29.2.37). The deceased could appoint several heirs, but only as to particular fractions or shares of the inheritance: e.g., "Be Titius heir to one third and Caius to two thirds." If the deceased did not specify the share of each heir, fractions were presumed to be equal. The heir inherited the rights and property of the deceased but also assumed all transmissible debts. This liability of the heir was not limited to the value of the inherited property; his liability, in principle, went beyond the estate of the deceased person (*ultra vires hereditatis*), but it was at some point and under some circumstances restricted (*intra vires hereditatis*). As a son cannot stop being a son, an heir could not be appointed for a limited period of time. This was the meaning of the rule: "Once an heir, always an heir" (*semel heres, semper heres*). This rule implied that the heir could neither make another person heir in his place nor appoint successive heirs, thus creating a successive interest in the inheritance. The provision "Be my heir my wife Titia and after her death my children" was invalid under Roman law. Usufruct and hereditary trust (*fideicommissum hereditatis*) were the legal institutions used to create outcomes of this sort.

Types of heirs

A man's heirs *par excellence* were his intrinsic or family heirs (*heredes sui*) – those persons, male or female, who would be under the power of the father (*paterfamilias*) if he were still alive. Family heirs were a man's children (including adoptive and posthumous), grandchildren whose fathers had predeceased them, and his widow, if she remained under his marital power. Family heirs succeeded automatically, without a voluntary act of acceptance, upon the death of the paterfamilias or, in accordance with the *lex Papia*

Poppaea (9 CE), at the moment of the opening of his will. They had no power of refusal because, to a large degree, they were owners of the family estate when the father was alive, and under Roman law the continuity of the family prevailed over individual interests. In this sense, family heirs were necessary heirs. Also a necessary heir, though not a family heir, was the testator's slave set free by the will and instituted as an heir under it. He, too, became heir automatically upon the opening of the will and had no power of refusal.

The praetor could allow family heirs to escape an insolvent inheritance and all kinds of hereditary liabilities by keeping their hands off the hereditary estate (*ius abstinendi*). In such cases, the inheritance was sold in the name of the deceased and not in the name of the heirs. In spite of their abstention, however, family heirs technically remained heirs. In the case of an insolvent inheritance, the praetor could also restrict the liability of the slave manumitted and appointed necessary heir by will, to the limit of whatever the slave had received or might later receive from the estate – thus shielding any property the slave had acquired from other sources.

All other heirs who were not family heirs were called extraneous or external heirs (*extranei heredes*) because they usually were not members of the testator's household. Unlike the family heir, the succession of the extraneous or external heir was neither automatic nor immediate. Heirs of this sort had the choice of accepting or refusing the inheritance, and they did not technically become heirs until they had declared their decision to enter on the inheritance (*aditio hereditatis*). In this sense, they were called voluntary or free heirs (*heredes voluntarii*). The external heir appointed in a will could accept the inheritance by a formal act (*cretio*) observed within one hundred days of the opening of the will. Gaius (2.166) recorded the prescribed formula: "Whereas Publius Mevius by his will has instituted me his heir, I deliberately accept and enter upon that inheritance (*adeo cernoque*)." Another way to accept the inheritance was to act as an heir, for instance, by using things belonging to the estate or paying the debts of the deceased (*pro herede gestio*). According to Justinian's law, if the external heir made an inventory of the inheritance, he would not be liable for the debts attaching to the estate or to the claims of legatees beyond the assets (*beneficium inventarii*).

Finally, in accordance with the kind of succession at issue, an heir could be testamentary, intestate, or compulsory. Testamentary heirs were those who inherited by testamentary appointment; intestate heirs were entitled by law to inherit from the estate of someone who had failed to leave a valid will; and compulsory heirs were those who were entitled by the law to inherit against a will that did not benefit them.

Hereditas iacens

If a person had neither family heirs nor necessary heirs, there would be an interval between the decedent's death and the entry of the external heir. During this period, of course, the estate could not simply be static: slaves belonging to the estate continued their activities, animals had to be fed, and so on. For this reason, Roman jurists considered this period of the estate a legal entity in its own right, as a sort of personification of the inheritance. The inheritance as such was able to contract, settle debts, and incur liabilities. Celsus said that if a slave who was part of an unclaimed inheritance was killed, the estate was deemed to be the owner of that slave (Celsus-Ulpian, D. 9.2.13.2). A curator of the estate might be appointed for particular cases when the instituted heirs were still deciding whether to accept (Ulpian D. 27.10.3).

During this period of *hereditas iacens*, things to be inherited were considered *res nullius* (nobody's property). Thus, theft of the physical objects of an estate was technically not possible, and a special usucaption called *usucapio pro herede* was allowed under early civil law, accelerating the process of acceptance of the inheritance and forcing heirs to make their decision (Gaius 2.52). According to this special usucaption, both movable and immovable objects of an estate could be acquired within one year by the usucaptor, even without title or good faith. This practice was ultimately forbidden by a senatorial resolution in Hadrian's era.

Bonorum possessio

To correct the old civil law of succession on several points and to protect it with new remedies, the praetor established a parallel system of succession called *bonorum possessio*, or an authorization by the praetor to take possession of the property of the deceased. Although the praetor could not appoint a civil heir (Gaius 3.32: *praetor heredes facere non potest*), the position of the possessor of the estate was very similar to that of the civil heir.

The praetor granted the possession of the deceased person's estate to claimants who were not necessarily civil heirs, and in a different order from that dictated by civil law. Indeed, sometimes possession of the estate was granted to someone who was also civil heir, so that he could enjoy praetorian remedies, and sometimes possession was granted in disregard of a civil law claim. Possession granted by the praetor provided a valid title for usucaption.

The grant of the bonorum possessio could be fully effective and permanent (*cum re*), or partially effective and temporary (*sine re*). This authorization was effective and permanent when the possessor of the estate retained possession even against claims by the civil heir; for instance, when the praetor gave possession of the estate to the emancipated son of the deceased. The position of the possessor in this case was similar to that of the "bonitary owner." On the other hand, the possession of the estate could also be granted only temporarily, and without the full range of legal protections – in particular, without protection against any claims by civil heirs. That would happen, for instance, when the praetor granted possession of the estate to someone in the belief that the deceased had made no will, and a will later emerged: in that case, the civil heir's claims would prevail over those of the possessor of the estate.

The possession of the estate could be granted by the praetor upon intestacy (*sine tabulis*), i.e., when there was no will; in accordance with the will, i.e., to the heir appointed in a testament (*secundum tabulas*); or despite the will (*contra tabulas*), i.e., to a different person than the one appointed in the testament. The details of each case will be explained below.

Intestate succession

The Twelve Tables (5.4–5) laid down the order of intestate succession, which reflected the structure of early Roman society: "If someone dies intestate and without family heirs (*heredes sui*), the nearest agnate shall have the property. If there is no agnate, the member of the family clan (*gens*) shall have the family property."

Although the Twelve Tables did not expressly mention it, family heirs succeeded in accordance with the principle of representation (*in stirpes*), which meant that the grandchildren represented the son when he was no longer alive or had lost the condition of family heir – for instance, in case the son had been emancipated by the deceased. Suppose that at the death of Titius, the following relatives were still alive: his brothers Tiberius and Sextus, his son Caius, his daughter Marca, and two sons of his deceased daughter Publia named Sempronius and Lucius. The heirs would be Caius, Marca, Sempronius and Lucius. Caius and Marca would take one-third each; and Sempronius and Lucius, one-sixth each.

If there were no family heirs, the inheritance fell to the nearest agnate in degree, to the exclusion of the other agnates. The nearest agnate was the closest collateral relative in the male line, i.e., from a common male ancestor (brothers, uncle, and nephew). Since women had no children under their power, and therefore no family heirs, the nearest agnate actually had the first claim in the case of female intestate succession. Illegitimate children had no agnatic relatives since they were not under the paternal power. The nearest agnate did not become heir automatically, but only after accepting the inheritance. Among agnates, the principle of representation did not apply, and agnates of the same degree took equal shares of the estate. In the case of the succession of a freedman without family heirs, the place of the agnate was taken by the patron (Gaius 3.40), because the freedman had no agnatic family.

Suppose that at the death of Titius, the following relatives were alive: his sister Publia, who was under marital power; two children of Publia under their father's *patria potestas*; Caia, daughter of a deceased brother of Titius; Tiberius, son of another deceased brother; and Manius, a cousin of Titius. The heirs would be Caia and Tiberius, because they would be the nearest agnates (niece and nephew, respectively). However, the *lex Voconia* (169 BCE) or its interpreters seem to have limited the inheritance rights of female relatives, allowing only the sisters of the deceased to inherit. Thus, after the enactment of this statute, the only heir in our example would be Tiberius, the nephew of the deceased. Although the freedman could have children, he could have no other relatives and therefore had no agnatic family. Thus, in the absence of family heirs, the inheritance of the freedman fell to the patron and the patron's agnatic descendants.

If there was neither a family heir (*heres suus*) nor an agnate, the Twelve Tables gave the estate to the family clan. We do not know exactly what that meant, but it probably implied that each member of the clan could take possession of the estate if no heir with a better claim had already done so.

Praetorian intestate succession

To correct the deficiencies of the old civil intestate succession system, the praetor introduced several edicts, by means of which he offered possession of the estate to different members of a class within a certain time frame. If that window of time had passed, members of the next class could apply for a grant of possession. There were four classes. The first class, *liberi,* consisted of the children of the intestate man, including the family heirs, but also emancipated children as well as children who had been given in adoption and later emancipated by the adoptive father. The principle of representation was applied, and the possessor of the estate was permanent (cum re) and effectively protected against any other potential heir.

The second class, *legitimi*, consisted of the civil heirs, i.e., those who could inherit in accordance with the Twelve Tables: the praetor offered the estate to the family heirs again, as well as to the agnates. The patron and his descendants in the male line were also called in the case of succession of a freedman who died without family heirs.

In the absence of members of the above-mentioned groups, the praetor offered the possession of the estate to the blood-relatives of the deceased (*cognati*) up to the sixth degree. This group of cognati included children in an adoptive family with respect to the estate of their biological parents, and female agnates beyond the degree of sisters (Gaius 3.29–31). The relation between mother and child was recognized in this group. Illegitimate children were not regarded as blood relatives of the father, but they were considered blood relatives of the mother. In the case of freedmen, blood relatives were taken into consideration only when the family relationship had been created after manumission.

In the final class, *vir et uxor*, the praetor offered the estate to the surviving spouse. If the wife was under marital power (*in manu*), she was considered a family heir of her husband; if she was not under marital power, she would be a family heir of her father.

During the Principate, two important senatorial resolutions improved the rights of succession between mother and children, both legitimate and illegitimate. The so-called *senatus consultum Tertullianum*, passed during the reign of Hadrian, granted a mother with three children (*ius liberorum*) a right of intestacy succession to her children's inheritance, along with the other agnates (after the proper heirs of a male child and the child's father, and brothers of the whole blood). The sisters and the mother forms one class. On the other hand, the so-called *senatuus consultum Orficianum* (178 CE) established that when a mother died intestate, her children would be the first to succeed her. Later legislation extended the right to grandchildren.

Collatio emancipati

The new praetorian order of succession incorporating emancipated children sometimes resulted in clear unfairness against the family heirs, who were not able to create their own estate. Suppose that Titius died leaving two sons, Caius and Sempronius. Caius remained under the paternal power until Titius's death, while Sempronius had been emancipated ten years before his father's death. Had Sempronius continued under the paternal power, as Caius did, all of Sempronius's acquisitions would have become part of the inheritance, since all things purchased by a son under parental power belonged automatically to the father.

The praetor remedied this injustice with a new edict in which he denied possession of the estate to those emancipated children who did not promise to share their own property with the other family heirs. Emancipated children thus could either receive a diminished share of the inheritance or make some payments to the other possessors to compensate for the value of their own assets. Of course, if the emancipated children thought possession of the estate under these new circumstances disadvantageous for them, they could abstain from applying for a share in it.

The major reform on intestacy of Emperor Justinian

Novel 118 (543 CE) and its supplementary Novel 127 (548) introduced a major reform through rules on intestacy that still play an important role in the civil law tradition. Justinian abolished the distinctions between agnates and blood relatives, as well as between male heirs and female heirs, and created the following order of succession: (a) descendants (with representation); (b) ascendants and brothers and sisters (the principle of representation applied only to children of a deceased sibling); (c) half-brothers and half-sisters (the principle of representation applied again exclusively to children); and (d) the other collateral relatives, with no representation and no limit of degree. That Novels 118 and 127 did not specifically mention the surviving spouse was interpreted by jurists as confirmation that Justinian did not change the position of the surviving spouse. If no claims were made, the inheritance went to the treasury.

Testamentary succession

A testament or will was a legal act in which a Roman citizen declared his wishes for after his death (see Modestinus, D. 28.1.1). The will served to appoint a respectable heir who would provide continuity to the family and, in some sense, to the personality of the deceased. Wills were also used to give unequal portions to different family heirs (basically, to different children), to pay debts to creditors, and to reward loyal relatives, friends, and servants. In general, Roman law gave the testator a high degree of freedom.

A will could contain important dispositions, such as legacies and other bequests, appointments of tutors, and manumission of slaves. But the "source and foundation" of the Roman will was its institution of an heir (Gaius 2.229). The appointment of one or several heirs was the only essential feature of a will. Without such an appointment, there was no valid will. Likewise, if no appointed heir or heirs accepted the inheritance, the whole testament failed.

The testament was essentially revocable, but nobody could leave two valid testaments. If two had been written, the later will prevailed over the earlier one, even when they were compatible. A subsequent testament always invalidated or "broke" the previous one (*testamentum ruptum*). The provisions of the will referred to the time of the testator's death and could be affected by the testator's acquisitions after making his will or by other circumstances (e.g., the birth of a new son or the death of an heir or coheir). Roman jurists developed a general disposition to do their best to preserve the validity and efficacy of a testament to protect a testator's last will (*favor testamenti*).

Forms of testaments

Originally, there were two forms of testament (Gaius 2.101). A will could be made either at assemblies of the Roman people (*comitia calata*), which were held twice a year for the purpose of making wills; or when war was imminent, before going into battle (*in procinctu*). According to Gaius (2.102), a third form (*per aes et libram*) was later developed to provide an easy way to make a will in case of imminent death. This new form consisted of a conveyance to a trustee. The testator, by means of a mancipation, transferred all of his property to a purchaser of the family estate (*familae emptor*) with instructions on how to distribute the inheritance after his death. The mancipatory ceremony required the presence of the transferor, the purchaser, five witnesses, and someone holding a scale.

In classical Roman law, only the mancipatory testament remained, but with some changes: first, it became a common practice to provide a written document with the testamentary instructions; second, the trustee and the scale-holder were considered additional witnesses; third, the document containing the instructions had to be sealed by seven witnesses (including the scale-holder and the trustee) who did not know the content of the testator's will. The document did not have to be signed or sealed by the testator himself, and it could have been drafted by someone other than the testator.

Over time, the praetor simplified the formalities and began to accept as a valid testament a written document sealed by seven witnesses, even without the ritual of the mancipation. The praetor granted the possession of the estate to any person appointed as heir in such a will. When a will that was valid according to civil law was followed by a testament valid according to praetorian law, the former was not technically broken (*testamentum ruptum*). The praetor simply granted definitively (*cum re*) the possession of the estate in accordance with the praetorian testament. The content of the testament was usually written down not by the testator himself but by a scribe or notary. The signature of the scribe was followed by the testator's subscription, which confirmed the content of the will and prevented the document from spurious additions, and the signatures of the witnesses.

Particular provisions regarding military wills were introduced beginning with Julius Caesar (Ulpian, D. 29.1.1pr.) to exempt soldiers from relevant testamentary formalities. Thus, military wills were considered valid even if they were not sealed by seven witnesses and did not appoint any heirs. They also did not need to be written in Latin, and the rule of exclusion of successions (between testate and intestate) was not applied. The last desires of a loyal fallen soldier were enforceable and had to be executed, even when these soldiers, in the poetic words of an imperial constitution of Constantine, "had written their intentions on the scabbards of their swords, or on their shields, with the crimson letters of their own blood, or had traced them in the dust with the points of their swords, at the time when they were dying in battle" (C.J. 6.21.15 of 337).

Different from the testament was the codicil, a written document that added to or supplemented an existing will. Codicils were free from the formalities relevant to wills, e.g., the seal of seven witnesses. An heir could not be appointed in a codicil, but a codicil could specify the name of an heir appointed generically in a will – e.g., if the will had stated that "the person whom I will make heir in my codicil shall be heir" (see Papinian, D. 28.5.78 [77]). In general, if the codicil was expressly confirmed and incorporated by the will, it could contain any provisions that a testament could contain: legacies, manumissions, appointments of tutors, and so on. Without confirmation in a will, a codicil could only create trusts (Gaius 2.270 a).

In 2015, Maria Novak published an excellent collection of papyri or wax tablets containing original or copies of preserved wills in Greek and Latin, accompanied with English translations, from the Hellenistic period until the end of Roman rule in the seventh century (see bibliography). Most of the documents were discovered in Egypt.

Testamentary capacity

Any Roman citizen who was above the age of puberty, independent (*sui iuris*), and mentally healthy, generally had the capacity to make a will (active *testamenti factio*). Since Romans under parental power owned nothing, however, they were not able to compose a testament. Some Latins with a right to commerce could, and noncitizens could make a will according to the law of their home country. From the time of Emperor Hadrian, women were allowed to make a will without restrictions, but if they were under guardianship, the consent of their tutors was required (Gaius 1.115a; 2.112–113; *Epitome Ulpiani* 20.15). Wills made by lunatics (except during an interval of lucidity) and spendthrifts were invalid.

Legal capacity to inherit under a will (passive *testamenti factio*) was more general. Only Roman citizens could be appointed heirs in the will of a Roman citizen. Romans under parental power or curatorship or below the age of puberty could accept or reject an inheritance with the consent of their father, curator, or tutor, respectively. As mentioned above, the testator's own slave could be appointed heir if he was freed under the same will. Persons of whose individuality the testator had no clear idea (uncertain persons) could not be appointed heirs (e.g., "the person who comes first to my funeral"). But a will might include children yet to be born at the time it was made (*postumi sui*). All abstract beings (idols) and corporate bodies were considered uncertain persons and therefore could not be instituted as heirs. Nevertheless, some exceptions were made over time in favor of the state or municipalities as well as charities. Some persons, although validly instituted heirs, were disqualified from taking possession of the estate (*ius capiendi*). That happened, for instance, with unmarried persons, males over age twenty-five, and females over twenty after the Augustan reform on marriage (Gaius 2.111).

Institution of the heir

The institution of an heir (or heirs) was the main purpose of making a will (Gaius 2.229). Thus, originally, the testator had to make the appointment of the heirs first, before any other provision or indication. This rule, however, gradually admitted of many exceptions. According to the Proculians, for instance, a tutor could be appointed prior to the institution of the heir because "nothing was taken out of the inheritance" (Gaius 2.231). The institution had to be expressed in a solemn and prescribed form: "Titius shall be my heir," or "Titius, Caius, and Sempronia shall be my heirs."

If the testator did not specify portions for coheirs, their shares had to be equal. When a testator did institute heirs to specific portions of the inheritance (e.g., half for Titius, a fourth for Caius, and a fourth for Sempronia), he had to cover the whole property. If the sum of the portions did not add up to one, the will would be interpreted to distribute the remainder among the testamentary heirs. For instance, if the testator declared: "Titius and Caius shall be my heirs of my *landed* property," jurists would interpret the will to give each instituted heir one half of the whole inheritance.

All family heirs had to be mentioned in the will, either to be instituted as heirs or to be expressly disinherited. Sons and posthumous children of both genders could be disinherited only by name (*nominatim*). But other family heirs (a wife under marital power, daughters, and grandchildren) could be disinherited by a general provision, e.g., "all other family members shall be disinherited." The omission of a son or posthumous child made the will null and void. If the other family members were omitted, the testament remained valid, but the omitted members would receive a share of the inheritance despite their omission and notwithstanding other provisions of the will. Consequently, the praetor would grant possession of the estate without will (*bonorum posssessio sine tabulis*) to the omitted sons and posthumous children, and possession of the estate against the will (*bonorum possessio contra tabulas*) to the other family heirs.

An heir could be appointed conditionally, i.e., depending on an event both future and uncertain: e.g., "Titius shall be my heir if he has at least three children when I die." The condition had to be satisfied before entry into the inheritance. Conditional institutions were submitted to some limits, however. Impossible, immoral, and illegal conditions, for instance, were struck: e.g., "Titius shall be heir if he touches the sun with his right hand," or "Titius shall be heir if he commits adultery," or "Titius shall be heir if he institutes Caius as heir." Institutions limited by a future but certain event (e.g., "Caius shall be my heir until he turns twenty-five") or submitted to a resolutory or dissolving condition (e.g., "Titius shall be my heir until he is married") were also struck as conflicting with the rule of "once an heir, always an heir" (*semel heres, semper heres*). Under classical law, the following testamentary provision was also considered to be against the "semel heres" rule: "My wife Titia shall be my unique heir; after her death, my children Caius and Sempronius shall be my heirs."

Substitutions

Substitutions were a special case of conditional institutions. A common substitute (*substitutus vulgaris*) could be appointed in a will so that he could take the estate in case the primary heir did not accept the inheritance or died prior to the testator. If the instituted heir took the estate, the substitute was excluded; if not, the substitute would take the estate along with its burdens: e.g., "Titius shall be my heir. If he is not, let Caius be my heir." The substitute could have a different share of the estate, and coheirs might be substituted for each other. Quite different was the case of the so-called pupillary substitution (*substitutio pupillaris*). Children could not make a will before reaching the age of puberty. Suppose, for instance, that a father instituted his only son as an heir, and the child died after receiving the estate but without reaching the age of puberty. In that case, the inheritance would automatically go to the nearest agnate, in accordance with the rules of intestate succession. To avoid intestate succession, the father could appoint an heir for his son (*heres pupilli*). Although appointed by the father, this substitute heir of the son was not necessarily the heir of the father.

Since the son might also die before the father, a testament could include both a common substitution, appointing an heir in case the son died prior to the father, and a pupillary substitution, appointing an heir of the son if he does not reach puberty. Both appointments of substitutes could even go to the same person. So, for instance: "My son Titius shall be my heir. If my son shall not be my heir [because he dies] or shall be my heir and die before reaching puberty, let Seius be my heir" (Gaius 1.79).

Usually, the pupillary substitution was written on a separate tablet of the father's testament that would be opened only if the child died before puberty. The reason for keeping the name of the pupillary substitute secret was to avoid giving that substitute incentive to kill the child in order to inherit. Postclassical lawyers considered the pupillary substitute an heir of the father, even if the son did become his father's heir.

Following the model of pupillary substitution, Justinian introduced a special substitution for insane descendants who, by reason of their insanity, were not able to make a will. Substitutes could be appointed by any ascendant, not just by the father, and the appointment was restricted to the descendants or brothers and sisters of the insane person (Inst. 2.16.1).

The *querela inofficiosi testamenti*

Important economic and social changes at the end of the Republic changed people's understanding of the purpose of a will. The custom to institute a single heir to take over the family farm was well founded and meaningful in an agrarian society governed by agricultural interests, but not in a society focused on commerce and economic relations. The meaning of disinheritance also shifted. In an agrarian society, disinheritance was a way to avoid the division of family land and to promote continuity of family farming. But at the end of the Republic, disinheritance was regarded as a means of punishing some relatives. Consequently, wills containing disinheritance without good reasons were considered "undutiful" (*testamentum inofficiosum*), i.e., wills against the moral standards of behavior expected of Roman citizens. From the middle of the first century BCE, the centumviral court, in charge of disputes concerning inheritances, allowed some close relatives to bring complaints against undutiful and irresponsible testators' wills (*querela inofficiosi testamenti*).

The *querela* protected the testator's closest relatives against disinheritance without justification. Through the querela, these relatives – including descendants, parents (and ascendants), and siblings – asked for the will to be rescinded on the ground that the testator's mind had been disturbed when he made his will (Inst. 2.18pr.), or that it had been made without due regard for natural claims (Marcianus, D. 5.2.2). The complaint failed when the testator had left those relatives entitled to lodge the querela at least a quarter of the intestate share of the estate. This amount was probably fixed following the model of the *lex Falcidia* (40 BCE), which secured for heirs a fourth of the testator's property free of legacies. For instance, if a testator disinherited his three children, each of them would have the right to bring the querela if he or she had not received at least one-twelfth of the testator's estate.

Justinian recognized the right of the closest relatives to be appointed heirs rather than simply receive a value of the estate. He provided aggrieved relatives with an action (*actio ad supplendam legitimam*) for supplementing their share when they did not receive the minimum amount (*portio legitima*). That action, however, affected neither the validity of a will nor any benefit under it. Justinian also increased the minimum amount available to these relatives to one-third of the intestate portion when the testator left up to four children, and to one-half if there were more children.

Hereditatis petitio and *interdictum quorum bonorum*

The civil heir had the *rei vindicatio* to make specific claims against possessors either in good or bad faith, as well as other ordinary actions to enforce contracts and obligations attending the estate. However, when the civil heir, either testamentary or intestate, wanted to claim the whole estate (or his share) against a possessor who contested his status as a true heir, the heir had to bring a *hereditatis petitio*. This was an action *in rem*, based on civil law, similar in many ways to the rei vindicatio. Just as the plaintiff of the rei vindicatio had to prove his status as owner, so the plaintiff of the hereditatis petitio had to prove his status as civil heir.

Since the hereditatis petitio was not available to the praetorian possessor of the estate if he was not also a civil heir, the praetor granted him the interdict *quorum bonorum* against anyone who held things belonging to the inheritance. The evidentiary advantages of the interdict were so significant that even civil heirs used to seek praetorian possession of the estate in order to avoid having to prove their status as heirs. On the other hand, the disadvantages were also obvious: the interdict could be used only to demand physical objects of the estate, and only against someone claiming to possess the estate as heir – not against the possessor who claimed to have bought the thing in question.

Legacies

A legacy was a gift of certain specific items from the testator to the legatee at the expense of the heir or heirs. In his *Institutes*, Florentinus defined a legacy (*legatum*) as "a deduction from the inheritance by which a testator wishes something to be transferred to somebody out of the total that would belong to the heir" (D. 30.116pr.). By legacy, the testator could transfer his own property and rights arising from claims, could create a usufruct or a dowry, and could release persons from debts, among other legal acts. Civil law allowed testators to give a share of their estate as a legacy (*legatum partitionis*). Even in this case, the legatee was not considered a universal successor, because he did not represent the deceased, could not sue or be sued as heir, and was not liable, like the heir, for debts of the estate. Legacies always had to be for the benefit of the legatee and not simply for the purpose of constraining the heir to do or not do something. Gaius (2.235) offers the following example of an invalid legacy whose purpose was to control the heir: "If my heir gives his daughter in marriage to Titius, let him pay Seius ten thousand sesterces." Legacies were revocable by the testator.

In early Roman law, a legacy could be bequeathed only in a valid testament after the appointment of an heir. Later, legacies could be made in a codicil confirmed by a will (Gaius 2.270a). Justinian allowed legacies even in unconfirmed codicils. The rules dictating who could be a beneficiary were similar to the rules of testamentary capacity. The *lex Voconia*, however, limited the testamentary capacity of women and was not applied to legacies. An heir could receive, in addition to his share in the estate, a specific thing as a legacy. Like the institution of heirs, legacies could be submitted to conditions and terms (*dies*). In order to protect heirs against an excessive charge of legacies on an estate, the *lex Falcidia* (40 BCE) provided that when legacies exceeded three-quarters of an estate, they were cut back proportionally.

Types of legacies

The two basic forms of legacy were the legacy *per vindicationem* and the legacy *per damnationem*. The first was a particular disposition with the following formal words (or similar phrasing: Gaius 2.193): "I give (*do*) and bequeath (*lego*) to Titius." The scope of this legacy was confined to things that could be vindicated: land, usufruct, predial servitudes, slaves, and specific physical things, among others. Only civil property belonging to the testator both at the time of the making of his will and at the time of his death could be bequeathed by vindication. In the case of fungible things, however (e.g., wine, oil, corn), jurists considered it sufficient if the property belonged to the testator at the time of his death (Gaius 2.196). The legacy: "I give and bequeath to Titius wine, oil, and corn in my storehouse" was valid, but the legacy of a slave still not usucapted at the time of the making of the will would be void. Ownership of the property left by legacy per vindicationem transferred from the testator to the legatee without need for any act of transfer by the heir. This explained why the legatee could claim his ownership by bringing the rei vindicatio directly against the heir or any other possessor, without any requirement for the heir to do something.

More common, general, and flexible than the legacy per vindicationem was the legacy *per damnationem*, by means of which the testator charged an obligation upon the heir. The solemn form of this legacy was, "Be my heir under a charge to give" (*heres meus dare damnas esto*). Anything that could be left by legacy per vindicationem could be bequeathed by legacy per damnationem, but the legacy per damnationem covered more: since the testator did not need to be the civil owner of the object of the legacy, the testator could make a legacy of something belonging to someone else, or of a future thing. He could even charge the legatee with the performance of a concrete act. "Be my heir Titius under the charge to build a house for my legatee Caius close to my farm and to give him all the animals born in my farm in the three years following my death"; or "Be my heir Titius under the charge of paying off all the debts of the legatee." The legatee could bring an action, called *actio ex testamento*, against the heir for the legacy or its value.

Mistakes in form made the legacy null and void at civil law. The formalities required for legacies, however, were attenuated after the enactment of a senatorial decree under the reign of Nero. The rule derived from it was that if a legacy was articulated in the wrong form, it should be construed as if it had been expressed in the most adequate form necessary for its validity. In post-classical law, the importance of words was relaxed. Justinian submitted all legacies to the same rules and remedies (C.J. 6.37.21).

Acquisition of legacies

A matter of some dispute among Roman jurists was when, exactly, the legatee acquired ownership over the legacy. The idea that ultimately prevailed was that it occurred upon the heir's entry into the inheritance, which, as mentioned above, occurred at the moment of the testator's death (or at the opening of the will) in case of family heirs, and at the moment of acceptance (*aditio hereditatis*) in case of external heirs. The nonclassical Latin term to refer to this moment of acquisition was *dies veniens.* Since a certain period of time could pass before the external heir accepted the estate, an expectation transmissible to his own heirs was acquired by the legatee the very day of the testator's death. Under the aforementioned *lex Papia Poppaea* (9 CE), this expectancy was delayed until the day on which the will was officially opened, but Justinian restored the original rule (C.J. 6.51.1). The nonclassical term to refer to this moment in which the legacy began to be transmissible was *dies cedens.* Obviously, the dies cedens and the dies veniens coincided in the case of family heirs or necessary heirs. If the legatee died before the testator, or before the opening of the will (dies cedens), the legacy was not transmitted to his heirs.

In the case of a legacy by vindication, following the prevailing opinion of the Sabinians, the legatee became owner automatically on the dies veniens. But if the legatee refused the legacy, jurists considered the legacy never to have been acquired by the legatee. In the case of a legacy per damnationem, the legatee became creditor on the dies veniens. If the legacy was submitted to a condition, the dies cedens was delayed until the fulfillment of the condition. In the legacy of usufruct, since the usufruct was nontransferable, the dies cedens occurred only upon entry by the heirs. Casuistry abounded.

The possessor of the estate was protected by the praetor with a special interdict, called *quod legatorum*, against the legatee who took possession of his legacy inopportunely and without the possessor's consent. During the proceeding, however, the possessor of the estate had to give security for the restoration of the legacy in case the legatee proved to be chargeable.

Fideicommissum

Fideicommissum, or trust, was an informal request made by the deceased to an heir or other beneficiary of his estate (e.g., a legatee or a recipient of a donation *mortis causa*) in favor of a third party (*fideicommissarius*). The trust might be left not only in a will but in any kind of codicil, even orally. Thus, not only testamentary heirs but also intestate heirs could be charged with a trust. Fideicommissa made possible the distribution of all the estate without the making of a will.

Fideicommissa constituted an alternative to legacies from the beginning of the Principate. There were many reasons for their introduction. No legal formality limited either the creation or the revocation of fideicommissa. They could benefit those who were unable to become heirs or legatees because of legal incapacity, or those who tried to avoid the Augustan marriage legislation. On the other hand, fideicommissa benefitted from the procedural advantages of the extraordinary cognition.

The object of a fideicommissum could be virtually anything, including the whole estate or a portion of it (the so-called *fideicommissum hereditatis*). In such cases, the fideicommissarius became successor to the whole inheritance or cosuccessor with the fiduciary heir. The fideicommissum hereditatis had obvious disadvantages for the heir. He could remain as a simple intermediary between the deceased and the fideicommissarius with the additional burden of being liable to the creditors of the deceased. In this situation, the acceptance of the inheritance by the heir was at risk. A resolution of the Senate, the *senatus consultum Trebelianum* (ca. 56 CE) placed the fideicommissarius in the position of an heir. The fideicommissarius would be responsible for the liabilities of the estate proportionally to his share of the estate. Moreover, all the actions in favor of or against the heir could now be granted by the praetor in favor of or against the fideicommissarius (Gaius 2.253). A second senatorial resolution, the *senatus consultum Pegasianum* (c. 73 CE) extended the restriction of the *lex Falcidia* to the fideicommissa. As a result, the heir could keep a quarter of the estate free of fideicommissa. Conversely, the fideicommissarius could compel the heir to accept the inheritance. Under Justinian, legacies and fideicommissa were fused (C.J. 6.43.2.1). The new system was closer to the flexibility of the fideicommissa than to the formalities of the classic legacies.

Further reading

Amelotti, Mario. *Il testamento romano*. Florence: Le Monnier, 1966.

Berger, Adolf. *Encyclopedic Dictionary of Roman Law*. Philadelphia, PA: The American Philosophical Society, 1953; reprint 1980.

Biondi, Biondo. *Successione testamentaria e donazioni*. 2nd ed. Milan: Giuffrè, 1955.

Buckland, William Warwick. *A Text-Book of Roman Law*. 3rd ed. Revised by Peter Stein, 282–404. Cambridge: Cambridge University Press, 1963.

Buckland, William Warwick, and Arnold D. McNair. *Roman Law and Common Law*. 2nd ed. Revised by F. H. Lawson, 143–192. Cambridge: Cambridge University Press, 1952.

Caseau, Béatrice and Sabine R. Huebner, eds. *Inheritance, Law, and Religions in the Ancient and Mediaeval Worlds*. Paris: Collège de France-CNRS, 2014.

Champlin, Edward. *Final Judgments: Duty and Emotion in Roman Wills, 200 B.C.–A. D. 250*. Berkeley: University of California Press, 1991.

Finnazi, Giovanni. *La sostituzione pupillare.* Naples: Jovene, 1997.

Frier, Bruce W., and Thomas A. J. McGinn. *A Casebook on Roman Family Law.* Oxford: Oxford University Press, 2001.

González Roldán, Yuri. *Il diritto ereditario in età adrianea: legislazione imperiale e senatus consulta.* Bari: Cacucci, 2014.

Grosso, Giuseppe. *I legati nel diritto romano.* 2nd ed. Turin: G. Giappichelli, 1962.

Johnston, David. *The Roman Law of Trusts.* Oxford: Clarendon Press, 1988.

Johnston, David. "Succession." In *The Cambridge Companion to Roman Law*, edited by David Johnston, 199–212. Cambridge and New York: Cambridge University Press, 2015.

Kaser, Max. *Das römische Privatrecht.* Vol. I, *Das altrömische, das vorklassische und klassische Recht*, 668–765. 2nd ed. Munich: Beck Verlag, 1971.

Mouritsen, Henrik. *The Freedman in the Roman World.* Cambridge: Cambridge University Press, 2011.

Mousourakis, George. *Fundamentals of Roman Private Law*, 279–308. Berlin, Heidelberg: Springer, 2012.

Müller-Ehlen, Martina. *Hereditatis petitio.* Cologne, Weimar, and Vienna: Böhlau Verlag, 1998.

Novak, Maria. *Wills in the Roman Empire: A Documentary Approach.* Warsaw: University of Warsaw, 2015.

Nicholas, Barry. *An Introduction to Roman Law*, 234–270. Oxford: Clarendon Press, 1975.

Rüfner, Thomas. "Intestate Succession on Roman Law." In *Comparative Succession Law. II. Intestate Succession*, edited by Kenneth Reid, Marius de Waal, and Reinhard Zimmermann, 1–32. Oxford and New York: Oxford University Press, 2015.

Rüfner, Thomas. "Testamentary Formalities in Roman Law." In *Comparative Succession Law. I. Testamentary Formalities*, edited by Kenneth Reid, Marius de Waal, and Reinhard Zimmermann. Oxford and New York: Oxford University Press, 2011.

Scherillo, Gaetano. *Corso di dirittto romano. Il testamento.* 2 vols. Milan: La Golliardica, 1965–67.

Schulz, Fritz. *Classical Roman Law*, 203–333. Oxford: Clarendon Press, 1951.

Spina, Alessia. *Ricerche sulla successione testamentaria nei responsa di Cervidio Scevola.* Milano: Giuffrè, 2012.

Terranova, Francesca, *Richerche sul testamento per aes et libram. I. Il ruolo del familiae emptor.* Turin: G. Giappichelli Editore, 2011.

Thomas, J. A. C. *Textbook of Roman Law*, 483–526. Amsterdam, New York, and Oxford: North-Holland Publishing Company, 1976.

Voci, Pasquale. *Diritto ereditario romano.* 2 vols. 2nd ed. Milano: Giuffrè, 1963, 1967.

Waelkens, Laurent. *Amne adverso. Roman Legal Heritage in European Culture*, 257–275. Leuven: Leuven University Press, 2015.

Watson, Alan. *The Law of Succession in the Later Roman Republic.* Oxford: Clarendon Press, 1971.

Zimmermann, Reinhard. "Compulsory Heirship in Roman Law." In *Exploring the Law of Succession*, edited by Kenneth Reid, Marius de Waal, and Reinhard Zimmermann, 27–48. Edinburgh: Edinburgh University Press, 2007.

Zulueta, Francis de. *The Institutes of Gaius. Part II. Commentary.* Oxford: Clarendon Press, 1953.

11 The law of obligations I

Contracts

The law of obligations is one of the most significant contributions of Roman law to legal culture, illuminating the civil law tradition more than any other branch of Roman law. Our modern legal framework regarding the law of obligations has been unquestionably shaped by Roman concepts, rules, and institutions. The very idea of obligation and contract, the duality of contract/delict, the different categories of liability, the balance between formalities and consent, among other things – these have constituted fundamental elements of most of the legal systems in both civil and common law traditions.

The central component of the law of obligations is the contract. Roman jurists did not produce an elaborate and systematic theory of contract, as happened in modern law. Rather, Roman jurists created and developed concrete contracts, usually in a casuistic fashion. For those reasons, the meaning of contract was a matter of continuous evolution, subject to the commercial and economic progress of Roman society. There was not a single, unitary law of contract but a law of (different) contracts. Medieval European lawyers of the *ius commune*, primarily canon lawyers and late Scholastics, took the first steps toward developing a general theory of contract in the civil law tradition.

Obligation

The Latin word *obligare* (to bind) was first used by the early Roman playwright Plautus (c. 254–184 BCE) in his plays *Truculentus* (at 214) and *Bacchides* (at 748). Much later, Cicero (*Ad Brutum* 1.18.3) used the word as a noun: *obligatio*. In his *Institutes* (3.13pr.), Justinian famously defined the obligation as a "legal tie that binds us to the necessity of making some performance according to the laws of our state."

Obligation referred to both the creditor's right (and action) and the debtor's duty: it was the duty enforceable by an action *in personam*. Obligation established a legal relation between two bound persons, the creditor and the debtor. A creditor, from *credere* (to trust), is anyone to whom anything is due by a debtor for any ground (Gaius, D. 50.16.11). A debtor is anyone who has the legal duty to perform something to the benefit of the creditor and, as a result, has a potential liability. The creditor believed (*credere*) that the debtor would accomplish the act that was due, and had a personal claim against the debtor.

Paul put it well: the essence of obligation does not consist in the fact that it makes someone property, but in the fact that it binds another person to give (*dare*) or do (*facere*) or perform (*praestare*) something (D. 44.7.3pr.). *Dare* refers to the transfer of civil ownership; *facere* involves all kinds of acts as well as omissions concerning the performance of obligations; *praestare* means to be a guarantee, and it vaguely refers to any liability beyond *dare* and *facere*. The main feature of the Roman obligation was its strictly personal character. This explains why Roman law did not recognize, in general, contracts in favor of third parties, cessions of rights and actions (assignment), and direct agency.

The liberation of the debtor from his obligation by performance of what he had undertaken to do was called *solutio* in classical law. The most usual form of performance of an obligation was by payment. Payment had to be made in full, together with accessories (e.g., fruits), at the agreed upon time and place, and to the creditor or his authorized representative (e.g., tutor, mandatary, and cashier). If the obligation was divisible (e.g., a payment of money), the creditor could accept partial payments. If the obligation was indivisible (e.g., constitution of a predial servitude), only substantial performance would do. The creditor might also accept a substituted performance, such as the payment of a jar of oil instead of money (Gaius 3.168: "aliud pro alio"). The payment could be made by a third party and even without the debtor's knowledge or against his will (Inst. 3.29pr.), except when it was a strict personal obligation and it mattered who made the performance (e.g., when a singer would be hired for a party).

Delay in the performance of an obligation was called default (*mora debitoris*). In the case of wrongful default, the debtor was liable for accidental destruction of the thing involved in the obligation, and if the obligation consisted of a money debt, he was liable for interest. When the creditor refused to accept the payment (*mora creditoris*), the debtor could deposit the payment in a public place (the court or a temple), and he would be released since he had paid.

Civil, praetorian, and natural obligations

Like ownership (*dominium*) or inheritance (*hereditas*), obligation was also originally an exclusively civil-law concept. When a debtor was bound by the praetor, not by civil law, to do something, jurists used other Latin words or expressions (e.g., *actione teneri, debere, adstringere*). Classical terminology, nevertheless, was obscure, and legal language on obligations became ambiguous and equivocal, especially in the postclassical period. In his *Institutes*, for instance, Gaius said nothing about praetorian obligations. Emperor Justinian, however (Inst. 3.13.1), affirmed that the distinction between civil and praetorian obligations was the leading classification of obligations, but he did not pay attention to this distinction thereafter. In general, it can be said that civil obligations were established by statutes or at least sanctioned by civil law, and they were enforceable by civil actions. On the other hand, praetorian obligations, also called honorary, were established by a praetor's own jurisdiction and were enforceable by praetorian actions, especially actions *in factum*.

A third category of nonenforceable obligations was *natural obligations*. Originally, these were obligations contracted by individuals who were under parental, marital, or dominical power: children, women *in manu,* and slaves. They were not enforceable obligations because persons under power could not bring an action to claim them. Just as natural possession was not enforceable by action, neither was natural obligation. Nonenforceability did not imply invalidity, however; natural obligations were valid. They were legally relevant and had legal effects. The most important effect was that if a debtor fulfilled his obligation, by law he could not bring an action to take reclaim his payment (*soluti retentio*) (Julianus, D. 41.1.16.4). Additionally, natural obligations could be used to offset a claim of the debtor; they could also be transformed into a new obligation (*novatio*), and a security could be provided to ensure its fulfillment.

Sources of obligations: contracts and delicts

Probably based on the Aristotelian distinction between voluntary and involuntary activities, Gaius in his *Institutes* (3.88) introduced a primary division of the sources of obligation: all obligations arise either from contract (*ex contractu*), i.e., an enforceable agreement, or from delict (*ex delicto*), i.e., a wrongful conduct. Although the boundaries between contract and delict have been tempered by the jurisprudence of subsequent legal cultures, the distinction continues to be at the heart of both civil law and common law traditions.

A legal elaboration of the idea of contract took place in the later Republic. Servius Sulpicius used the noun *contractus* in relation to betrothal (Aulus Gellius 4.4). Labeo's attempt to restrict the concept of contract to bilateral agreements was probably isolated, but it cannot be underestimated (Ulpian-Labeo, D. 50.16.19). Labeo identified the Latin *contractus* with the Greek *synallagma* and therefore considered contractual only those obligations in which the parties were mutually obliged (*ultro citroque obligatio*). Later, the jurist Pedius (Ulpian-Pedius, D. 2.14.1.3) acknowledged that every contract is founded on an agreement: "There is no contract, there is no obligation which does not contain in itself an agreement." From Gaius's time onward, contract meant an enforceable agreement in accordance with civil law. Originally, informal nonenforceable agreements were called pacts (*pacta*), but with the recognition of some enforceable pacts, the distinction between pacts and contracts became confused and meaningless. I use the term "contract" according to Gaius's broad conception, although I am aware of its limitations: Gaius's approach was unfamiliar to classical jurists, and he was rightly considered a pre-postclassical jurist. His doctrine, however, deeply influenced Justinian's compilers and ultimately prevailed in the civil law tradition.

Different from contract was delict (in Latin *delictum* and sometimes *maleficium*). A delict was a wrongful conduct that caused harm to someone. As with contracts, the Romans did not elaborate a doctrine of delicts. Rather, they identified and regulated a series of individual delicts in both civil and praetorian law, and they protected the injured person with penal actions. Delicts were always private, unlike crimes, which were offenses punished by public criminal law. Redress of a delict had a penal character and was ordered originally by civil law. Gradually, however, the praetor established some redresses for situations not covered by civil law: the so-called praetorian delicts.

The dichotomy of contract/delict was not exclusive. Gaius (3.91) refers to a case of a payment that was not due but was made anyway – a payment that thus appeared to be founded neither on contract nor on delict. It is therefore not surprising that this famous dichotomy was partially altered by Gaius himself in his *Res cottidianae sive aurea* (D. 44.7.1pr.), a revised version of the *Institutes* attributed to him: "Obligations arise from contract, from delict, or by some provisions of law from various types of causes." This text added a residual third category of obligations that embraced those that arose without agreement or wrong (e.g., a payment of money that was not due).

Justinian's *Institutes* (3.13.2) offered a more detailed classification of the sources of obligations, basically following Gaius's order. According to Justinian's Institutes, obligations could arise from a contract (*ex contractu*), as though from a contract (*quasi ex contractu*), from a wrong (*ex maleficio*), or as though from a delict (*quasi ex maleficio*). Justinian's compilers subdivided the "various types of causes" Gaius mentioned in *Res cottidianae* into those that were closer to contracts and those that were closer to delicts. Quasi contractual obligations included the payment of money not due (*solutio indebiti*) and the management of another's affairs (*negotiorum gestio*). Their common denominator was probably the existence of some kind of business without an agreement between the parties. Examples of quasi-delictual obligations were those derived from pouring or throwing things out of buildings and from stealing or damaging property entrusted to a sea carrier, innkeeper, or stable keeper, among others. The common denominator of quasi delicts was the imposition of liability regardless of fault.

Types of contracts

Gaius (3.89) offered a fourfold classification of contracts, which Justinian followed (Inst. 13.3.2). According to Gaius, contracts were concluded by the delivery of a thing (*re*), by the uttering of formal words (*verbis*), by a documentary form (*litteris*), or by formless consent (*consensu*). Thus, based on how they were concluded, contracts could be real (e.g., a loan for consumption), verbal (e.g., a stipulation), literal (e.g., a ledger entry), or consensual (e.g., a sale).

The distinction between unilateral and bilateral contracts was also important. Unilateral contracts were those that created duties for one of the parties and, as a result, rights to the other (e.g., a stipulation or loan of money). The old Roman law was founded on unilateral obligations, probably because they constituted the most elementary type of obligations. Bilateral contracts were those that created reciprocal obligations, producing both rights and duties for each party (e.g., sale and partnership). The purpose of the bilateral obligation could not be fully achieved by means of two different interconnected unilateral contracts. For this reason, bilateral contracts constituted a masterpiece of late Republican jurisprudence.

Bilateral contracts were called *imperfect* (e.g., a mandate or deposit) when the obligations of one party were only contingent – for instance, in case of expenses or damages. Reciprocity was called *perfect* (e.g., a sale, lease, or partnership) when the obligations of both parties were inevitable. Thus, in a perfect contract it was not possible to have a sale in which the buyer had no obligation to pay or the seller no obligation to deliver, while in an imperfect contract it was possible to have a contract of deposit in which no obligation bound the depositor: e.g., if Titius gave a ring to Caius to care for but could demand its return with no expenses or damages.

Verbal contract: stipulation

The most important verbal contract was, by far, the stipulation, because of its elasticity and formal simplicity. Founded on Roman *fides*, a stipulation was an oral obligation by means of which a promisor became a debtor after answering a question formulated by the stipulator; e.g., "Do you promise to give me three hundred sesterces?" "Yes, I promise." The answer had to be completely coherent with the question and had to use the same verb as in the question: "Do you swear?" "I swear"; "Will you do?" "I will do"; "Do you pledge?" "I pledge" (Gaius 3.92). Both the stipulator and the promisor had to be present and agree at the same time and in the same place in a continuous proceeding (Venuleius, D. 45.1.137pr.). No witnesses were required.

Two or more persons could act as stipulators or promisors in one and the same stipulation. If Titius promised Caius and Sempronius to pay one hundred sesterces, both Caius and Sempronius might claim the payment from Titius, and Titius might fulfill his obligation by paying either Caius or Sempronius. On the other hand, if Caius and Sempronius promised to pay Titius one hundred sesterces, Titius might claim the payment from either one of them. The payment from either Caius or Sempronius destroyed the obligation.

The content of a stipulation had to be clear and specific, and any ambiguity would be construed against the stipulator (Ulpian, D. 45.1.38.18). The promisor could not change the terms of the contract; any addition, condition, limit, or restriction in his answer to the stipulator's question made the whole stipulation void. Because of the oral nature of the stipulation, neither a mute nor a deaf person could contract a stipulation (Ulpian, D. 45.1.1pr.).

The old form of stipulation (*sponsio*), religious in origin, was permitted only to Roman citizens and had to be made in Latin. Later, however, it was available to noncitizens. Greek and probably other languages also were accepted, for commercial reasons. The stipulation was unilateral, since only the promisor was bound; the stipulator acquired a right of bringing action. This action was the *condictio* when the object of the stipulation was the payment of a fixed amount of money or an individual thing (*res certa*). In other cases, the remedy was the action *ex stipulatu* (e.g., an action arising from Titius's promise to repair the roof of Caius's house).

The stipulation was abstract in content in the sense that if all formalities required by the stipulation were fulfilled, the debtor was obliged, without regard to the ground (*causa*) of the stipulation. In the stipulation, "Titius, do you promise to give me one thousand sesterces?" "Yes, I promise," the ground could be payment of annual rent, payment of the price of an item purchased by Titius, or making of a donation, among other things. These grounds, however, were not relevant if they were not expressly mentioned, because of the formal and abstract character of the stipulation. Sometimes, however, the praetor could grant an *exceptio doli* when the stipulation was not founded on a legal ground, or the stipulator did not act in good faith.

Stipulations could be used to create any kind of obligation in all areas of private law, including civil procedures: payments, a fine for not fulfilling a contract, constitution of a dowry, cautions, sureties, constitution of servitudes, and usufructs in provincial lands, among other things. Actually, stipulation was a contractual template or a way of contracting rather than a contract in the strictest sense. Stipulations could be expressed in a written document (*cautio*) for evidentiary purposes; however, especially after the Antonine Constitution (212 CE), the written document, in accordance with Greek practice, replaced the oral declaration, which gradually lost all significance. Emperor Leo (C.J. 8.37.10 of 472) dispensed with the old Roman oral ritual of the stipulation if the parties agreed at the same time and in the same place.

Stipulations bound only stipulators and promisors. Thus, stipulations in favor of third persons (e.g., Titius promised Caius to pay one hundred sesterces to Sempronius) were invalid unless the third person was under the power of the stipulator (Ulpian, D. 45.1.38.17). Some rationales supporting the prohibition of this kind of stipulation in favor of others can be found in the formal consistency between the question and the answer required by the stipulation, in the usual lack of an actionable interest of the stipulator to be involved in such a stipulation, and especially in the Roman reluctance to accept the validity of agreements in which third parties acquired rights.

Acceptilatio

According to the Roman rule, all obligations created by words (*verbis*) had to be released by other words (Gaius 3.170). Thus, the Roman jurists created an oral contractual form of release, called *acceptilatio*. Gaius (3.169) says that it was a sort of "imaginary payment" whose formula was as follows: "What I promised you, have you received?" "I have." Later, Greek words were also accepted. Acceptilatio could not be subject to a condition or *dies*, but a conditional stipulation could be released by acceptilatio – e.g., "Do you promise to give me one hundred sesterces if it rains tomorrow?" "I promise." Although acceptilatio served in later law as partial release (Ulpian, D. 2.15.2), in Gaius's time it was questioned (3.172).

Originally acceptilatio was restricted to verbal obligations, but the effects of acceptilatio were expanded to all kinds of obligations, both civil and praetorian, thanks to the new stipulation formulated by the Republican jurist Aquillus Gallus: the so-called *stipulatio Aquiliana*. The Aquilian stipulation could cover all kinds of debts – those arising from both civil law and praetorian law, those present and future, and those due and not yet owed. The Aquilian stipulation was essentially a general settlement of all specific debts of a particular debtor to a creditor. By means of this stipulation, whose formula has been preserved (Florentinus, D. 46.4.18.1 and Inst. 3.29.2), the parties transformed by novation all previous obligations, whatever they were, into a single verbal obligation that could be released by acceptilatio (Ulpian, D. 2.14.4). Acceptilatio could also affect property relations.

Novation

Novation implied the extinction of an existing obligation and its replacement with a new one. Ulpian (D. 46.2.1pr.) defines the novation as the "transformation and conversion of an earlier debt into another obligation, whether civil or natural." For instance, Caius could stipulate from Titius the payment of what Sempronius owes him: "Titius, do you promise to pay me whatever Sempronius owed me?" "I promise."

The old obligation could arise from any kind of contractual or testamentary obligation, while the new one had to arise from a stipulation (later also a literal contract). The new obligation had to consist of the same debt (*idem debitum*) as the previous one, but it also had to add something new (*aliquid novi*); otherwise, the new obligation would be redundant and unnecessary (e.g., if Titius promised to give Caius a concrete sculpture twice). All securities and liabilities derived from the previous obligation were destroyed. The intention of the parties to novate (*animus novandi*) and the fact that the new stipulation had to refer to the old debt linked the old and the new obligations, while the new elements justified the transformation. The new obligation could change the identity of the creditor or of the debtor, the legal ground (causa) of the obligation, or the required form, or it could introduce new conditions or a new date.

The novation often operated as a form of payment by changing the creditor. If Titius owes Caius, and Caius owes Sempronius, Caius can ask Titius to promise to pay Sempronius what Titius owes him. Thus, Caius can satisfy his debt to Sempronius by substituting Titius for himself. This novation by change of the creditor required the consent of the three parties. The novation by change of the debtor (*expromissio*), however, did not require the consent of the old debtor. Thus, Titius could promise Caius to pay him all that Sempronius owes Caius, without asking permission of Sempronius, whose debt will be extinguished by novation.

Under Justinian's law, the intention to novate (*animus novandi*) became predominant. To produce a novation, Justinian demanded that the contracting parties expressly state their intention to novate; otherwise, the previous obligation would subsist, and the second one would be added to it (C.J. 8.41.8; Inst. 3.29.3a).

Adstipulatio

One of the most important applications of stipulations was as an accessory to another obligation. This could happen when a promisor of a previous stipulation made the same promise to a new stipulator: e.g., "Do you promise me what you promised Sempronius?" "Yes, I promise." This obligation was called *adstipulatio* since an additional stipulator was added to an existing obligation. The adstipulator could stipulate for the same debt or less but never for more than the principal stipulator. The adstipulatio did not produce a novatory effect, probably because of the lack of an intention by any of the parties to novate (*animus novandi*).

Adstipulatio was mainly applied when a person wanted to assure that a payment would be made after his death. Thus, the adstipulator was like a trustee who might claim from the promisor what was owed to the principal stipulator. The adstipulator could release the promisor from his obligation by means of acceptilatio. With the rise of the contract of mandate, which could be applied with a similar purpose, and the development of some new remedies, the adstipulatio became obsolete and disappeared.

Adpromissio

Much more frequent and significant than the adstipulatio was the addition of a new promisor to an existing obligation, *adpromissio*. Adpromissio was a means to creating suretyship or personal securities by stipulation. Roman law knew three types of *adpromissiones*: the *sponsio*, the *fidepromissio*, and the *fideiussio*. These names derived from the Latin verb used in the form of the stipulation (Gaius 3.116). None of the three guarantees had novatory effect.

Sponsio was the oldest and was confined to Roman citizens. Sponsio and fidepromissio, the latter available to noncitizens, were basically subject to the same rules. Both sponsio and fidepromissio could guarantee only debts created by means of a stipulation, and in both cases the liability of the guarantor was limited to two years and not transmissible to his heirs. The full validity of the adpromissio did not depend on the effectiveness of the principal stipulation. For instance, if the promisor in the principal stipulation was a woman acting without the permission of her tutor, the woman was free from obligation, but the guarantor was not (Gaius 3.119). Originally, the principal stipulation and the adpromissio were concluded in one continuous and uninterrupted act. This requirement was abandoned in classical times, and it was even permitted to conclude the adpromissio in the absence of the principal debtor. The sponsio and fidepromissio disappeared at the beginning of the postclassical period.

The third form of surety, the fideiussio, was created at the end of the Republic or at the beginning of the Principate to improve the system of surety. Fideiussio was the only form that survived in Justinian's time. Unlike the sponsio and the fidepromissio, the fideiussio was not restricted to principal obligations that arose from stipulations, and it had no expiry date. In Justinian's time, fideiussio was supplemented with three privileges, some of them based on classical roots: (a) the surety became subsidiary in the sense that before bringing any action against the guarantors, the creditor first had to bring action against the principal debtor (*beneficium excusionis*); (b) the liability of the guarantors was limited by the debt resulting from the division of the principal debt (*beneficium divisionis*); and (c) the guarantor who had paid the principal debt could bring the same actions that the creditor could have brought against the principal and/or his guarantors (*beneficium cedendarum actionum*).

Literal contract

An entry in the cashbook of a Roman citizen created a new obligation that replaced the previous obligation from another contract. This new *literal obligation*, as Gaius called it (3.128), relieved the creditor from the burden of proving the original obligation. The mechanism of the contract, available only for money debts, is obscure. According to Gaius (3.128), there were two kinds of entries: (a) when the previous obligation between the parties was entered and thereby transformed into a new literal obligation; and (b) when the previous obligation still due was entered as discharged, and the same amount was entered as being owed by a third party who became liable for the debt of the previous debtor. The literal contract could produce the same effect as a novation by stipulation.

The conciseness of Gaius's account suggests that the literal contract had already disappeared in his time, probably because the accounting system itself became obsolete. The *Institutes* of Justinian (3.13.2) referred to it, probably to justify the creation of a new literal contract with the purpose of granting full validity of a debt derived from the mere existence of a written document.

Real contracts

The common characteristic of so-called real contracts was that the binding element arose upon the transfer of a thing (*res*). The delivery, therefore, was an essential part of the creation of the contract: delivery was neither a consequence of the contract nor a constitutive element of its performance. In other words, the agreement established by the parties became fully effective only upon delivery of the thing; without agreement and delivery (*datio*), there was no binding obligation (Paul, D. 2.14.17pr.). The obligation arising from these contracts was the restoration of the items given. Sometimes, however, the party was also liable for damages, e.g., when a depositary lost the deposited object.

The prototype of real contracts and one of the cornerstones of daily life was the loan for consumption (*mutuum*). This is the only specific real contract Gaius deals with in his *Institutes* (3.90). Justinian (Inst. 3.14), however, refers to four real contracts: the just-mentioned loan for consumption but also the loan for use (*commodatum*), the deposit (*depositum*), and the pledge (*pignus*). It is commonly thought that the four real contracts Justinian mentioned were already recognized as contracts in the classical period and that Gaius's approach was only transitional. The loan for consumption and loan for use were contracted for the benefit of the recipient; the deposit was basically in the interest of the depositor; the pledge provided advantages to two parties, but specifically it was in the interest of the creditor.

Mutuum

Probably derived from *mutare* (to change), the mutuum was the loan of consumption of money or other things normally used by being consumed (oil and corn, among others). The mutuum was a real, unilateral, and gratuitous contract. It was real because the loan could not be concluded until the lender (or creditor) had handed the money or the fungible thing over to the borrower (or debtor). A simple agreement to lend money without delivering it to the borrower did not properly constitute a mutuum but was only a pact for lending money (*pactum de mutuo dando*). The agreement between the parties was of course essential for the constitution of a mutuum, but it was not enough and remained therefore unenforceable.

The mutuum was unilateral because the only obligation was on the side of the debtor, who had to restore not the thing itself but an equivalent in quantity and quality. Therefore, the mutuum gave rise to only one action from the lender against the recipient of the loan, not vice versa. The mutuum was gratuitous because it was done free of charge, and no claim for interest could be enforced. This suggests that the simple mutuum was largely used between friends, relatives, and acquaintances.

If the lender wanted to receive any interest on capital loaned, which was standard, the parties had to enter into an additional stipulation. This stipulation could also include incidental provisions concerning the time and place of performance. The stipulation was usually made before the delivery of money; it therefore did not produce a novatory effect because novation, as mentioned above, required that the existing obligation precede the stipulation. This transaction, therefore, was actually not only real (*re*) but also formal (*verbis*). As a matter of fact, however, the stipulation seemed to absorb the mutuum (Pomponius, D. 46.2.7). Maximum interest rates were legally fixed and varied from period to period. During the late Republic and the Empire, the maximum rate was 12 percent per year.

The condictio was the personal action that the creditor could bring against the debtor when the latter did not fulfill his obligation of restoring the equivalent thing. The action was called *actio certae creditae pecunia* where the object of the loan was money, and *condictio triticaria* where other fungible things were involved. Because of the very nature of money or other fungible things, performance would not be rendered impossible if such goods were accidentally lost. The debtor therefore was responsible for his inability to return the borrowed things, even when no fault was attributable to him (*genera non pereunt*).

The Roman idea of mutuum as a verbal contract distinct from both the agreement of lending money and the stipulation of interest became precarious and problematic and was not generally accepted by modern law.

Commodatum

Commodatum involved lending for use an object that was nonconsumable. The scope of consumable things was narrower than that of fungible things. Nonfungible things are usually also consumable, but there are exceptions. For instance, cash on a table or a key to open an apartment are not consumables (they can be used many times), but they are fungibles, since they can be replaced by equivalent things. Originally, the loan for use was restricted to movables but later was expanded to include immovable things.

Like the mutuum, the commodatum was a real and gratuitous contract. Unlike the mutuum, the lender expected that the very same thing would be restored to him in the same condition and not just its equivalent in quantity and quality. In contrast to the hire (*locatio conductio rei*), the loan for use was strictly gratuitous. In contrast to precarium, a commodatum could not be revoked at will. A commodatum did not involve any transfer of ownership, and therefore the lender did not have to be the owner (e.g., a usufructuary). The borrower was not protected by the possessory interdicts, since he was not a praetorian possessor but a mere holder.

Usually, a commodatum was for the exclusive benefit of the borrower, and it therefore normally occurred between friends, relatives, or acquaintances without involving any commercial or economic interest. It was a matter of friendship, outside the province of the law. At the end of the Republic, however, the praetor granted an action *in factum* to the lender to sue the borrower for recovery (Ulpian, D. 13.6.11pr.). By the time of the codification of the Edict, the lender could choose between the old action in factum and a new one in ius (Gaius, 4.47), probably based in good faith. The borrower also might sue with the *actio contraria* against the lender for the recovery of extraordinary expenses and damages caused through the fault of the latter. For instance, if a lender knowingly lent defective containers, and the wine or oil contained in them was spoiled or spilled, the borrower could bring the actio contraria against him (Gaius, D. 13.6.18.3). This contra claim was only secondary, but it made the commodatum no longer a necessary unilateral contract, like the stipulation and the mutuum, but a bilateral one. Because of the accidental character of this bilateralism, modern lawyers consider the commodatum an imperfect bilateral contract.

Since the commodatum was in the interest of the borrower, his liability for the use of the thing was extensive, including not only fraud (*dolus*) and negligence (*culpa*) but also the so-called custody liability. Custody liability consisted of a guarantee to keep the object safe because it belonged to another person. Specifically, it referred to the liability of the borrower in case of theft. Custody did not presuppose fault and excluded damages that were beyond human capacities (*vis maior*). If the borrower used the thing improperly, however, or fell into default (*mora*), he was liable for all the risk, including damages caused by superior force (*vis maior*) or accident (*casus fortuitus*).

Depositum

The deposit was a contract by means of which a depositor handed over a movable thing to the depositary for safekeeping. The deposit is one of the more primitive legal institutions, reflecting the basic human need of entrusting valuable things to the care of another person when one cannot watch over them.

Like the commodatum, the deposit was a real, gratuitous, and imperfectly bilateral contract in which there was no transfer of ownership. Like the commodatary, the depositary was not protected by possessory interdicts but was just a holder. Unlike the commodatum, however, the depositum was concluded for the benefit and in the interest of the depositor. The depositary did not profit; he was only an unselfish and benevolent holder. He could not use the deposited thing (to do so was a theft), and he had to restore on demand the very same thing (not an equivalent) and its fruits and accessories to the depositor, even when the parties established a fixed period of deposit. Because of his lack of benefit, a depositary was liable only for fraud (dolus), not for negligence (culpa) and safekeeping (custodia). The action against the depositary was the *actio depositi* based in good faith. A contra claim against the depositor was also recognized for reimbursement of expenses and damages.

Three kinds of deposits had special rules. (1) The so-called *depositum miserabile* was a deposit made in time of fire, riots, and other calamities. Since the depositor was not able to choose the depositary, the liability of the latter increased to double the value of the thing in case of damages or fraud. (2) Sequestration was a provision in cases of dispute concerning a particular thing. The parties could hand over the thing to an impartial person until the issue had been settled (Florentinus, D. 50.16.110). The depositary (*sequester*) had to restore the thing to the person in whose favor the controversy was decided. The praetor granted the sequester interdictal protection so that the sequester could protect the thing with some degree of autonomy in relation to the parties. (3) Irregular deposit (*depositum irregulare*) was the deposit of money or other fungibles; consequently, the depositary had to return not the very same thing but an equivalent. This kind of deposit was like a mutuum in that it involved the transfer of ownership, but it had the advantages of bilateral contracts based on good faith, including the possibility of awarding interest in some cases. The institution had a Hellenistic origin and seems to be postclassical.

Pignus

An archetype of real security, the *pignus* (pledge) was a real contract that consisted of handing over a movable or immovable thing to secure a debt. Pignus implied transfer of possession but not ownership. The real contract gave rise to a limited right in rem in the property owned by the pledgor. The pledgor could be a debtor, but also a third party. Suppose that Titius lent a thousand sesterces to Caius, and the latter secured this debt by handing over his ring to Titius. In this case, the pledgor and the debtor are the same person (Caius). It is possible, however, that not Caius but Sempronius (now the pledgor) secured Caius's debt by handing over furniture to Titius (pledgee). The pledgee (creditor) became the praetorian possessor of the pledged thing and was protected by possessory interdicts.

The pledgee could not use the pledged thing and had no rights over its fruits, unless it was agreed as an interest (*antichresis*). He was liable for fraud (dolus), negligence (culpa), and safekeeping (custodia). Once the underlying obligation had been extinguished, the pledgee had to restore the thing to the pledgor. If the pledgee did not give back the pledged thing, the pledgor could sue the pledgee for restoration of the thing with a personal action (*actio pigneraticia in personam*). Of course, if the pledgor was the civil owner of the pledged thing, he could also bring a *rei vindicatio* against the pledgee. But for the pledgor, it was easier to bring the *actio pigneraticia* because it required only proof of the pignus, not proof of civil ownership. On the other hand, the pledgee could bring a contra claim against the pledgor (*actio pigneraticia contraria*) for damages caused in the pledged thing and for reimbursement of necessary expenses. The pledgee had a right of retention (*ius retentionis*) until the pledgor compensated for damages and expenses.

It was usual in classical law to agree that the creditor should be entitled to sell the pledged thing if the debtor did not pay the debt by the agreed-upon date. In later classical law, the right to sell (*ius distrahendi*) was conceived as a right of the creditor, unless it was expressly excluded. After the sale, if the price of the pledged thing exceeded the debt for which the pledge was given, the pledgor had the right to the excess (*superfluum*). The parties might also agree to the transfer of ownership from the pledgor to the pledgee if the debtor did not pay his debt by a certain day (the so-called *lex commissoria*). Because this agreement could produce excessive interest to the creditor when the plegded thing was more valuable than the amount of the debt, Emperor Constantine prohibited the *lex commissoria* (C.J. 8.34.3).

Hypothec

Despite its Greek name, *hypothec* has a Roman origin. It was a real security, similar to the pignus, but without transfer of possession (*pignus conventum*). Anything – movable or immovable, corporeal or incorporeal (e.g., usufruct), even future things (e.g., a future harvest) – could constitute a hypothec. Hypothecs were usually created by simple agreement whereby a debtor granted his creditor a real right over a thing as security for the discharge of a debt. Hypothecs also could be constituted directly by operation of law without private agreement in order to secure certain legal relations: so-called legal hypothecs. Claims of the imperial treasury, for instance, were secured by a legal hypothec on the entire property of the fiscal debtor.

The origin of the institution of hypothec is connected to the leasing of land. It was common practice for a tenant to pledge his properties, such as farming implements, cattle, or slaves, to his landowner as security for future rent. The praetor gave the landowner the so-called *interdictum Salvianum* (Gaius 4.147) to claim possession of the items in question if the rent was not paid. Later, the praetor extended the protection of the landowner by granting an action in rem (called *actio Serviana*) against anyone who had the possession, even if he was not the tenant. An additional development extended the protection of the *actio Serviana* to all pledges, whether possession had been transferred or not.

The great advantage of the hypothec over the pignus was that hypothec did not deprive the pledgor of possession, and as a result, successive hypothecs could be established over the same property to secure different debts to the same or different creditors. The generally applicable Roman rule was that the hypothec constituted earliest in time prevailed in law (*prior tempore potior iure*). Thus, each consecutive creditor had to be informed about the precedent hypothecs and the value of the charged debts. Only the first creditor in line could exercise the right to sell the charged property to satisfy his debt. Successive creditors could only take the position of a previous one offering the payment of his debt (*ius offerendi et succedendi*).

A way to register hypothecs did not appear until the end of the fifth century. This lack of publicity was probably the greatest disadvantage of the Roman system of hypothecs.

Fiducia

In contrast to the loan for use, deposit, pledge, and hypothec, *fiducia* was a formal transaction that implied the transfer of ownership. Gaius did not mention fiducia as a contract, but it is possible that it became a real and formal contract in the classical period. Fiducia was created by a mancipation or *in iure cessio* with an additional agreement (*pactum fiduciae*) according to which the thing had to be restored to the transferor (usually a debtor) under specific circumstances. The recipient acquired full ownership and was protected with the vindication. If the transferor was not the owner, the recipient could gain ownership by usucaption after one year, even if it was land (Gaius 2.59). The transferor could bring an *actio fiduciae* against the recipient when the latter failed to restore the thing to him. On the other hand, the transferor had a contra claim (*actio fiduciae contraria*) to recover damages and expenses caused by the thing mancipated.

Gaius (2.60) divided the fiducia into two classes: *cum creditore* and *cum amico*. *Fiducia cum creditore* was the earliest form of real security the Romans knew. It consisted of the transfer of ownership of a debtor's property to the creditor. The reconveyance could be demanded only on payment of the debt. The fiducia afforded a powerful real security in favor of the creditor, but it involved a great risk for the debtor who had lost ownership. Furthermore, like the pignus, and in contrast to the hypothec, fiducia could be produced only once.

Fiducia cum amico was a transfer of ownership to a friend for different purposes (e.g., use, safekeeping, managing) and under different circumstances, with a trust for reconveyance. In contrast to *fiducia cum creditore*, the *fiducia cum amico* required return of property on demand. Suppose that Titius decided to transfer the ownership of his slave Stikus to Caius because Titius planned to be out of town for three years. According to the fiduciary agreement, Caius would have to restore the slave when Titius returned. The advantage of this agreement was that Caius would be protected as an owner against third parties. The disadvantage was that Titius surrendered ownership based on nothing more than trust.

Fiducia disappeared in postclassical times when the required mancipation and the *in iure cessio* also disappeared. The compilers eliminated the expression *fiducia cum creditore* and replaced it by pignus; the expression *fiducia cum amico* was replaced by the terms deposit, loan for use, or precarium.

Innominate contracts

Originally, Roman jurists recognized as contracts only a restricted number of legal transactions. The expression "innominate contracts" refers to a group of transactions, primitively not contractual, which came into existence only after one of the parties performed his obligation. In a sense, they were similar to real contracts. These transactions became contractual at some point, probably in the classical period, and were labeled innominate because the actions to protect them were not individualized by a concrete name.

Innominate contracts constituted a later development of the classical agreements in which the simple agreement itself had no binding force. Suppose that Titius agreed with Caius that he would give an amphora of wine in exchange for Caius's amphora of oil. In early law, after giving his amphora of wine to Caius, Titius had no legal remedy to demand Caius's amphora of oil. The only action that Titius could bring against Caius was the condictio (in some cases, the actio de dolo) in order to recover his amphora of wine, because his transfer had no legal ground (*datio sine causa*). Later, the praetor granted an action in factum to the party who had already performed his obligation to the other party in order to force the other party to carry out his part of the agreement. Justinian introduced an *actio praescriptis verbis* based in good faith to protect all kinds of bilateral contracts in which a party, after performing his obligation, claimed the performance of the reciprocal obligation by the other party.

Innominate contracts embraced the following types (Paul, D. 19.5.5pr.): *do ut des* (e.g., I will give you four loaves of bread so that you will give me a jar of vinegar); *do ut facias* (e.g., I will give you an amphora of oil so that you will teach me Greek for two days); *facio ut des* (e.g., I will heal your slave's broken arm so that you will give me a toga); and *facio ut facias* (e.g., I will repair your roof so that you will keep my slave safe for a month). Of course, the possibility of services consisting in an abstention (e.g., use my well to draw water) (*non facere*) should also be taken into consideration.

Relevant innominate contracts were the *permutatio*, the *aestimatum*, and the *precarium*. A permutatio (barter) was the exchange of one thing for another. According to the Sabinians, barter should be considered a sale, and therefore a consensual contract, but the Proculeian doctrine prevailed that without a price there was no sale (Paul, D. 18.1.1.1.). According to Justinian, a barter was a real contract that demanded performance for one of the parties. An aestimatum was a transaction by means of which an owner transferred a thing to another person who had to either restore it or pay a fixed amount of money within a fixed term, while retaining any profit the recipient had obtained from selling it at a higher price. Finally, the precarium was a gratuitous grant of the use and enjoyment of a thing, revocable at will (Ulpian, D. 43.26.1pr.).

Consensual contracts

Consensual contracts were those in which a simple agreement was binding. They were all bilateral (but the mandate only imperfectly so) and concluded by formless consent. Consent sufficed of itself (Gaius 3.136): no transfer of the item or symbolic act was required. Hence, such contracts could be formed between parties at a distance (*inter absentes*), i.e., by letter or messenger (Gaius 3.136), unlike oral obligations, for instance. In consensual contracts, the parties were reciprocally liable for what each was bound to perform for the other (Gaius 3.137). Consensual contracts were of great commercial and economic importance and constituted one of the most significant accomplishments of Republican jurisprudence.

Classical Roman law recognized four consensual contracts: sale (*emptio venditio*), hire (*locatio conductio*), partnership (*societas*), and mandate (*mandatum*). All consensual contracts were based on good faith, and this foundation in good faith allowed the contracting parties a greater degree of flexibility in defining the content of their obligations. On the other hand, these arrangements gave the judge wide discretion in taking into account particular circumstances in case of conflict between the parties.

Sale (*emptio venditio*)

The sale was the most important of all consensual contracts. It was the contract by means of which goods were exchanged for money. A sale was concluded when the buyer and the seller agreed by formless consent upon the thing to be sold and the price to be paid for it.

The sale by itself did not transfer ownership: mancipation, in iure cessio, or traditio was required. Sale was, therefore, neither a conveyance nor a contract for transferring ownership, which remained strictly separate. Consequently, the sale of a thing not belonging to the seller could be valid. Similarly, payment of the price was not a condition for the passing of ownership. However, until the buyer paid the price, he was not entitled to bring contractual action (*actio empti*) against the seller.

The object of a sale could be anything not legally excluded from private transaction (Paul, D. 18.1.34.1). Noncorporeal things and rights (e.g., servitudes, inheritance) and even future things could be sold – e.g., the sale of next year's crop or the unborn child of a slave woman. The use of land or the labor of workers could not be sold, however.

The price of a sale had to be money. In classical law, parties were free to fix the price, but it had to be certain (*certum*) and real (*verum*). Certainty required only that the price could be at least indirectly identified (e.g., "what you paid for it"). "Reality" meant that the price had to be genuine, authentic, though its adequacy with an objective value was irrelevant. Postclassical and Justinian laws, however, limited the parties' freedom to establish a price.

Two main obligations arose from a sale: (a) the seller's obligation to deliver the free and undisturbed possession of the thing (*vacua possessio*) to the buyer, and (b) the buyer's obligation to pay the price. These two obligations were intrinsically connected. If the thing perished by accident after the conclusion of the sale, the buyer assumed the risk (*periculum est emptoris*) and had to pay the price. The seller, however, was liable for safekeeping (custodia), for instance, in case the thing was stolen before the delivery. Both the seller and buyer were liable for fraud (dolus) and negligence (culpa). The seller had the *actio venditi* against the buyer who did not pay the established price at the fixed time; the buyer, on the other hand, had the *actio empti* to force the seller to deliver the thing.

Liability for eviction and latent defects

When the seller was the owner of the thing, and the thing was delivered in accordance with the law, the buyer acquired ownership. However, eviction occurred when the seller sold a thing that did not belong to him, and the buyer, as a result, was deprived of his possession by the real owner. Originally, liability for eviction was established by different optional stipulations, but further development of the seller's liability led the Roman jurists to consider that the contract of sale as such implied warranty for eviction.

The seller was not liable for any defects in the things unless that was expressly established by stipulation. However, a liability for latent defects was introduced by the magistrates with jurisdiction over the market of the city of Rome (*aediles curules*). Sellers of slaves and beasts of burden had to disclose certain nonobvious and manifest physical and mental defects. Sellers also had to note other specific circumstances: for instance, whether the slave was a fugitive, a vagabond, or burdened with noxal liability. If nondisclosed defects appeared, the buyer could either claim a rescission of the sale by the *actio redhibitoria* or claim a reduction of the price paid for the slave or animal by the *actio quanti minoris.* The seller's liability was strict. It did not depend on his knowledge or ignorance but only on the existence of the defect. This liability for latent defects was extended later to other sales outside the Roman market, and Justinian's compilers expanded it to all kinds of sales, including sales of land.

Letting and hiring (*locatio conductio*)

Locatio conductio was a bilateral and consensual contract of letting and hiring for a price. It was a general contract that included a wide diversity of transactions. The main feature linking all such transactions was the fact that the *locator* placed (*locare*) a thing (or services) at the disposal of the *conductor* for him to carry along (*conducere*): a landowner placed land at the disposal of the lessee for the latter to use it; an artisan placed his services at the disposal of an employer to make repairs at the employer's house; a customer placed a piece of cloth at the disposal of a tailor to make a toga; a Roman citizen placed ten jars of wine at the disposal of a carrier for transportation to another city.

In many ways, locatio conductio was similar to sale. Both were consensual and bilateral contracts based on good faith and involving money. Gaius (3.144) affirms that sometimes the similarities ran so deep that the distinction was not clear. This occurred, for instance, when a thing was let in perpetuity. In the curious example of the contract for supplying gladiators (Gaius 3.146), the prevailing opinion held that the contract was a hire for the gladiators who came out unhurt and a sale for the gladiators who were killed or disabled. The contract for making a ring was a sale if the gold belonged to the goldsmith, but a hire if the customer supplied the gold (Gaius 3.147).

There was an important practical difference between sale and hire. In sales, it was always the buyer who paid the price to the seller. In hires, however, either the locator or the conductor could pay the remuneration. So, the position of the locator or conductor was not as clear as the positions of the buyer and seller, and it was not as important. Both the locator and conductor were liable for fraud (dolus) and negligence (culpa). In general, the risk in case of accidental destruction was on the locator (*periculum est locatoris*), and, therefore, the conductor was liable for safekeeping of the thing (custodia). However, a more equitable and flexible distribution of risk, subject to special agreement between the parties, was gradually introduced by the jurisprudence of the classical period (Labeo-Paul, D. 19.2.62; Florentinus, D. 19.2.15.6). Two actions arose from any locatio conductio, with a similar structure to the actions deriving from sale: the locator had the *actio locati* to enforce his claim, and the conductor the *actio conducti.*

Although there was only a singular contract of hire, the Romans did not apply the same rules to all forms of it. This allowed for grouping the contract into three different categories.

a *Locatio conductio rei*: This was a contract whereby the locator agreed to give the conductor a movable or immovable thing (e.g., a piece of land, an animal) for use, or use and enjoyment, while the conductor promised to pay a recompense in money (*merces*). The lessor (locator) had to be the owner and was liable to the lessee (conductor) if the latter was evicted by the real owner. The lessor had to refund the lessee any expenses for the benefit of the thing. He also had to pay taxes and other charges. The lessee had only the use of the thing, neither civil nor praetorian possession. He could sue only the lessor, not a third person. The lessee could not change the character of the thing and had to restore it at the end of the contract to its original condition.

b *Locatio conductio operarum:* This was a subcategory of the locatio conductio rei in which, instead of offering a thing, the locator offered his own services (*dare operas*) for a limited time without allusion to a specific result to be achieved. The locator (e.g., domestic or manual worker) agreed to provide some services (usually at a day's wage) for a remuneration to be paid by the conductor. The conductor did not have to pay the wages to the locator when the latter could not perform the services because of illness or lack of ability. However, the conductor had to pay the wages if the locator was not responsible for his labor not being performed, e.g., in case of a collapse of a mine (Paul, D. 19.2.38pr.). Professions and liberal arts (e.g., lawyers, physicians, and orators) were excluded from this type of contract.

c *Locatio conductio operis*: In this contract, the locator agreed to place at the disposal of the conductor some materials for the conductor to perform a specific task or work or produce a final result (*opus factum*) or certain effect (e.g., making a dress, building a house, or transporting goods and persons). The conductor had to complete the work within the agreed-upon time frame; if no deadline was fixed, the work had to be done in a reasonable time (Labeo, D. 19.2.58.1). Subcontracting was allowed, but the principal conductor continued to be responsible for the final result. The locator had the obligation to accept the completed work, giving approval where necessary (Florentinus, D. 19.2.36), and pay the remuneration (*merces*) in the appropriate way.

Partnership (*societas*)

Partnership was a consensual and bilateral contract based on good faith by means of which two or more individuals (partners) agreed to cooperate with some resources (skills, money, property, work, experience, or a combination of them) for a common purpose. Usually, making a profit was a major element of the common purpose, but it was not essential (e.g., three neighbors could agree to buy land to preserve its natural features). Unlike sale and hire, partnership implied that partners shared a common interest founded on a special relation of friendship (*affectio societatis*).

Each partner had to make a contribution. Otherwise, there would be not a partnership but a donation. Contributions could be different in kind and amount, however, and shares also could be unequal (Proculus, D. 17.2.6.80). Following the opinion of Servius Sulpicius Rufus, which prevailed, a partner could have a larger share in profits than in losses (Gaius 3.149). If no shares were agreed upon, they were presumed to be equal (Ulpian, D. 17.2.29pr.). Each partner was liable for fraud (dolus) and negligence (culpa), and in general they had to demonstrate the same diligence and care that they would exercise in their own affairs (Gaius, D. 17.2.72).

The common purpose of the contract of partnership could be only a single transaction, as, for instance, an agreement to share the expenses of a journey (*societas unius rei*); some kind of specific business, such as transportation or building construction (*societas alicuius negotiationis*); or merger of all the assets of the partners (*societas omnium bonorum*). A partnership did not give rise to legal personality. Thus, partnerships created legal relations only between and among the partners, not with respect to third persons. If Titius, Caius, and Sempronius were partners, and Titius borrowed money from Lucius to do something concerning the partnership's purpose, Lucius had rights only against Titius, not against the other partners, even though they authorized the transaction between Titius and Lucius.

The action *pro socio* was the general remedy for partnership. As partners usually were also joint owners, the *actio communi dividundo* to divide common ownership was also available. The main causes for termination were the death or *capitis deminutio* of one of the partners, the renunciation of the partnership, and the bringing of an action pro socio by any partner. All these causes reflect the strictly personal and friendly character of partnership.

Mandate (*mandatum*)

A contract of mandatum (from Latin *manum dare*, to entrust something) was concluded when one party (the mandatary) agreed to perform a service at the request of the other party (the mandator). The mandatary became bound to perform the service and the mandator to repay expenses and compensate damages incurred by performing the service. The service had to be gratuitous, possible, lawful, and not contrary to morality. For instance, there could not be a mandate to steal from Titius or to insult him (Gaius 3.157).

A mandatum was based on friendship and, therefore, was most like the contract of partnership. To act as one's procurator in litigation and to act as an adstipulator were, among other things, friendly services that contributed to the development of the contract of mandate. Relations with liberal professions, such as architects, land surveyors, and lawyers, also fell within the ambit of this contract. According to Roman social standards, work for money was undignified and objectionable because the services of an honorable Roman citizen could not be estimated fairly; they were priceless. Where remuneration was fixed, the contract was locatio conductio, not a mandate. In later classical law, however, the gratuitous character of the mandate started fading in importance, especially when an honorarium could be sought by the mandatary by extraordinary cognition.

A mandatum was consensual. A simple unilateral request or mere good advice was not enough to conclude a mandatum. Moreover, a validly established mandate was dissolved if revoked before the mandate was acted on (Gaius 3.159). A mandatum had to concern the mandator: a mandate in the exclusive interest of the mandatarius (or a third party) was superfluous and treated as advice; e.g., the mandate to invest your money in the purchase of land rather than lend it out at interest (Gaius, D. 17.1.2.6). The reason for this was that a person's own interest could be managed only by his own judgment and not by mandate from another (Gaius, 3.156).

A mandatum was not about agency. The mandatary did not act as the mandator's representative, and the mandatary's dealings with third parties did not create rights and liabilities for the mandator. For instance, if for any reason Titius asked Caius to lend money to Sempronius (*mandatum pecuniae credendae*), Caius had the condictio against Sempronius and the *actio mandati contraria* against Titius for expenses and damages, but Titius had no action against Sempronius.

The mandatary had to execute the service and to hand over all benefits deriving from his performance. He was not allowed to exceed the purpose and terms of the mandate (*fines mandati*). He was liable for fraud (dolus), like the depositary, and in later law for ordinary negligence (culpa). The mandator had an action on mandate (*actio mandati*) against the mandatary for restitution of whatever he received on account of or in the performance of his service. The mandatary could sue the mandator only with the *actio mandati contraria* for reimbursement of expenses and compensation for damages. Because the actio mandati contraria was only contingent, the mandatum is considered to be imperfectly bilateral.

Mandatum ended with the death of either party, by revocation by the mandator, or by renunciation of the mandatary.

Quasi contracts

As already mentioned, quasi contracts were legally enforceable obligations broadly similar to contracts that did not arise either from contract or from delict. Quasi contract was a residual category that encompassed obligations arising from unjustified enrichment, unauthorized management of another's affairs, relations between and among co-owners, the tutor's business concerning the ward's affairs, and an heir's instructions in a will (Inst. 3.27). We can find some similarities between the position of a tutor or a manager of another's affairs and the position of a mandatary, the joint owners or heirs, and the contract of partnership, as well as between a mutuum and an undue payment (*solutio indebiti*). We will pay attention only to *negotiorum gestio* and undue payment. In both cases, obligations arose not from an agreement between parties but from a performance that entailed rights and duties.

Negotiorum gestio

Negotiorum gestio was the management of another's affairs without his request, instruction, or authorization: repairing a neighbor's roof, settling a debt for him, becoming a surety, purchasing oil or wine for a friend, and defending him in a trial, among other things. Negotiorum gestio was based on friendship, helpfulness, and solidarity (*humanitas*), and it was especially useful in case of absence or emergency. For this reason, negotiorum gestio was gratuitous but not a gift, since expenses must be reimbursed to the manager (*gestor*) by the principal (*dominus negotii*).

Negotiorum gestio was quite similar to mandate but without an initial agreement. Thus, if the principal gave his consent after having knowledge of the business, the negotiorum gestio became mandate. Like the mandatary, the manager had to perform his service to the end and in the best interest of the principal, not his own interest (e.g., to make a donation or perform a contractual duty). The result of the manager's service did not necessarily have to be useful, successful, or beneficial. It was enough that the service was reasonable (*utiliter coeptum*). The manager was liable for fraud (dolo) and negligence (culpa).

The principal could bring the *actio negotiorum gestorum* against the manager to claim restitution of anything acquired by him during his management, as well as for damages derived from negligence (*actio directa*). On the other hand, the manager had the *actio contraria* for reimbursement of expenses or compensation for damages.

Undue payment (*solutio indebiti*)

One of the most important categories of unjust enrichment, *solutio indebiti*, was the mistaken payment of a debt in discharge of an obligation that in fact did not exist. The legal act, not founded on contract (Gaius 3.91), but considered a quasi contract, was almost identical to the mutuum, except that the payment was made in discharge and not to create an obligation.

Both the giver and the receiver had to act in good faith and in error. If the giver paid knowing that the money was not due, the payment was not recoverable (Ulpian, D. 12.6.1) and therefore was treated as a donation. If the receiver acted in bad faith, the payment was treated as a theft. Payment of a debt of money due by a third person was an undue payment unless paid in the name of the third person. Paul says, however, that no recovery is possible against a man who has received his own property (a slave, for instance), even from a person other than the true debtor (D. 12.6.44). A conditional debt remained undue as long as the condition was not satisfied (Pomponius, D. 12.6.16pr.). However, where a debt fell due on an unfixed day (*dies incertus*), recovery was not possible because the day had to come first (Pomponius, D. 12.6.16pr.). The fulfillment of a natural obligation could not be considered undue payment (Africanus, D. 12.6.38.1).

The giver could recover the payment by a personal action: the *condictio indebiti* (Gaius 3.91). The plaintiff had to prove the fact of the payment and that the obligation was not due. Restitution had to be with fruits and accessories, and interest could not be claimed.

Pacta

A *pactum* (plural, *pacta*) was "the agreement and consent of two or more persons concerning the same matter" (Ulpian, D. 2.14.1.2). All kinds of agreements that did not fall within a defined category of contract could be considered a pactum. Originally, pacts were not actionable, and they gave rise only to a defense (Ulpian, D. 2.14.7.4). These kinds of agreements were called naked pacts (*pacta nuda*). For instance, the formless agreement by which the creditor assumed the obligation not to sue the debtor (*pactum de non petendo*) was an archetypical naked agreement. If the creditor, contrary to this agreement, brought action against the debtor, the latter could repeal it by a defense, the *exceptio pacti*.

At times, however, pacta were enforceable and gave rise to an action (Ulpian, D. 2.14.7.5). Enforceable pacts were the so-called *pacta adiecta*, i.e., an additional agreement to a contract in order to modify part of its content – e.g., the agreement by means of which a tenant would be liable for whatever occurred due to a higher force (*vis maior*) (Ulpian, D. 19.2.9.2) and the aforementioned *lex commissoria* in the sale, among others. If the additional agreement was made at the time of the original contract, the agreement was enforceable by the very contractual action. When the agreement was introduced subsequently, it was not enforceable by means of an action, but only an exception.

Sometimes, the praetor granted an action in factum for the enforcement of some agreements that were not additional to contracts. That occurred, for instance, in the case of an informal agreement to pay an already existing debt at an agreed-upon, fixed date (*constitutum debiti*). The debt could be one's own or that of a third person, so it constituted a form of surety. The agreement had no novatory effect because it was not a stipulation. The advantage of bringing the action in factum (called *actio de pecunia constituta*) was that it was strengthened by an additional promise of a penalty of one half of the original debt.

Other praetorian agreements were the undertaking of a person to act as an arbitrator in a dispute between two or more persons (*receptum arbitri*); the obligation assumed by a banker to pay the debt of his client at a fixed date (*receptum argentarii*); and the undertaking of a ship's master, an innkeeper, or a liveryman that their customers' goods confided to them would be safe (*receptum nautarum, cauponum, stabulariorum*).

Further reading

Berger, Adolf. *Encyclopedic Dictionary of Roman Law.* Philadelphia: The American Philosophical Society, 1953; reprint 1980.

Betti, Emilio. *La struttura dell'obbligazione romana e il problema della sua genesi.* Milan: Giuffrè, 1955.

Birks, Peter. *The Roman Law of Obligations.* Edited by Eric Descheemaeker. Oxford: Oxford University Press, 2014.

Buckland, William Warwick. *A Text-Book of Roman Law.* 3rd rev. ed. Revised by Peter Stein, 405–603. Cambridge: Cambridge University Press, 1963.

Diósdi, György. *Contract in Roman Law: From the Twelve Tables to the Glossators.* Translated by J. Szabó. Budapest: Akadémiai Kiado, 1981.

d'Ors, Álvaro. *Derecho privado romano.* Edited by Xavier d'Ors. 10th ed. Pamplona: Eunsa, 2004.

du Plessis, Paul J. *Letting and Hiring in Roman Legal Thought: 27 BCE–284 CE.* Leiden: Brill, 2012.

Fiori, Roberto. *La definizione della locatio conductio: giurisprudenza romana e tradizione romanistica.* Naples: Jovene, 1999.

Grosso, Giuseppe. *Il sistema romano dei contratti.* 3rd ed. Torino: G. Giappichelli, 1963.

Ibbetson, David J. *A Historical Introduction to the Law of Obligations.* Oxford and New York: Oxford University Press, 1999.

Ibbetson, David J. "Obligatio in Roman law and Society." In *The Oxford Handbook of Roman Law and Society*, edited by Paul J. du Plessis, Clifford Ando, and Kaius Tuori, 569–580. Oxford: Oxford University Press, 2016.

Kaser, Max. *Das römische Privatrecht.* Vol I, *Das altrömische, das vorklassische und klassische Recht*, 474–667. 2nd ed. Munich: Beck Verlag, 1971.

McGinn, Thomas A. J., ed. *Obligations in Roman Law: Past, Present, and Future.* Ann Arbor: University of Michigan Press, 2012.

Mousourakis, George. *Fundamentals of Roman Private Law*, 183–251. Berlin and Heidelberg: Springer, 2012.

Nicholas, Barry. *An Introduction to Roman Law*, 158–207. Oxford: Clarendon Press, 1975.

Paricio Serrano, Javier, ed. *Derecho romano de obligaciones. Homenaje al profesor José Luis Murga Gener.* Madrid: Centro de Estudios Ramón Areces, 1994.

Santoro, Raimondo. *Il contratto nel pensiero di Labeone.* Palermo: Palumbo, 1983.

Schulz, Fritz. *Classical Roman Law*, 455–633. Oxford: Clarendon Press, 1951.

Thomas, J. A. C. *Textbook of Roman Law*, 312–383. Amsterdam, New York, and Oxford: North-Holland Publishing Company, 1976.

Watson, Alan. *Contract of Mandate in Roman Law.* Oxford: Oxford University Press, 1961.

Watson, Alan. *The Law of Obligations in the Later Roman Republic*. Oxford: Clarendon Press, 1965.

Wegmann Stockebrand, Adolfo. *Obligatio re contracta. Ein Beitrag zur sogenannten Kategorie der Realverträge im römischen Recht*. Heidelberg: Mohr Siebeck, 2017.

Zimmermann, Reinhard. *The Law of Obligations. Roman Foundation of the Civilian Tradition*. Oxford and New York: Oxford University Press, 1996.

Zulueta, Francis de. *The Institutes of Gaius. Part II. Commentary*. Oxford: Clarendon Press, 1953.

12 The law of obligations II

Delicts

Along with contracts, the other significant branch of the law of obligations is that of delicts, i.e., private wrongs for which redress was provided by civil law. Just as Roman lawyers did not develop a general theory of contracts, neither did they produce an elaborate doctrine of delicts. The Roman law of delicts consisted of a set of reprehensible behaviors (e.g., theft, injury, wrongful loss) that were originally punished under civil law with a fine, compensation for the loss and damages, or both. Later, as social life developed, the praetor granted actions and ordered redress for some situations not covered by civil law (e.g., fraud, duress, robbery). These private wrongs were classified as praetorian delicts. Penalties for both civil and praetorian delicts might have corresponded to the value of the damaged or stolen thing, a multiple of a given value, or a fixed amount of money.

Although delicts and crimes both incurred punishment, they were essentially distinct. Crimes fell within the province of public law, while delicts fell within private law. Crimes were major offenses (e.g., treason, murder, and sacral wrongs, among others) punishable by a public penalty following conviction in a special court. In contrast to delicts, crimes usually implied offense against the entire community, not simply harm to particular interests; liability for delicts could not be canceled by informal agreement (pactum). Modern lawyers can learn more from the law of delicts than from Roman criminal law because Roman jurists did not develop criminal law as fully. Indeed, legal literature did not begin to pay significant attention to crime until the second century CE.

In early law, redress for delicts consisted of delivering the body of the wrongdoer into the hands of his victim. This penal character of redress explains many particularities of the law governing delicts as opposed to contracts – for instance, the fact that the death of the wrongdoer ended liability for the delict. Proceedings against the wrongdoer's heir were accepted under praetorian law only when the heir had derived some benefit from the wrong. Another important reason for the essentially punitive character of the law of delicts was that the guilty wrongdoers were viewed as acting with intent to defraud (dolus). Hence, persons not able to perceive the fraudulent nature of some of their actions (*doli capaces*), such as lunatics (*furiosi*) and prepubescent children, could not commit delicts. Gaius (3.208), however, says that if a child was approaching puberty and understood that what he was doing was wrong, he could be held liable for theft. Women and slaves were able to commit delicts. After the promulgation of the *lex Aquilia* (286 BCE), negligence (culpa) sufficed for the characterization of a delict. This recognition of culpable negligence was one of the greatest contributions of Roman law to Western legal culture.

The law of delicts progressed from enabling a victim to exact personal revenge, to requiring an agreement for satisfaction. Revenge thus became redeemable, and it was gradually transformed into a claim for monetary compensation or compulsory payment of a fine. In these cases, the victim had to abstain from revenge by accepting a compensation paid by the wrongdoer or his relatives. The amount to be paid in redress was sometimes prescribed directly by statutory law and sometimes decided by the judge in his discretion.

By the time of classical law, the Roman law of delicts and compensations was solidly established as a form of civil proceedings imposing penalties for wrongdoers. More than twenty delicts were known to the Romans in the early Principate. Among these twenty, theft in the broader sense (*furtum*), injury (*iniuria*), and wrongful loss (*damnum iniuria datum*) were probably the most important civil delicts, and fraud (dolus) and duress (*metus*), the most significant praetorian delicts. This chapter will address only these categories.

Penal actions (*actiones poenales*)

Roman jurists classified as penal those actions derived from delicts to punish the wrongdoer. In general, the three main features of most penal actions were passive intransmissibility, cumulative liability, and noxal liability. All these features were expressions of the strictly personal character of the penalty.

Passive intransmissibility meant that the penal action did not survive beyond the wrongdoer's death. Gaius (4.112) says, "There is no more certain rule of law than that penal actions … never lie or are granted against the wrongdoer's heir." On the other hand, penal actions could be granted in favor of the victim's heirs, except in cases where the action was strictly personal (e.g., offenses against the good reputation of a Roman citizen).

Cumulative liability meant that if joint perpetrators caused the wrong, each one would have to compensate the victim. The more persons who had participated in the delict, the more compensation would be paid out to the victim. The reason for this cumulative compensation was that the penalty was about punishment as well as recompense. Each wrongdoer had to be punished by the law, so the number of perpetrators was irrelevant to the monetary penalty leveled against each of them.

As mentioned in chapter eight, noxal liability meant that where the wrongdoer was a person under parental or dominical power, the paterfamilias could either pay the penalty as if he himself had committed the delict or surrender the offender to the injured party (Gaius 4.75). Noxal liability was established either by statute (e.g., applied by the *lex Aquilia* to wrongful damage of property) or by praetor's edict (e.g., for outrage or robbery) (Gaius 4.76).

Actiones mixtae and *rei persecutoriae*

Some actions were purely penal in nature – i.e., their purpose was exclusively to punish the wrongdoer without taking into consideration compensation for damages. This was the case, for instance, with actions in response to theft and injury. Purely penal actions needed to be complemented by so-called reipersecutory actions (*actiones rei persecutoriae*), whose exclusive purpose was the restitution of an item or compensation for damages – in the case of theft, for instance, recovery of the thing stolen.

A common reipersecutory action was the *rei vindicatio*, which could be brought against the thief and any other possessor of the stolen thing for recovery of the item or its value. When the thing stolen was money or had been destroyed, the condictio rather than the rei vindicatio fulfilled the reipersecutory function. Since compensation and penalty were different in nature, reipersecutory actions could be added to penal actions.

In later law, however, some actions called *actiones mixtae* served both the penal and the compensatory two functions. They penalized the wrongdoer but also compensated the injured party. Justinian (Inst. 4.6.19) provided the example of an action for robbery in which the penalty was quadruple the value of the thing stolen: triple its value was considered the penalty, and the simple value of the thing was paid in compensation for damages.

Theft (*furtum*)

Furtum (according to Romans, from *ferro*, to carry away) was a delict against property, which appeared as early as the Twelve Tables (VIII 12–17). The jurist Paul defined furtum as the "fraudulent interference (*contrectatio*) with a thing, whether with the thing itself or the use or possession of it, with a view to profit" (D. 47.2.1.3). The handling had to be intentional and fraudulent (dolus). When someone took an item while believing, in good faith, that the owner had consented, this was not a theft, because the requisite intention to defraud was lacking. Thus, children and insane persons could not commit theft.

Only movable things and persons in power could be objects of furtum (Gaius 3.199). Furthermore, a stolen thing could not be a *res nullius* or *res extra commercium*. To steal divine things was a *sacrilegium*; to steal or misappropriate public things was a crime of *peculatus*, subject to prosecution in public criminal proceedings. Furtum required that someone actually owned the thing stolen (*res furtiva*), but that owner did not have to be the victim: for example, a thief could steal a book that someone had borrowed, but the book had to be actually owned by someone to be considered stolen. The stolen thing could not be acquired by usucaption as long as it had not yet returned to the possession of its owner.

Within furtum a basic distinction was made between cases where the thief was caught in the act (*furtum manifestum*) and cases where he was caught later (*nec manifestum*) (Gaius 3.183). The distinction, which appears in the Twelve Tables (VIII.14), was still preserved in Justinian's law as an expression of classicism. The question of flagrancy was a matter of discussion among Roman jurists (Gaius 3.184). For some, manifest theft had to be detected at the very moment it was being committed. For others, however, it was enough if the thief was detected in the *place* where the theft had occurred, e.g., if the thief was still in the vineyard where grapes had been stolen. Others considered a theft to be manifest so long as the thief had not yet arrived at his final destination. Still others considered a theft manifest if someone saw the thief at any point in time with the stolen items in hand.

This discussion was not simply theoretical, because the penalty for manifest theft was capital punishment. According to the Twelve Tables (VIII, 12–13), if the manifest thief was caught stealing by night or tried to defend himself with arms, he could lawfully be killed. The person who suffered the theft had to call neighbors as witnesses. In all other cases of manifest theft, if the thief was a free man he was assigned by the magistrate to the person from whom he had stolen. If the thief was a slave, he was put to death. In the later Republican period, these penalties for manifest theft were replaced with payment of four times the value of the property stolen. For nonmanifest theft, however, the penalty of double the value of the stolen item was imposed by the Twelve Tables (VIII.18b) and maintained by the praetor (Gaius 3.190).

Gaius (3.186–88) mentioned some special cases. If a stolen thing was found at someone's house after a formal inspection with witnesses, a threefold penalty was imposed on the owner of the house (*furtum conceptum*). If the owner of the house was not the actual thief, he could bring an action against the person who had deposited the stolen thing, even if the latter was also not the thief. The same penalty was imposed on the homeowner who refused to let his house be searched (*furtum prohibitum*). In general, recipients of stolen things were liable for nonmanifest theft.

In the classical period, the delict of furtum included not only ordinary stealing and embezzlement but also selling something belonging to another; unauthorized intentional use (*furtum usus*) of another's property that was entrusted but used in an inappropriate manner (e.g., if the depositary used the deposited thing); collecting money from another's debtor as a payment; and physical help (e.g., holding a ladder) and advice and collaboration in theft (e.g., a suggestion on the way to execute the theft [*ope consiliove*]). The actual owner could commit furtum when he took something from the person who had the right to hold it (*furtum possessionis*): e.g., a pledgor stealing the pledged item from the pledgee (Gaius 3.200). Destruction of a thing was not considered furtum.

Anyone with some legitimate interest in the stolen thing could bring action for manifest or nonmanifest theft (*actio furti manifesti* or *actio furti nec manifesti*), even if he was not the owner (Gaius 3.203). If a thief who perpetrated a manifest theft was assisted by an accomplice, the action for manifest theft lay against the thief, and the action for nonmanifest theft against the accomplice. In applying the principle of accumulation, if the value of the stolen thing was one hundred sesterces, the person from whom the thing was stolen would obtain six hundred sesterces altogether: four hundred as a penalty for manifest theft, and one hundred each from the thief and the accomplice. The action for theft was a purely penal action that expired with the death of the thief. In addition to this action, the owner of the stolen thing could bring a reipersecutory action for the recovery of the thing or its value.

Robbery (*rapina*)

Regarded originally as a type of furtum, robbery (*rapina*) – i.e., theft by violence – was later considered a delict in itself, prosecuted separately by the praetor. To punish robbery, a special action (*actio vi bonorum raptorum*) was introduced, probably by the *praetor peregrinus* Licinius Luculus in 76 BCE. The edict text, quoted by Ulpian (D. 48.7.2pr.), also included banditry, but it is possible that this expansion of the edict took place in the postclassical period.

Since robbers usually were not caught in the act, the penalty imposed for robbery was that of the nonmanifest theft, that is, double the value of the thing. This penalty was clearly too light, especially in times of social convulsion. By introducing this new action, the praetor increased the penalty to four times the value of the stolen thing, but only if the action were brought within a year of the robbery; otherwise, only the value of the stolen thing could be recouped. For recovery of the stolen thing or its value, the victim could bring a reipersecutory action in addition to a penal action. Gaius (4.8) mentioned this action for robbery as a mere penal action. However, since the value of the thing was included in the damage award, Justinian classified this action for robbery as a mixed action (Inst. 4.6.19). In addition to the private delict of robbery, in certain cases of private violence (e.g., offensive assaults, the use of arms), criminal proceedings were added.

Wrongful loss (*damnum iniuria*)

The delict of "loss wrongfully caused" (*damnum iniuria datum*) was developed in the *lex Aquilia de damno* (D. 9.2 and Gaius 3.210–219), a plebiscite of unknown date, but probably enacted before 217 BCE. The *lex Aquilia* became the ground of redress for damage to property and therefore was regularly commented on by Roman jurists.

The *lex Aquilia* introduced general provisions on wrongful damage to property and largely superseded old provisions and specific cases mentioned by the Twelve Tables and other statutes (Ulpian, D. 9.2.1). Two of its three chapters are relevant to the development of this delict. Chapter one of the *lex*

Aquilia condemned the killing of slaves (male and female) and grazing animals – sheep, oxen, horses, mules, goats, and donkeys, among others, but not wild animals. Wild beasts, even if tamed, and dogs, whose legal position often changed with the law, were outside this category (Gaius, D. 9.2.2.2). The penalty that this statute imposed on a violator was the highest value that the slave or animal had had in the year before the killing. Chapter three was more general. It penalized cases not covered by chapter one in which a man caused loss to another by burning (*urere*), breaking (*frangere*), or destroying (*rumpere*) his property. The penalty imposed was the highest value of the damaged thing within the previous thirty days.

The action of the *lex Aquilia* was available to the owner (Ulpian, D. 9.2.11.6). Originally its scope was limited. For instance, the loss inflicted on the owner had to be the result of a wrongful, physical, and direct act of a wrongdoer upon a tangible thing (*corpore corpori*). Damages caused indirectly (e.g., opening the door of a stable with the result that a horse would bolt) or simple omissions created no liability under the statute. Furthermore, interested parties, such as a usufructuary or pledgee, who may have suffered economic loss, were not originally protected under the *lex Aquilia*.

By way of interpretation and praetorian extensions, however, the application of the *lex Aquilia* was expanded to new situations created by a developing society. By the later Republic, Roman jurists interpreted chapter three to cover all cases of damages not falling within chapter one. They read the Latin term *rumpere* (to destroy) as equivalent to *corrumpere* (to spoil, to ruin, and to hurt), including all kinds of deterioration or damage to an item. On the other hand, the word *iniuria* was understood not only as unlawful but also involving both fraud (dolus) and negligence (culpa).

Justinian described the standard civil action derived from the *lex Aquilia* as a mixed action (Inst. 4.16.9), because the perpetrator of the damage had to pay the highest value the thing had had during a period of time and not its value when it was damaged. The *actio legis Aquiliae* could be combined with other actions deriving from contracts. For instance, if a depositary damaged an item deposited with him, the depositor could bring two actions: the action resulting from the deposit and the action concerning the Aquilian law. As a penal action, the Aquilian action was not passively transmissible, and when there were more than one perpetrator, all of them had to pay the complete penalty. The compensation, which originally depended on the objective value of the thing, was later fixed, taking into consideration the actual interest of the injured party, including consequential damages (*damnum emergens*) and lost profit (*lucrum cessans*).

On the basis of Aquilian law, the praetor granted praetorian actions (sometimes *utiles*, sometimes *in factum*) in cases where damages had been caused only indirectly: e.g., by locking up a slave in a barn so that he died of starvation, driving a mule so hard that it was injured, or pushing one man so that he damaged the property of another. Ulpian (D. 9.2.9pr.) reports a decision of Labeo arguing that the praetorian action should be granted against a midwife who provided medicine to a female slave for her to take by herself, from which the slave died. If the midwife had administered the medicine with her own hands, the *lex Aquilia* would have been applied against her directly, but because the female slave received the medicine to administer herself, the application of the statute required the praetorian extension: the medicine was the cause of the death, but it could not be said that the midwife at any point killed the female slave. If one man held a slave while the other killed him, the first was liable by the praetorian action (*actio in factum*) because he furnished a cause of death, while the second was liable by the ordinary action of the Aquilian law (Ulpian, D. 9.2.11.1).

The praetor also extended protection to interested parties other than the owner who had suffered economic loss (e.g., the possessor in good faith, the usufructuary, the pledgee). Praetorian law was supplemented by criminal sanctions introduced by the *lex Cornelia de iniuriis* (81 BCE) for beating, striking, or flogging a person or entering a dwelling by force. This statute reflected the new legal inclination to regulate *iniuria* through criminal law.

Loss caused by animals

A delict on loss caused by animals was already included in the Twelve Tables (VIII.6): "si quadrupes pauperiem fecisse dicetur …" (If a four-footed animal is said to have caused damages …). The Latin word *pauperies* (probably from the Latin *pauper*, poor) was understood by Ulpian (D. 9.1.1.3), many centuries later, to refer to damages caused without fault on the part of the doer. Of course, when animals inflicted some damages, according to the Ulpian argument, they were incapable of committing any legal wrong because they lacked rational powers.

The victim of the damages could bring an *actio de pauperie* against the owner of the animal at the time of the joinder of the issue (not at the time when the damage had been done). The noxal character of the action allowed the owner of the animal to surrender it instead of paying the compensation. The *actio de pauperie* was applied only to domestic four-footed animals, but it was later extended to other domestic animals (chicken, ducks, and geese) through praetorian actions (Paul, D. 9.1.4). If the animal was under control of the owner, the Aquilian action was applied but not the *actio de pauperie.* For example, if the owner had a dog on a leash and caused it to bite someone, chapter three of Aquilian action was applied; if the owner was not holding the dog's leash when it caused the damage, the action *in factum* extending the Aquilian law was applied (Julian-Ulpian, D. 9.2.11.5). If the dog was not under the control of the owner when it caused the damage, then the *actio de pauperie* was applied. The determination of the regulation applying specifically to dogs presented some difficulties because there existed an early *lex Pesolania* of which little is known (P.S. 1.15.1). Where wild animals escaped from captivity and caused damages, the victim had no action (Ulpian, D. 9.1.1.10) because the wild animal became a *res nullius* when it escaped, and thus there was no owner to sue.

According to Ulpian, the general rule was that the *actio de pauperie* applied when an animal caused damages "moved by some wildness contrary to nature" (Ulpian, D. 9.1.1.7). The concept was extremely flexible, and cases were resolved in a pragmatic fashion. For example, when a horse given to kicking actually kicked someone, or an ox that was prone to goring gored someone, the *actio de pauperie* was applied (Servius-Ulpian, D. 9.1.1.4). It was also applied when the horse kicked at someone who was stroking or patting it. But if the horse kicked someone because it was pricked or hit or wounded (Ulpian, D. 9.1.1.7), the *actio de pauperie* was not applicable. Justinian extended the application of the *actio de pauperie* to damages caused by wild animals (Inst. 4.1.9).

The magistrate responsible for the safety of the public roads (*aedilis curulis*) issued an edict on wild animals (*edictum de feris*). In this edict of unknown date, he granted an action against those who had brought wild beasts (dogs, boars, wolves, bears, panthers, and lions, among others) near a public road where there was frequent traffic, or who kept them there at the risk of injuring someone (Ulpian, D. 21.1.40–42). The person in charge of the beasts, not necessarily the owner, was liable for creating a risk to others without taking into consideration whether or not he could prevent an injury. If a freeman attacked by such an animal was dead, the edict imposed a penalty of two hundred solidi; if he was injured, the judge had discretion to apply some other penalty. In case of damages to property, the person in charge of the animals would be liable for twice the value of the damage done. Noxal surrender was not applicable. It is possible that provocation of the beast by the injured victim excluded liability (Ulpian, D. 21.1.42).

Injury (*iniuria*)

The delict of outrage or injury (*iniuria*) was a product of the development of Roman delictual obligations. Grounded on the Twelve Tables (VIII.1a–4) and expanded by praetorian edicts and jurisprudential interpretation, the delict of injury punished any intentional and unlawful infringement of the body, honor, or reputation of a free person. Specifically, it penalized any conduct in which contumely (*contumelia*) was involved.

Contumelia means "scratching" or "deriding" (Ulpian, D. 47.10.1pr.). It covered any affront to another's reputation, honor, and good name. Every contumely was inflicted on the person and could be perpetrated either by acts (e.g., assault) or by words (e.g., insult). Contumely could be inflicted on someone personally (e.g., an abusive letter seen only by the victim) or through others (e.g., when the affront was to one's children or when the corpse of a departed person to whom one was heir was treated insolently). There could be no injury against a slave. Ulpian says that if someone inflicted an outrage against a slave, it was done to his master, and the master could bring the action for insult in his own right (D. 47.10.15.35). The praetor also granted an action to the master against the person who thrashed or tortured the master's slave (Ulpian, D. 47.10.15.34).

The delict of injury demanded intentionality. It had to have been committed deliberately. Negligent acts or accidents did not produce injury, although a mistake regarding the identity of the victim did not exclude liability for outrage. For instance, Titius perpetrated an affront against Caius, thinking that he really was Sempronius; what really mattered was that Titius had insulted Caius (Paul, D. 47.10.18.3).

Originally, the delict was concerned with physical assaults. The Twelve Tables (VIII.1–4) made some provisions for different forms of physical aggression: magical incantation with the purpose of producing physical harm, amputation or mutilation, and assault, among other things. Because of inflation, pecuniary penalties became ridiculously inadequate. Aulus Gellius (20.1.12–13) refers to the episode of a wicked and cruel man called Lucius Veratius, who used to amuse himself by striking freemen in the face with his open hand. A slave followed him with a purse full of money; after hitting someone, Lucius Veratius would order twenty-five asses to be counted out at once, according to the provision of the Twelve Tables.

Hence, the praetor issued a general edict introducing an all-inclusive action for injuries (*actio iniuriarum*). A series of special edicts extended the action to other forms of outrageous behavior: public abuse against another, violation of chastity, and defamation. The *actio iniuriarum* was penal in nature and therefore cumulative against joint wrongdoers. It also offered the alternative of surrender when the delict had been committed by a person in power or by a slave. It had to be brought within one year after the wrongful act had occurred. It was not only passively nontransmissible but also actively so, in the sense that if the victim died, his heirs could not bring action, owing to the strictly personal character of the outrage (Gaius 4.112). The praetor allowed the plaintiff to make his own assessment of the injury, and the judge, after taking into consideration significant circumstances, could condemn to the limit of that assessment but never beyond it (Gaius 3.22).

An injury could be deemed to be aggravated (*atrox iniuria*) either by an actual deed (e.g., flogging a man), by the place in which the outrage was effected (theater or marketplace), or by the status of the victim (e.g., a magistrate or a senator) (Gaius 3.25). Like the delict of wrongful loss, the civil delict of injury was supplemented by criminal prosecutions for personal assaults and for entry into dwellings by force as introduced by the *lex Cornelia de iniuriis* (81 BCE). In later law, criminal procedures were usually preferred.

Duress (*metus*)

Civil law did not provide a satisfactory solution for private transactions effected by duress. The principle applied was that consent under coercion, fear, or force was still legally valid consent. Paul (D. 4.2.21.5) says that if someone entered upon an inheritance under duress, he became heir because even though he would have refused if he had had free choice, nevertheless, when compelled, he had the intention to enter (*tamen coactus, volui*). Stipulations under duress were usually valid (Inst. 4.13.1).

In 79 or 78 BCE, a praetor named Octavius introduced the first edict punishing the use of duress to compel the victim to conclude a transaction, to make a payment, or to assume an obligation. The person who acted under duress could bring an action to claim back what he had been compelled to hand over (the *formula Octaviana* or *actio qud metus causa*). According to Gaius, the duress relevant in this edict was not that experienced by a weak-minded man but that which would reasonably have an effect upon a strong-willed man (D. 4.2.6). Fear of death, enslavement, or imprisonment fell into the edictal category, but not the mere fear of being sued or being exposed to infamy (Ulpian, D. 4.2.7pr.).

The action *quod metus causa* was a penal action with some peculiarities. On the one hand, the defendant was liable for four times the value that had been extorted, which was a high penalty according to Roman standards. On the other hand, the action could be brought not only against the extortionist, but against any third party who had acquired the extorted thing, even in good faith. The reason for this extension of the action is that its main purpose was not punishment of the extortionist for criminal behavior but restoration of the extorted thing. Thus condemnation under the *actio quod metus causa* did not involve infamy and included a clause by means of which the defendant had the option of avoiding the payment of the condemnation – e.g., the fourfold value of a ring – by simply restoring the extorted item to the plaintiff. The argument Ulpian provided (D. 4.2.14.5 in fine) is that "Duress exercised by one person ought not to be the means of another's advantage." When more than one person was involved in the delict of duress, each was liable for the entire penalty. If the extorted thing was restored, however, the others were released, since, again, the main purpose of the action was the restoration of the extorted thing, not punishment.

Suppose that Titius forced Caius to give his ring to Sempronia, Titius's fiancée, and Sempronia, after breaking up with Titius, sold the ring to Marcus. Caius could bring the action *quod metus causa* against Marcus for four times the value of the ring. Since Marcus was a simple purchaser in good faith, he probably would restore the ring to its owner, Caius, instead of paying the high penalty. Furthermore, since Marcus was not an extortionist, he would not be condemned for infamy.

If the extortionist sued the person who had acted under duress, the praetor granted the defendant an *exceptio metus*. Like the action *quod metus causa*, this exception could be used not only against the extortionist but against any plaintiff in good faith who sought the fulfillment of any obligation made under duress. Suppose that Titius promised by a stipulation made under duress to give a thousand sesterces to Caius, the extortionist. If Caius brought an action for the stipulation against Titius for the payment of this amount, the praetor could grant an *exceptio metus* to the defendant because the transaction was made under duress. On the other hand, if Titius, under duress from Caius, promised by means of stipulation to pay one thousand sesterces to Sempronius, and the latter asked Titius for the amount, the praetor would also grant Titius the *exceptio metus* to avoid allowing anyone to benefit from the imposition of duress.

Fraud (*dolus*)

The definition of *dolus* by Labeo, adopted by Ulpian, is "any craft or deceit employed for the circumvention or entrapment of another person" (D. 4.3.1.2). In accordance with civil law, and only in the case of duress, the existence of fraud did not invalidate a legal transaction, probably because Roman citizens were expected to be clever enough not to be deceived.

In the first century BCE, however, the praetor introduced an exception in the edict to protect the defendant in an action aimed at enforcing a fraudulent transaction. Later, the praetor granted restitution *in integrum* (restoration to the original condition) to the defrauded party when the fraudulent transaction had been executed. Finally, the praetor introduced an action for fraud (*actio de dolo*), a residual remedy granted only when no other action was available after a praetorian inquiry (Ulpian, D. 4.3.1.1.). In transactions based on good faith (e.g., consensual contracts), for instance, the judge would take into account any fraudulent behavior. In these cases, an actor in good faith was protected against fraud by the same action derived from the transaction, so the *actio de dolo* was not required. The action for fraud could be granted, for instance, when the owner of a piece of land, before delivering possession, had imposed a servitude on it or destroyed some of its buildings (Labeo-Ulpian, D. 4.3.7.3); when the promisor of a slave under stipulation had poisoned him before delivery; or when the promisor handed over a slave who really did not belong to him (Paul, D. 19.5.5.2). The *actio de dolo* also could be granted when the heir who had to deliver a slave at his convenience to the legatee knowingly gave a thief, and the thief stole from the legatee (Africanus, D. 30.110).

The *actio de dolo* sought compensation for actual loss, and it had to be granted within a year from the date of the fraudulent transaction. The defendant could avoid payment of the penalty by restoring what he had obtained fraudulently (*clausula arbitraria*). In contrast to the action for duress, the action for fraud lay only against the fraudulent party. For this reason, the penalty for fraud also entailed infamy. In cases involving more than one defrauder, if one paid the compensation or restored the thing obtained fraudulently, all were freed (Ulpian, D. 4.3.17pr.). As with other penal actions, this action was actively but not passively transmissible, unless and insofar as an heir had been enriched by a fraudulent transaction (Ulpian, D. 4.3.17.1). Agreements excluding liability for fraud were void.

Quasi delicts

Quasi delicts were the last category in the Justinian classification of obligations. As Justinian's *Institutes* explains (Inst. 4.5pr.), some obligations could not properly be called delictual, and yet they did not arise from contract. Consequently, the wrongdoer's liability would seem to be quasi-delictual, and a pecuniary penalty could be imposed on him at the judge's discretion.

Quasi delicts were isolated forms of no-fault liability with a still-unclear common factor. From the point of view of the victim, they constituted a sort of insurance or guarantee established by public policy and granted by praetorian actions (*actiones in factum*). Of the four quasi delicts mentioned by Justinian, three are related to vicarious responsibility.

The first quasi delict punished the judge who reached the wrong decision or committed some irregularities in the decision-making process, either intentionally or negligently. The second quasi delict penalized the occupant of a building from which objects were thrown or poured out onto a street, road, or public area, no matter by whom. Passersby who suffered personal or property damages could bring a praetorian action against the occupant for double the value of the damage done, even when the occupant had no personal fault. If the wrongdoer was different from the occupant, an *actio iniuriarum* or an action based on the Aquilian law could be brought directly against the wrongdoer. If a free person was killed, a popular action could be brought for a fixed penalty. If the victim suffered only personal damages, the judge would determine the penalty after taking into consideration all relevant losses and circumstances.

The third quasi delict penalized the placement or suspension of objects from a building in such a way as to endanger passersby on a public road or common way. A passerby could bring an action with a fixed penalty against the occupant of a building, no matter who in fact had placed the object in the dangerous position. Because the prevention of potential dangers was a matter of public interest, any member of the community could bring the action (*quivis ex populo*). If the suspended object actually fell, it was considered to have been thrown, and the aforementioned action was brought.

Finally, a master of a ship, an innkeeper, or a stable keeper was liable for theft of things and damages to his clients (passengers or guests) by his employees or slaves. Innkeepers were also liable for damages caused by permanent residents. The justification of the penalty lay in the negligence of the person in charge of selecting his employees. The action granted to the clients was for twice the value of the thing damaged or lost.

Further reading

Bauman, Richard A. *Crime and Punishment in Ancient Roman Law*. London and New York: Routledge, 1996.

Berger, Adolf. *Encyclopedic Dictionary of Roman Law*. Philadelphia, PA: The American Philosophical Society, 1953; reprint 1980.

Brasiello, Ugo. *La repressione penale nel diritto romano*. Napoli: Jovene, 1937.

Buckland, William Warwick, and Arnold D. McNair. *Roman Law and Common Law*. 2nd ed. Revised by F. H. Lawson, 338–398. Cambridge: Cambridge University Press, 1952.

Castresana Herrero, Amelia. *Nuevas lecturas de la responsabilidad aquiliana*. Salamanca: Ediciones Universidad de Salamanca, 2001.

Cursi, Floriana M. *Iniuria cum damno. Antigiuridicità e colpevolezza nella storia del danno aquiliano*. Milan: Giuffrè, 2002.

Cursi, Floriana M. *Danno e responsabilità extracontrattuale nella storia del diritto privato*. Naples: Jovene, 2010.

du Plessis, Paul J. "Damaging a Slave." In *Judge and Jurist: Essays in Memory of Lord Rodger of Earlsferry*, edited by Andrew Burrows, David Johnston, and Reinhard Zimmermann, 157–166. Oxford: Oxford University Press, 2013.

Fargnoli, Iole. *Ricerche in tema di furtum: qui sciens indebitum accipit*. Milan: Giuffrè, 2006.

Frier, Bruce W. *A Casebook on the Roman Law of Delict*. Atlanta, GA: Scholars Press, 1989.

Giménez Candela, Teresa. *Los llamados cuasidelitos*. Madrid: Trivium, 1999.

Harries, Jill D. *Law and Crime in the Roman World*. Cambridge and New York: Cambridge University Press, 2007.

Kaser, Max. *Das römische Privatrecht*. Vol. I, *Das altrömische, das vorklassische und klassische Recht*, 609–633. 2nd ed. Munich: Beck Verlag, 1971.

Mommsen, Theodor. *Römisches Strafrecht*. Leipzig: Duncker & Humblot, 1899.

Mousourakis, George. *Fundamentals of Roman Private Law*, 251–271. Berlin and Heidelberg: Springer, 2012.

Nicholas, Barry. *An Introduction to Roman Law*, 207–227. Oxford: Clarendon Press, 1975.

Nippel, Wilfried. *Public Order in Ancient Rome*. Cambridge and New York: Cambridge University Press, 1995.

Paricio Serrano, Javier, ed. *Derecho romano de obligaciones. Homenaje al profesor José Luis Murga Gener*. Madrid: Centro de Estudios Ramón Areces, 1994.

Pólay, Elemér. *Iniuria Types in Roman Law*. Translated by József Szabó. Budapest: Akademiai Kiadó, 1986.

Robinson, Olivia F. *The Criminal Law of Ancient Rome*. Baltimore, MD: Johns Hopkins University Press, 1995.

Robinson, Olivia F. *Penal Practice and Penal Policy in Ancient Rome*. London and New York: Routledge, 2007.

Santalucia, Bernardo. *Diritto e processo penale nell'antica Roma*. 2nd ed. Milan: Giuffrè, 1998.

Schulz, Fritz. *Classical Roman Law*, 572–609. Oxford: Clarendon Press, 1951.

Sirks, Boudewijn. "Delicts." In *The Cambridge Companion to Roman Law*, edited by David Johnston, 246–271. Cambridge and New York: Cambridge University Press, 2015.

Thomas, J. A. C. *Textbook of Roman Law*, 349–383. Amsterdam, New York, and Oxford: North-Holland Publishing Company, 1976.

Watson, Alan. *The Law of Obligations in the Later Roman Republic*. Oxford: Clarendon Press, 1965.

Zimmermann, Reinhard. *The Law of Obligations: Roman Foundations of the Civilian Tradition*, 902–1142. Oxford: Clarendon Press, 1996.

General bibliography

I Sources of Roman law

The *editio maior* of the Digest was edited by Theodor Mommsen, *Digesta Iustiniani Augusti*, 2 vols. (Berlin: Weidmann, 1868–70), and that of the Code of Justinian by Paul Krüger, *Codex Iustinianus* (Berlin: Weidmann, 1877). However, the most commonly used edition of the *Corpus Iuris* is the stereotype edition: *Corpus Iuris Civilis*: Vol. I., *Institutiones*, edited by Paul Krüger, and *Digesta. Editio minor*, edited by Theodor Mommsen and Paul Krüger, 16th ed. (Berlin: Weidmann, 1954); Vol. II, *Codex Iustinianus*, edited by Paul Krüger, 11th ed. (Berlin: Weidmann, 1954); and Vol. III, *Novellae*, edited by Rudolph Schoell and Wilhelm Kroll, 6th ed. (Berlin: Weidmann, 1954). This edition has been repeatedly reprinted.

Valuable recent translations into English of the Institutes of Justinian are: J. A. C. Thomas, *The Institutes of Justinian: Text, Translation, and Commentary* (Amsterdam, New York, and Oxford: North Holland Publishers, 1975); and Peter Birks and Grant McLeod, *Justinian's Institutes* (Ithaca, NY: Cornell University Press, 1987).

Alan Watson is the editor of an English translation of the Digest: *The Digest of Justinian*, 4 vols. (Philadelphia: University of Pennsylvania Press, 1985), including the Latin text of Mommsen's *editio maior*. Later, only the English translation was published in two volumes: *The Digest of Justinian. English Translation edited by Alan Watson* (Philadelphia: University of Pennsylvania Press, 1998). Bruce W. Frier is the editor of a new annotated translation of Justinian's Code: *The Codex of Justinian,* 3 vols. (Cambridge and New York: Cambridge University Press, 2016).

A Spanish translation of the *Corpus Iuris Civilis* was edited in 1889 by Ildelfonso García Corral: *Cuerpo de Derecho civil*, 6 vols. (Madrid: Lex Nova, reprint 1989). A translation of the Digest into Spanish was edited and coordinated by Álvaro d'Ors, *El Digesto de Justiniano*, 3 vols. (Pamplona: Aranzadi, 1968, 1972, 1975). A new translation of the Digest into French entitled *Les 50 Livres du Digeste de l'empereur Justinien, nouvelle traduction française* was made by Dominique Gaurier (Paris: La Mémoire du Droit, 2017). Some German professors, led by Okko Behrends and Rolf Knütel, are working on a German translation of the *Corpus Iuris Civilis*. Until now, five volumes have been published under the general title: *Corpus Iuris Civilis. Text und Übersetzung* (Heidelberg: C. F. Müller, 1990–2012).

The commonly used edition of the *Theodosian Code* is that edited by Theodor Mommsen and Paul Meyer, based in part on the work of Paul Krüger: *Codex Theodosianus. Theodosiani libri XVI: cum Constitutionibus Sirmondianis et Leges novellae ad Theodosianum pertinentes*, 2 vols., 3rd ed. (Berlin: Weidman, 1962). An English translation was edited by Clyde Pharr, *The Theodosian Code and Novels and the Sirmondian Constitutions* (Princeton, NJ: Princeton University Press, 1952).

Good editions of Gaius's *Institutes* include: *Gai Institutiones*, edited by Emil Seckel and Bernhard Kübler (Leipzig: Teubner, 1935); *Gai Institutiones. Editio minor*, edited by Martin David (Leiden: Brill, 1948); and the still unfinished *editio maior, Gai Institutiones*, edited by Martin David, Hein L. Nelson (books I and II, 1954–68), and Hein L. Nelson and Ulrich Manthe (book III, 1992–2007). Book IV has been not yet published.

Available translations into English are: *The Institutes of Gaius*, 2 vols., edited by Francis de Zulueta (Oxford: Clarendon Press, 1946–53) with an excellent commentary; and *The Institutes of Gaius*, edited by William M. Gordon and Olivia Robinson (London: Duckworth, 1988). The *Institutes* of Gaius have been translated into many languages.

Pre-Justinian sources (Roman statues, works of classical jurists, and legal documents) were collected by Carl Georg Bruns in *Fontes Iuris Romani Antiqui* (Tubingen: I. C. B. Mohr, P. Siebeck, 1909 and 1912; reprint Aalen: Scientia, 1958). Later Italian Romanists prepared a useful edition, which is commonly used: *Fontes Iuris Romani Antejustiniani* (FIRA), edited by Salvatore Riccobono, Giovanni Baviera, Contardo Ferrini, Giuseppe Furlani, and Vincenzo Arangio Ruiz, 3 vols., 2nd ed. (Florence: Barbera, 1968). The first volume collected statutes (*leges*), the second, works of jurists (*auctores*), and the third legal transactions (*negotia*).

Other documents of legal practice, such as the new Pompeian tablets, have been published after the Italian collection of FIRA; see Giuseppe Camodeca, *Tabulae Pompeianae Sulpiciorum (TPSulp.): Edizione critica dell'Archivio Puteolano dei Sulpicii* (Rome: Quasar, 1999); and Joseph Georg Wolf, *Neue Rechtsurkunden aus Pompeji. Tabulae Pompeianae Novae* (Darmstadt: Wissenschaftliche Buchgesellschaft, 2010). A revised version of FIRA is in progress: *Revisione ed integrazines dei Fontes Iuris Romani Anteiustiniani. Studi preparatory. I. Leges*, edited by Gianfranco Purpura (Turin: Giappichelli Editore, 2012); and *Studi preparatori vol II. Auctores. Negotia* edited by Gianfranco Purpura (Turin: Giappichelli Editore, 2013).

Very helpful is the collection of Roman statutes and documents translated from Greek or Latin into English by Allan Chester Johnson, Paul Robinson Coleman-Norton, and Frank Card Bourne, *Ancient Roman Statutes* (Austin: University of Texas Press, 1961). Excellent is the collection edited by Michael H. Crawford, which includes the texts of epigraphically attested and other known Roman statutes, with introduction, bibliography, critical material, translation, and commentary: *Roman Statutes*, 2 vols. (London: Institute of Classical Studies, University of London, 1996). A Spanish translation of Roman legal sources was edited by Rafael Domingo, et al., *Textos de Derecho Romano*, 2nd ed. (Cizur Menos: Thomson Aranzadi, 2002). Always useful is the collection of Roman documents gathered by Paul Frédéric Girard and Félix Senn, *Textes de droit romain*, vol. I. *Commentaires*, 7th ed. (Paris: Dalloz, 1967) [juristic writings]; vol. II. *Les lois des Romains,* 7th ed. by Vincenzo Giuffrè (Naples: Jovene, 1977) [inscriptions/papyri].

The most accurate, but still insufficient, reconstruction of the praetor's edict was made by Otto Lenel, *Das Edictum Perpetuum. Ein Versuch zu seiner Wiederherstellung*, 3rd ed. (Aalen: Scientia, 1927, reprint 1956). The reconstruction of the edict was based on the reconstructions of the works of the Roman jurists from the fragments contained in Justinian's Digest: Otto Lenel, *Palingenesia Iuris Civilis*, 2 vols., 2nd ed. (Graz: Akademische Druck- u. Verlagsanstalt, 1960). These two works of Lenel continued to be a basic point of departure for any research in classical Roman law. Nonetheless, they demand a full revision. For a new reconstruction of the first two edictal titles, see Rafael Domingo, *Estudios sobre el primer título del edicto del pretor*, 3 vols. (Santiago de Compostela: Universidad de Santiago de Compostela, 1989, 1993, 1995).

Literary and legal sources are available online at www.thelatinlibrary.com. General information about all things concerning Roman law can be found on the website edited by Ernest Metzger: www.iuscivile.com.

II Textbooks on Roman law

The worldwide leading handbook and most comprehensive modern (but not updated) account on Roman law is that of Max Kaser, *Das römische Privatrecht:* vol. I, *Das altrömische, das vorklassische und klassische Recht*, 2nd ed. (Munich: Beck Verlag, 1971) and vol. II, *Die nachklassischen Entwicklungen*, 2nd ed. (Munich: Beck Verlag, 1975). This work was completed with a specific third volume on civil litigation: Max Kaser and Karl Hackl, *Das römische Zivilprozessrecht*, 2nd ed. (Munich: Beck Verlag, 1996). A translation into English of these three monumental volumes would be very helpful. Ulrike Babusiaux, Christian Baldus, Wolfgang Ernst, Franz-Stefan Meissel, Thomas Rüfner, and Johannes Platschek have coedited the new *Handbuch des römischen Privatrechts* (Tübingen: Mohr Siebeck forthcoming). The aim of the project is to create a definitive reference work on Roman private law, much as Kaser's handbook has been for decades, in line with the current state of research and presenting prospects for future research.

A recent original textbook that covers a great variety of topics beyond traditional private law was edited by David Johnston, *The Cambridge Companion to Roman Law* (Cambridge and New York: Cambridge University Press, 2015). Another fresh, useful, and unconventional volume, aimed at bringing to bear on Roman law the full range of resources of contemporary legal history, was edited by Clifford Ando, Paul J. du Plessis, and Kaius Tuori, *The Oxford Handbook of Roman Law and Society* (Oxford and New York: Oxford University Press, 2016).

The leading textbook in English was for decades that of William Warwick Buckland, *A Textbook of Roman Law from Augustus to Justinian*, 3rd ed., edited by Peter Stein (Cambridge: Cambridge University Press, 1963). Excellent, challenging, and sometimes even provocative is Fritz Schulz, *Classical Roman Law* (Oxford: Clarendon Press: 1951; 2nd ed., edited by Wolfgang Ernst [Aalen: Scientia, 1992]). Elegant and very well balanced is the textbook written by Barry Nicholas, *An Introduction to Roman Law* (Oxford and New York: Oxford University Press, 1962; reprint 1975, and 2008 with an introductory foreword, revised bibliography, and glossary of Latin terms by Ernest Metzger). Always helpful and interesting is J. A. C. Thomas, *Textbook of Roman Law* (Amsterdam, New York, and Oxford: North-Holland Publishing Company, 1976).

A good account of Roman law from a historical perspective is offered by H. F. Holowicz and Barry Nicholas, *Historical Introduction to the Study of Roman Law*, 3rd ed. (Cambridge: Cambridge University Press, 1972). A comprehensive handbook on the law of obligations including the civil legal tradition is that of Reinhard Zimmermann, *The Law of Obligations: Roman Foundations of the Civilian Tradition* (Oxford and New York: Oxford University Press, 1996). A textbook with a good selection of primary text in English translation is that of A. Arthur Schiller, *Roman Law. Mechanisms of Development* (The Hague, Paris, and New York: Mouton Publishers, 1978). To know how Roman law affected the Roman citizens in their day-to-day activities, see John A. Crook, *Law and Life of Rome (90 BC–AD 212)* (Ithaca, NY: Cornell University Press, 1984).

The popular *Borkowski's Textbook on Roman Law* has been edited by Paul du Plessis, 5th ed. (Oxford and New York: Oxford University Press, 2015). Recent textbooks include David Johnston, *Roman Law in Context* (Cambridge and New York: Cambridge University Press, 1999); Andrew M. Riggsby, *Roman Law and the Legal World of the Romans* (New York and Cambridge: Cambridge University Press, 2010); George Mousourakis, *Fundamentals of Roman Private Law* (Berlin and Heidelberg: Springer, 2012); and Laurent Waelkens, *Amne Adverso: Roman Legal Heritage in European Culture*, translated by Line Leys (Leuven: Leuven University Press, 2015).

Brief entries on Roman law concepts and terminology can be found in Adolf Berger, *Encyclopedic Dictionary of Roman Law* (Philadelphia, PA: America Philosophical Society, 1953; reimpr., Clark, NJ: The Law Exchange, Ltd., 2004). Excellent entries also can be found in the *Encyclopedia of Ancient History*, edited by Roger S. Bagnall, Kai Brodersen, Craige B. Champion, and Andrew Erskine (Oxford: Blackwell, 2012); *The Oxford Encyclopedia of Ancient Greece and Rome*, edited by Michael Gagarin and Elaine Fantham (New York, Oxford: Oxford University Press, 2010); and *The Oxford International Encyclopedia of Legal History*, edited by Stanley Nider Katz (Oxford: Oxford University Press, 2009), among others.

Solid and clear Spanish textbooks on Roman law include the following: Álvaro d'Ors, *Derecho privado romano*, 10th ed., edited by Xavier d'Ors (Pamplona: Eunsa, 2004); Juan Iglesias, *Derecho romano*, 17th ed., edited by Juan Iglesias Redondo (Barcelona: Ariel 2008); Alejandro Guzmán, *Derecho privado romano*, 2 vols. (Santiago de Chile: Editorial Jurídica de Chile, 1996); Manuel J. García Garrido, *Derecho privado romano* (Madrid: Ediciones Académicas, 2010); Amelia Castresana, *Derecho romano. El arte de lo bueno y de lo justo* (Madrid: Tecnos, 2015); Alejandrino Fernández Barreiro y Javier Paricio, *Fundamentos de Derecho privado Romano*, 2nd ed. (Madrid and Barcelona: Marcial Pons, 2016). On Roman public law, see: Antonio Fernández de Buján, *Derecho público romano* 19th ed. (Madrid: Thomson Civitas, 2016). On obligations, see: Javier Paricio Serrano, ed. *Derecho romano de obligaciones. Homenaje al profesor José Luis Murga Gener* (Madrid: Centro de Estudios Ramón Areces, 1994). For a selection and commentary of more than a thousand legal maxims and aphorisms, see Rafael Domingo, Javier Ortega, Beatriz Rodríguez Antolín, and Nicolás Zambrana, *Principios de Derecho Global. 1000 reglas y aforismos jurídicos comentados*, 3rd ed. (Cizur Menor: Thomson Aranzadi, 2006).

Classical and recent Italian accounts on Roman law abound. See, among others: Pietro Bonfante, *Corso di diritto romano*, 5 vols. (Roma: Sampaolesi, 1925–33); Vincenzo Arangio Ruiz, *Istituzioni di diritto romano*, 14th ed. (Naples: Jovene, 1960); Giovanni Pugliesse, in collaboration with Francesco Sitzia and Letizia Vacca, *Istituzioni di diritto romano* (Padova: Piccin, 1986); Mario Talamanca, *Istituzioni di diritto romano* (Milan: Giufrè, 1990); Alberto Burdese, *Manuale di diritto privato romano*, 4th ed. (Turin: UTET, 1993); Antonio Guarino, *Diritto privato romano*, 12th ed. (Naples: Jovene, 2001); Eva Cantarella, *Diritto romano. Istituzione e storia* (Milan: Modadori, 2010); and Matteo Marrone, *Istituzioni di diritto romano*, 3rd ed. (Palermo: Palumbo Editore, 2014).

In French, see: Édouard Cuq, *Les institutions juridiques des romains*, 2 vols. (Paris: Libraire Plon, Libraire Marescq Ainé, 1902); Jean Gaudemet, *Droit privé romain* (Paris: Montchrestien, 2000); Paul Freédéric Girard, *Manuel élémentaire de droit romain*, 8th ed. (Paris: Dalloz 2003); Michel Villey, *Le droit romain* (Paris: Presses Universitaires de la France, 2012); Bruno Schmidlin, *Droit privé romain* I, 2nd ed. (Basel: Helbing Lichtenhanh Verlag, 2012); Jean-Philippe Dunand, Bruno Schmidlin, and Bénédict Winiger, *Droit privé romain* II, *Obligations*, 2nd ed. (Basel: Helbing Lichtenhanh Verlag, 2012); and René Robaye, *Le droit romain*, 5th ed. (Leuven: Academia, 2016).

In German, along with the textbook by Max Kaser mentioned above, the following accounts are very helpful: Paul Jörs, Wolfgang Kunkel, and Leopold Wenger, *Römisches Recht*, 4th ed., edited by Heinrich Honsell, Theo Mayer-Maly, and Walter Selb (Berlin, Heidelberg, and Vienna: Springer, 1987); Theo Mayer-Maly, *Römisches Recht*, 2nd ed. (Berlin and Vienna: Springer, 1999); Alfons Bürge, *Römisches Recht* (Darmstadt: Wissenschaftliche Buchgesellschaft, 1999); Detlef Liebs, *Römisches Recht*, 6th ed. (Göttingen:

Vanderhoek & Ruprecht, 2004); Max Kaser and Rolf Knütel, *Römisches Privatrecht. Ein Studienbuch*, 20th ed. (Munich: Beck Verlag, 2013); Heinrich Honsell, *Römisches Recht*, 8th ed. (Berlin and Heidelberg: Springer, 2013); Peter Apathy, Georg Klingenberg, and Martin Pennitz, *Einführung in das römische Recht*, 6th ed. (Vienna: Böhlau, 2016).

Casebooks on Roman law include: Bruce W. Frier, *A Casebook on the Roman Law of Delict* (Atlanta, GA: Scholars Press, 1989); Bruce W. Frier and Thomas A. J. McGinn, *A Casebook on Roman Family Law* (Oxford: Oxford University Press, 2001); Herbert Hausmaninger and Richard Gamauf, *A Casebook on Roman Property Law*, translated by George A. Sheets (Oxford and New York: Oxford University Press, 2003).

III Other general works on specific areas

(a) On history of Roman law

Otto Karlowa, *Römische Rechtsgeschichte* (unfinished), 2 vols. (Leipzig: Verlag von Veit & Co., 1885, 1901); Arangio Ruiz, *Storia del diritto romano*, 7th ed. (Naples: Jovene, 1957); Wolfgang Kunkel, *An Introduction to Roman Legal and Constitutional History*, 2nd ed., translated by J. M. Kelly (Oxford: Clarendon Press, 1973), updated edition in German, Wolfgang Kunkel and Martin Schermaier, *Römische Rechtsgeschichte*, 14th ed. (Vienna and Cologne: Böhlau, 2004); Franz Wieacker, *Römische Rechtgeschichte* I, *Quellenkunde, Rechtsbildung, Jurisprudenz und Rechtsliteratur* (Munich: Beck Verlag, 1988) and II, *Die Jurisprudenz vom frühen Prinzipat bis zum Ausgang der Antike*, edited by Joseph Georg Wolf (Munich: Beck Verlag, 2006); Mario Talamanca, ed., *Lineamenti di storia del diritto romano*, 2nd ed. (Milan: Giuffrè, 1989); Antonio Guarino, *Storia del diritto romano*, 12th ed. (Naples: Jovene, 1998); Aldo Schiavone, *The Invention of the Law in the West*, translated by Jeremy Carden and Anthony Shugaar (Cambridge, MA, and London: The Belknap Press of Harvard University Press, 2012); Wolfgang Waldstein and Michael Rainer, *Römische Rechtsgeschichte*, 11th ed. (Munich: Beck Verlag, 2014).

(b) On Roman legal sources and methodology

Paul Krüger, *Geschichte der Quellen und Litteratur des römischen Rechts*, 2nd ed. (München: Verlag von Duncker & Humblot, 1912); Fritz Schulz, *Einführung in das Studium der Digesten* (Tübingen: J. C. B. Mohr, 1916); Hermann Kantorowicz, *Einführung in die Textskritik* (Leipzig: Dietrrich, 1921); Leopold Wenger, *Die Quellen der römischen Recht* (Vienna: Österreichische Akademie der Wissenschaften, 1953); Franz Wieacker, *Textstufen klassicher Juristen* (Göttingen: Vandenhoeck & Ruprecht, 1960); Max Kaser, *Zur Methodologie der römischen Rechtsquellenforchung* (Vienna, Cologne, and Graz: Böhlau, 1972); Max Kaser, *Römische Rechtsquellen und angewandte Juristenmethode* (Vienna: Böhlau, 1986); Franz Wieacker, *Römische Rechtgeschichte* I,

Quellenkunde, Rechtsbildung, Jurisprudenz und Rechtsliteratur (Munich: Beck Verlag, 1988) and II, *Die Jurisprudenz vom frühen Prinzipat bis zum Ausgang der Antike*, edited by Joseph Georg Wolf (Munich: Beck Verlag, 2006); Wolfgang Kaiser, *Authentizität und Geltung spätantiker Kaisergesetze* (Munich: Beck, 2007).

(c) On the spirit of Roman law

Rudolph von Ihering, *Geist des römischen Rechts auf den verschiedenen Stufen seiner Entwicklung*, 3 vols. (Schwabe: Basilea, 1954); Fritz Schulz, *Principles of Roman Law*, 2nd ed. (Oxford: Clarendon Press, 1967); David Daube, *Roman Law, Linguistic, Social and Philosophical Aspects* (Edinburgh: Edinburgh University Press, 1969); Peter G. Stein, *The Character and Influence of the Roman Civil Law* (London: Hambledon, 1988); Juan Iglesias, *Espíritu del Derecho romano*, 2nd ed. (Madrid: Editorial Centro de Estudios Ramón Areces, 1991); and Alan Watson, *The Spirit of Roman Law* (Athens: University of Georgia Press, 1995).

(d) On the Roman constitution and public law

Theodor Mommsen, *Römisches Staatsrecht*, 3 vols., 2nd ed. (Leipzig: Verlag Von S. Hirzel, 1876, 1888); Francesco de Martino, *Storia de la costituzione romana*, 6 vols. (Naples: Jovene, 1958–90); Wolfgang Kunkel, *An Introduction to Roman Legal and Constitutional History*, 2nd ed., translated by J. M. Kelly (Oxford: Clarendon Press, 1973); Andrew Lintott, *Imperium Romanum: Politics and Administration* (London and New York: Routledge, 1993); Alberto Burdese, *Manuale di diritto pubblico romano*, 3rd ed. (Turin: UTET, 1995); Wolfgang Kunkel and Roland Wittmann, *Staatsordnung und Staatspraxis der römischen Republik* II, *Die Magistratur* (Munich: Beck Verlag, 1995); Andrew Lintott, *The Constitution of the Roman Republic* (Oxford: Oxford University Press, 1999); Callie Williamson, *The Laws of the Roman People: Public Law in the Expansion and Decline of the Roman Republic* (Ann Arbor: University of Michigan Press, 2005); Dean Hammer, *Roman Political Thought* (Cambridge and New York: Cambridge University Press, 2014); and Benjamin Straumann, *Crisis and Constitutionalism: Roman Political Thought from the Fall of the Republic to the Age of Revolution* (Oxford and New York: Oxford University Press, 2016).

(e) On Roman jurisprudence and Roman jurists

Fritz Schulz, *History of Roman Legal Science* (Oxford: Clarendon Press, 1953); Richard A. Bauman, *Lawyers in Roman Republic Politics: A Study of the Roman Jurists in Their Political Setting, 316–82 BC* (Munich: Beck Verlag, 1983); Richard A. Bauman, *Lawyers in Roman Transitional Politics: A Study of the Roman Jurists in the Political Setting in the Late Republic and*

Triumvirate (Munich: Beck Verlag, 1985); Bruce W. Frier, *The Rise of the Roman Jurists: Studies in Cicero's Pro Caecina* (Princeton, NJ: Princeton University Press 1985); Detlef Liebs, *Die Jurisprudenz im spätantiken Italien (260–640 n. Chr.)* (Berlin: Duncker & Humblot, 1987); Detlef Liebs, *Römische Jurisprudenz in Africa: mit Studien zu den pseudopaulinischen Sentenzen* (Berlin: Akademie Verlag, 1993); Richard A. Bauman, *Lawyers and Politics in the Early Roman Empire: A Study of Relations Between the Roman Jurists and the Emperors from Augustus to Hadrian* (Munich: Beck Verlag, 1989); Tony Honoré, *Emperors and Lawyers*, 2nd ed. (Oxford: Oxford University Press 1994); Wolfgang Kunkel, *Die römischen Juristen. Herkunft und soziale Stellung*, reimpr. 2nd ed. (Cologne and Vienna: Böhlau, 2001); Rafael Domingo, ed., *Juristas universales* I, *Juristas antiguos* (Madrid, Barcelona: Marcial Pons, 2004); Detlef Liebs, *Hofjuristen der römischen Kaiser bis Justinian* (Munich: Bayerische Akademie der Wissenschaften and Beck Verlag. 2010).

(f) On Roman law and society

David Daube, *Roman Law: Linguistic, Social, and Philosophical Aspects* (Edinburgh: Edinburgh University Press, 1969); Kaius Tuori, *Ancient Roman Lawyers and Modern Legal Ideals. Studies on the Impact of Contemporary Concerns in the Interpretation of Ancient Legal History* (Frankfurt: Vittorio Klostermann, 2007); John W. Cairns and Paul J. du Plessis, *Beyond Dogmatics. Law and Society in the Roman World* (Edinburgh: Edinburgh University Press, 2007); Clifford Ando, *Law, Language, and Empire in the Roman Tradition* (Philadelphia: University of Pennsilvania Press, 2011); Paul J. du Plessis, ed., *New Frontiers: Law and Society in the Roman World* (Edinburgh: Edinburgh University Press, 2013); Paul du Plessis, Clifford Ando, and Kaius Tuori, eds., *The Oxford Handbook of Roman Law and Society* (Oxford: Oxford University Press, 2016); Kaius Tuori, *The Emperor of Law. The Emergence of Roman Imperial Adjudication* (Oxford: Oxford University Press, 2017).

(g) On medieval Roman law

Friedrich Carl von Savigny, *Geschichte des römischen Recht in Mittelalter*, 7 vols. (Wiesbaden-Biebrich: Becker & Co., 1834; facsimile edition, Bad Homburg: Hermann Gentner, 1961); Paul Vinogradoff, *Roman Law in Medieval Europe* (London and New York: Harper & Brothers, 1909); Francesco Calasso, *Medio Evo del diritto* (Milan: Giuffrè, 1954); Ennio Cortese, *Le grandi linee della storia giuridica medievale* (Rome: Il Cigno Galileo Galilei, 2001); Hermann Lange, *Römisches Recht in Mittelalter* I, *Die Glossatoren* (Munich: Beck Verlag, 1997) and II, *Die Kommentatoren*, in collaboration with Maximiliane Kriechbaum (Munich: Beck Verlag, 2007); Charles Radding and Antonio Ciaralli, *The Corpus Iuris Civilis in the Middle Ages: Manuscripts and Transmissions from the Sixth Century to the Juristic Revival* (Leiden: Brill, 2006).

(h) On the contribution of Roman law to European culture

Paul Koschaker, *Europa una das römische Recht*, 3rd ed. (Munich: Beck Verlag, 1958); Herbert Felix Jolowicz, *Roman Foundations of Modern Law* (Oxford: Oxford University Press, 1957; reprint 1978); Harold J. Berman, *Law and Revolution: The Formation of the Western Legal Tradition* (Cambridge, MA: Harvard University Press, 1983); Franz Wieacker, *A History of Private Law in Europe*, translated by Tony Weir (Oxford and New York: Oxford University Press, 1995); Peter Stein, *Roman Law in European History* (Cambridge and New York: Cambridge University Press, 1999); Raoul C. van Caenegem, *An Historical Introduction to Private Law*, translated by D. E. L. Johnston (Cambridge and New York: Cambridge University Press, 1992); Manlio Bellomo, *The Common Legal Past of Europe, 1000–1800* (Washington, DC: Catholic University of America Press, 1995); Raoul C. van Caenegem, *European Law in the Past and the Future: Unity and Diversity Over Two Millennia* (Cambridge and New York: Cambridge University Press, 2002); Laurent Waelkens, *Amne Adverso. Roman Legal Heritage in European Culture*, translated by Line Leys (Leuven: Leuven University Press, 2015).

(i) On civil litigation

Giovanni Pugliese, *Il proceso civile romano* II, *Il proceso formulare* (Milan: Giufrè, 1963); John M. Kelly, *Roman Litigation* (Oxford: Clarendon Press, 1966); John M. Kelly, *Studies in the Civil Judicature of the Roman Republic* (Oxford: Oxford University Press, 1976); José Luis Murga, *El proceso clásico* (Zaragoza: Universidad de Zaragoza, 1980); Carlo Augusto Cannata, *Profilo istituzionale del proceso privato romano* I, *Les legis actiones*; II, *Il proceso formulare* (Turin: Giappichelli, 1980–82); Leopold Wenger, *Institutes of Roman Law of Civil Procedure*, rev. ed., translated by Otis Harrison Fisk (Littleton, CO: Fred B. Rothman & Co., 1986); Max Kaser and Karl Hackl, *Das römische Zivilprozessrecht*, 2nd ed. (Munich: Beck Verlag, 1996); Ernest Metzger, *A New Outline of Roman Trial* (Oxford and New York: Oxford University Press, 1997); Roberto Fiori, *Ea res agatur: I due modelli del processo formulare repubblicano* (Milan: Giuffrè, 2003); Ernest Metzger, *Litigation in Roman Law* (Oxford and New York: Oxford University Press, 2005); Francesco de Angelis, (ed.), *Spaces of Justice in the Roman World* (Leiden: Brill, 2010); Detlef Liebs, *Summoned to the Roman Courts: Famous Trials from Antiquity* (Los Angeles and London: University of California Press, Berkeley, 2012).

(j) On family law and slavery

Alan Watson, *The Law of Persons in the Later Roman Republic* (Oxford: Clarendon Press, 1967); Alan Watson, *Roman Slave Law* (Baltimore and London: The Johns Hopkins University Press, 1987); Susan Treggiari, *Roman Marriage: Iusti Coniuges from the Time of Cicero to the Time of Ulpian*

(Oxford: Clarendon Press, 1991); Angelika Mette-Dittmann, *Die Ehegesetze des Augustus: eine Untersuchung im Rahmen der Gesellschaftspolitik des Princeps* (Stuttgart: F. Steiner, 1991); Jane F. Gardner, *Being a Roman Citizen* (London and New York: Routledge, 1993); Judith Evans Grubbs, *Law and Family in Late Antiquity: The Emperor Constantine's Marriage Legislation* (Oxford and New York: Oxford University Press, 1995); Jane F. Gardner, *Family and "familia" in Roman Law and Life* (Oxford and New York: Oxford University Press, 1998); Hans-Georg Knothe and Jürgen Kohler, eds., *Status Familiae: Festschrift für Andreas Wacke zum 65. Geburtstag am 28. April 2001* (Munich: Beck, 2001); Judith Evans Grubbs, *Women and the Law in the Roman Empire: a Sourcebook on Marriage, Divorce and Widowhood* (London and New York: Routledge, 2002); Hugh Lindsay, *Adoption in the Roman World* (Cambridge and New York: Cambridge University Press, 2009); Beryl Rawson, ed., *A Companion to Families in the Greek and Roman Worlds* (Malden, MA: Wiley-Blackwell, 2011); Christian Laes, *Children in the Roman Empire: Outsiders Within* (Cambridge and New York: Cambridge University Press, 2011); Judith Evans Grubbs and Tim Parkin, eds., *The Oxford Handbook of Childhood and Education in the Classical World* (Oxford and New York: Oxford University Press, 2013); Sandra R. Joshel and Lauren Hackworth Petersen, *The Material Life of Roman Slaves* (Cambridge and New York: Cambridge University Press, 2015); John Witte, Jr. and Gary S. Hauk, eds., *Christianity and Family Law: An Introduction* (Cambridge and New York: Cambridge University Press, 2017).

(k) On property law

Friedrich Carl von Savigny, *Das Recht des Besitzes. Eine civilistische Abhandlung*, 6th ed. (Giessen: G. F. Heyer, 1837); Max Kaser, *Eigentum und Besitz in älteren römischen Recht*, 2nd ed. (Cologne: Böhlau, 1956); György Diósdi, *Ownership in Ancient and Preclassical Roman Law* (Budapest: Akadémiai Kiadó, 1970); Alan Rodger, *Owners and Neighbours in Roman Law* (Oxford: Clarendon Press, 1972); Alan Watson, *The Law of Property in the Later Roman Republic* (Oxford: Clarendon Press, 1968; reprinted Aalen: Scientia Verlag, 1984); Bruce W. Frier, *Landlords and Tenants in Imperial Rome* (Princeton, NJ: Princeton University Press, 1980); Michael J. Rainer, *Bau- und nachbarrechtliche Bestimmungen im klassischen römischen Recht* (Graz: Leykam, 1987); Peter Birks, ed., *New Perspectives in the Roman Law of Property. Essays for Barry Nicholas* (Oxford: Clarendon Press, 1989); Luigi Capogrossi Colognesi, *Proprietà e diritti reali* (Rome: Il Cigno Galileo Galilei, 1999); Stefania Romeo, *L'appartenenza e l'alienazione in diritto romano: tra giurisprudenza e prassi* (Milan: Giuffrè, 2010); Letizia Vacca, *Possesso e tempo nell'acquisto della proprietà: saggi romanistici* (Padua: CEDAM, 2012); Christopher Pierson, *Just Property: A History in the Latin West* (Oxford: Oxford University Press, 2013); Paul Erdkamp, Koenraad Verboven, and Arjan Zuiderhoek, *Ownership and Exploitation of Land and Natural*

Resources in the Roman World (Oxford and New York: Oxford University Press, 2015).

(l) On succession upon death

Biondi, Biondo. *Successione testamentaria e donazioni* (2nd ed. Milan: Giuffrè, 1955); Mario Amelotti, *Il testamento romano* (Florence: Le Monnier, 1966); Pasquale Voci, *Diritto ereditario romano*, 2 vol., 2nd ed. (Milano: Giuffrè, 1963, 1967); Gaetano Scherillo, *Corso di dirittto romano. Il testamento*, 2 vols. (Milan: La Golliardica, 1963, 1967); Alan Watson, *The Law of Succession in the Later Roman Republic* (Oxford: Clarendon Press, 1971); David Johnston, *The Roman Law of Trusts* (Oxford: Clarendon Press, 1988); Francesca Terranova, *Richerche sul testamento per aes et libram. I. Il ruolo del familiae emptor* (Turin: G. Giappichelli Editore, 2011); Yuri González Roldán, *Il diritto ereditario in età adrianea: legislazione imperiale e senatus consulta* (Bari: Cacucci, 2014); Kenneth Reid, Marius de Waal, and Reinhard Zimmermann, eds., *Comparative Succession Law II, Intestate Succession* (Oxford and New York: Oxford University Press, 2015); Maria Novak, *Wills in the Roman Empire: A Documentary Approach* (Warsaw: University of Warsaw, 2015).

(m) On obligations

Emilio Betti, *La struttura dell'obbligazione romana* (Milan: Giuffrè, 1955); Giuseppe Grosso, *I sistema romano dei contratti*, 3rd ed. (Torino: G. Giappichelli, 1963); Alan Watson, *The Law of Obligations in the Later Roman Republic* (Oxford: Clarendon Press, 1965); György Diósdi, *Contract in Roman Law: From the Twelve Tables to the Glossators*, translated by J. Szabó (Budapest: Akadémiai Kiado, 1981); Raimondo Santoro, *Il contratto nel pensiero di Labeone* (Palermo: Palumbo, 1983); Javier Paricio Serrano, ed., *Derecho romano de obligaciones. Homenaje al profesor José Luis Murga Gener* (Madrid: Centro de Estudios Ramón Areces, 1994); Reinhard Zimmermann, *The Law of Obligations: Roman Foundation of the Civilian Tradition* (Oxford and New York: Oxford University Press, 1996); David J. Ibbetson, *A Historical Introduction to the Law of Obligations* (Oxford and New York: Oxford University Press, 1999); Teresa Giménez Candela, *Los llamados cuasidelitos* (Madrid: Trivium, 1999); Amelia Castresana Herrero, *Nuevas lecturas de la responsabilidad aquiliana* (Salamanca: Ediciones Universidad de Salamanca, 2001); Floriana M. Cursi, *Iniuria cum damno. Antigiuridicità e colpevolezza nella storia del danno aquiliano* (Milan: Giuffrè, 2002); Floriana M. Cursi, *Danno e responsabilità extracontrattuale nella storia del diritto privato* (Naples: Jovene, 2010); Thomas A. J. McGinn, ed., *Obligations in Roman Law: Past, Present, and Future* (Ann Arbor: University of Michigan Press, 2012); Peter Birks, *The Roman Law of Obligations*, edited by Eric Descheemaeker (Oxford: Oxford University Press, 2014); Adolfo Wegmann Stockebrand, *Obligatio re contracta. Ein*

Beitrag zur sogenannten Kategorie der Realverträge im römischen Recht (Tübingen: Mohr Siebeck, 2017).

(n) On Roman law of nations

Alan Watson, *International Law in Archaic Rome* (Baltimore, MD: Johns Hopkins University Press, 1993); Dieter Nörr, *Aspekte des römischen Völkerrechts: die Bronzetafel von Alcántara* (Munich: Bayerische Akademie der Wissenschaften, 1989); Dieter Nörr, *Die Fides in römischen Völkerrecht* (Heidelberg: Müller Juristischer Verlag, 1991); Max Kaser, *Ius gentium* (Vienna, Cologne, and Weimar: Böhlau, 1993); David J. Bederman, *International Law in Antiquity* (Cambridge and New York: Cambridge University Press, 2004); Karl-Hein Ziegler, *Völkerrechtsgeschichte*, 2nd ed. (Munich: Beck, 2007); Benedict Kingsbury and Benjamin Straumann, eds., *The Roman Foundations of the Law of Nations: Alberico Gentili and the Justice of Empire* (Oxford and New York: Oxford University Press, 2010); Benjamin Straumann, *Roman Law in the State of Nature: The Classical Foundations of Hugo Grotius' Natural Law* (New York and Cambridge: Cambridge University Press, 2015).

(o) On criminal law

Theodor Mommsen, *Römisches Strafrecht* (Leipzig: Duncker & Humblot, 1899); Ugo Brasiello, *La repressione penale nel diritto romano* (Naples: Jovene, 1937); Wolfgang Kunkel, *Untersuchungen zur Entwicklung des römischen Kriminalverfahrens in vorsullanischer Zeit* (Munich: Verlag der Bayerischen Akademie der Wissenschaften, 1962); Bernardo Santalucia, *Studi di diritto penale romano* (Roma: L'Erma di Bretschneider, 1994); Wilfried Nippel, *Public Order in Ancient Rome* (Cambridge and New York: Cambridge University Press, 1995); Olivia F. Robinson, *The Criminal Law of Ancient Rome* (Baltimore, MD: Johns Hopkins University Press, 1995); Richard A. Bauman, *Crime and Punishment in Ancient Roman Law* (London and New York: Routledge, 1996); Bernardo Santalucia, *Diritto e processo penale nell'antica Roma*, 2d ed. (Milan: Giuffrè, 1998); Olivia Robinson, *Penal Practice and Penal Policy in Ancient Rome* (London and New York: Routledge, 2007); Jill D. Harries, *Law and Crime in the Roman World* (Cambridge and New York: Cambridge University Press, 2007); Bernardo Santalucia (ed.), *La repressione criminale nella Roma repubblicana: fra norma e persuasion* (Pavia: IUSS Press, 2009).

IV Periodicals

Leading journals on Roman law are: (a) *Zeitschrift der Savigny-Stiftung für Rechtsgeschichte* (Romanistische Abteilung) (Vienna, Cologne, and Weimar: Böhlau Verlag); (b) *Tijdschrift voor rechtsgeschiedenis* (Leiden: Brill); (c) *Revue internationale des droits de l'Antiquité* (University of Liège); (d) *IVRA.*

Rivista Internazionale di diritto romano et antico (Naples: Jovene); (e) *Studia et Documenta Historiae et Iuris* (Rome: Lateran University Press); (f) *Index: International Survey of Roman Law* (Naples: Jovene); (g) *Bullettino dell'Istituto di Diritto Romano Vittorio Scialoja* (Milan: Giuffrè); (h) *Revista de Estudios Histórico-Jurídicos* (Pontificia Universidad Católica de Valparaíso, Chile); (i) *Seminarios Complutenses de Derecho Romano* (Madrid: Fundación Ursicino Álvarez); (j) *Revista General de Derecho Romano* (Madrid: Iustel).

V Internet resources

The Roman law resources site www.iuscivile.com, edited by Ernest Metzger, provides information on Roman law sources and literature, the teaching of Roman law, and the persons who study Roman law. The site is available in English and German. The Grenoble Roman law site edited by Yves Lassard and Alexandr Koptev provides links not only to Latin texts but also to modern language translations: https://droitromain.univ-grenoble-alpes.fr. There is also the new online Project LEPOR (Leges Populi Romani), led by Cyril Masset and Zakaria Abbadi, replacing Giovanni Rotondi's *leges publicae Populi Romani* (1912): http://www.cn-telma.fr/lepor/introduction. The Laws database of the Project Volterra consists of a series of tables containing the texts of imperial pronouncements and related information covering the years 193–455 CE: https://www.ucl.ac.uk/volterra/database/database-description. Literary and legal sources are available online at www.thelatinlibrary.com.

Index

Made in the USA
Las Vegas, NV
19 September 2026

06d93e1a-4f65-4e75-a740-1fdb4e9e64b2R01